Digital Transformation in The Recording Industry

The recording industry has famously been transformed by technology throughout its entire history.

The book presents an analysis of these changes using Porter's five forces model. The author highlights the evolution of buyers' and suppliers' power, the emergence of new competitors, product innovation and rivalry between companies in the industry driven by economic, political, social and legal factors.

As an early mover in the social diffusion of copyright-sensitive content, the recording industry reflected in this book serves as an important reference for the analysis of other cultural and creative sectors.

Anna Anetta Janowska is a Doctor of Economics, a cultural economist, and works as an Assistant Professor in the Department of Public Policy at the Warsaw School of Economics. Her scientific interests revolve around the impact of digital technologies on the cultural and creative sectors, with a particular focus on cultural policy, mainly in relation to the situation of artists and creators.

Routledge Research in the Creative and Cultural Industries

Series Editor: Ruth Rentschler

This series brings together book-length original research in cultural and creative industries from a range of perspectives. Charting developments in contemporary cultural and creative industries thinking around the world, the series aims to shape the research agenda to reflect the expanding significance of the creative sector in a globalised world.

Public Relations as a Creative Industry
Elisenda Estanyol

Co-Leadership in the Arts and Culture
Sharing Values and Vision
Wendy Reid and Hilde Fjellvær

Cultural Work and Creative Subjectivity
Recentralising the Artist Critique and Social Networks in the Cultural Industries
Xin Gu

Advertising as a Creative Industry
Regime of Paradoxes
Izabela Derda

Professionalization in the Creative Sector
Policy, Collective Action, and Institutionalization
Edited by Margaret J. Wyszomirski and WoongJo Chang

Digital Transformation and Cultural Policies in Europe
Edited by Ole Marius Hylland and Jaka Primorac

For more information about this series, please visit: www.routledge.com/Routledge-Research-in-the-Creative-and-Cultural-Industries/book-series/RRCCI

Digital Transformation in The Recording Industry

Evolution of Power: From the Turntable to Blockchain

Anna Anetta Janowska

Routledge
Taylor & Francis Group
LONDON AND NEW YORK

First published 2024
by Routledge
4 Park Square, Milton Park, Abingdon, Oxon OX14 4RN

and by Routledge
605 Third Avenue, New York, NY 10158

Routledge is an imprint of the Taylor & Francis Group, an informa business

British Library Cataloguing-in-Publication Data
A catalogue record for this book is available from the British Library

Library of Congress Cataloging-in-Publication Data
Names: Janowska, Anna Anetta, author.
Title: Digital transformation in the recording industry : evolution of power : from the turntable to blockchain / Anna Anetta Janowska.
Description: Abingdon, Oxon ; New York, NY : Routledge, 2024. | Series: Routledge research in the creative and cultural industries | Includes bibliographical references and index. |
Identifiers: LCCN 2023035845 (print) | LCCN 2023035846 (ebook) | ISBN 9781032539829 (hardback) | ISBN 9781032539836 (paperback) | ISBN 9781003414605 (ebook)
Subjects: LCSH: Sound recording industry. | Music—Economic aspects. | Copyright—Music.
Classification: LCC ML3790 .J36 2024 (print) | LCC ML3790 (ebook) | DDC 338.4/778—dc23/eng/20230802
LC record available at https://lccn.loc.gov/2023035845
LC ebook record available at https://lccn.loc.gov/2023035846

ISBN: 9781032539829 (hbk)
ISBN: 9781032539836 (pbk)
ISBN: 9781003414605 (ebk)

DOI: 10.4324/9781003414605

Typeset in Sabon
by codeMantra

Contents

Acknowledgements

The author would especially like to thank Professor Anna Zorska, whose advice and support during the preparation of the original text was so valuable, and Professor François Moreau, whose book on the recording industry was my first important reference. A huge thank you to Professor Karol Borowiecki for encouraging me to write this book. Thank you Joanna Frej for the precious comments.

Thanks also to my friends Annick Cornil, Magda Sobczyńska, Professor Helena Santos, Kasia Michalik-Jaworska and my whole dear family for their constant support.

To Marcin for love and music.

Introduction

The changes that have been taking place in the economy and society globally for several decades are referred to as the information economy, knowledge-based economy, digital economy, creative economy, or the third wave (Toffler, 1980) and postmodernity (Bauman, 2000). Undoubtedly, a new economic system is still being formed, accompanied by the shaping of a new lifestyle, work style, and civilisation.

Industries that have rapidly and significantly felt the effects of these profound socio-economic changes, primarily driven by the rapidly developing information and communication technologies (ICT), are referred to as creative industries (Gov.UK, 2001). Their role in the global economy is increasingly significant. According to a UNCTAD report (UNCTAD, 2018), the size of the global creative goods market more than doubled between 2002 and 2015, from $208 billion to $509 billion, growing at an average rate of around 7% during those years despite the 2007–2009 financial crisis, which had a negative impact on other sectors of the economy.

The recording industry is part of the cultural and creative sectors (Stachowiak, 2017). Its total revenues in 2022 amounted to $26.2 billion, representing a 9% growth (IFPI, 2023) compared to the previous year. It is an industry that was among the first to undergo transformations related to digital technologies, and the first within the cultural and creative sectors. These changes primarily affected two aspects: the reproduction of works (copying) and their distribution. Firstly, digitisation and later the dematerialisation of music products, separating content from the physical carriers it was previously associated with, resulted in marginal reproduction costs (copying) approaching zero (Rifkin, 2015; Shy, 2004). Consumers gained the ability to store their music collections, primarily on compact discs, in the memory of computers and portable music devices for easier and mobile access.

Secondly, the cost of distributing such a product in digital form over the Internet also became close to zero due to the decreasing prices of home computer equipment, mobile devices including mobile phones and later smartphones, as well as the costs of fixed and mobile internet access. Another element that accelerated these changes was the innovative technology of

DOI: 10.4324/9781003414605-1

mp3, which allowed music files to be compressed into small sizes, facilitating easy and fast transmission over the Internet.

The first and most visible consequence of the synergistic effects of these changes was the development of peer-to-peer (P2P) networks, which allowed users to share music files online without compensating the rights holders, including the creators, for the use of their works as required by copyright law. In the music industry, these activities were referred to as informal circulation of culture (Filiciak et al., 2012) or internet piracy. They were considered the main cause of the crisis in the recorded music sector, as the popularity of P2P platforms coincided with a significant decline in CD sales. Revenues from physical music sales dropped from around $22 billion in 1999 to $4.6 billion in 2022, and overall recorded music revenues, including digital, reached their lowest point of $13.1 billion in 2014 (IFPI, 2023).

Another consequence of these technological changes was a transformation in the entire structure and functioning of the industry. The product itself underwent a significant shift, as did the balance of power among the various entities operating in the music industry, including suppliers, producers, and consumers, as well as the methods of acquiring recorded music and its consumption. New business models emerged, mainly focused on distribution. In the distribution process, new powerful entities from the IT industry also entered the value chain, expanding their operations into the recorded music sector. This highlights the sector's significant importance for the overall economy and its significant impact on the evolution of the recording industry.

A lot of research has been conducted on the subject of cultural and creative sectors, including the phonographic/recording industry, primarily in English-language publications. Many of them have addressed the impact of the digital revolution on the functioning of this industry. They have extensively analysed intellectual property issues, piracy, the development of P2P networks, and described various business models that can operate in this market. The recent innovations such as blockchain and AI have also been discussed, along with their potential impact on the recording industry. Numerous references to this literature can be found in this book.

The main objective of this study is to diagnose the changes that have occurred in the recording industry under the influence of the ongoing technological revolution, particularly the analysis of power dynamics among the various entities operating in the industry. The main thesis is that the changes in the music industry, although seemingly revolutionary, ultimately reinforced the existing order. They further complicated the relationships between entities, strengthening the role of the most powerful players, including new major players, and introducing new barriers to entry for weaker entities.

The verification of the thesis will be aided by obtaining answers to the following research questions:

1 What was the power structure in the recording industry before the digital and ICT revolution?

2 How has the power structure in the recording industry changed under the influence of the digital and ICT revolution?
3 How has the product of the recording industry evolved under technological and socio-cultural transformations?
4 How has music consumption changed in relation to the digital and ICT breakthrough?
5 What was the impact of external factors, such as economic, political, social, legal, and particularly technological factors, on the development of the recording industry?
6 How did the international expansion of record companies and the globalisation of the industry unfold, and what had the greatest influence on them?
7 What are the relationships between copyright law and technological development in the music industry?
8 What legal and regulatory solutions have been proposed to balance the negative phenomena in the recording industry caused by the digital and ICT revolution?
9 Can the latest technology, blockchain, create new possibilities for managing rights to recorded music, its distribution, and monetisation?
10 What potential consequences could arise from a change in the approach to the value of recorded music for the industry's functioning model?

The adopted research perspective in this publication is the perspective of cultural economics. It is a relatively young discipline (Bille et al., 2020; Towse and Hernández, 2020) that is part of economics. However, the applied research method, the five forces model developed by M.E. Porter, originates from management sciences and has been primarily used for industry (sector) analysis, specifically for assessing competition in sectors of the economy. The model is part of strategic analysis used in organisations to develop strategies for operating in a specific sector.

The model consists of the following elements:

- bargaining power of buyers – in the case of the recording industry, this includes both individual consumers and business clients;
- bargaining power of suppliers, i.e., creators and performers of recorded music;
- threat of new entrants, which can be both new record companies and new intermediaries, especially in the area of recorded music distribution;
- threat of substitute products – these can be new artists, provided they are substitutable, as well as new music formats or consumption methods;
- competition among existing industry rivals – in the recording industry, this applies to dominant entities, such as international record label giants, as well as a multitude of small independent labels and music distributors.

Since the subject of this analysis is the industry itself, specifically the phonographic/recording industry (phonographic/recording sector), the chosen model seems to be an appropriate tool for diagnosing the changes that have occurred in it, particularly over the past 20 years and still ongoing.

The book consists of four chapters. Chapter 1 serves as an introduction, outlining the framework of analysis that will be conducted in the subsequent parts of the book. It begins by defining concepts such as industry and sector. The definition of the phonographic/recording industry is presented, along with its place among other related industries, particularly in relation to cultural industries. The characteristics of the phonographic industry's product, the companies operating in it, and the demand side of the industry, including individual and institutional consumers, are then presented in detail. Copyright issues emerge as important elements throughout the text and are referenced frequently. The historical perspective covers the macro-environment of the phonographic industry, as well as its internationalisation and globalisation. The macro-environment factors, including economic, technological, political, social, and legal aspects, contribute to the PEST(L) analysis, traditionally used to characterise the industry's broader environment. The analysis of the macro-environment delineates the framework of the industry's functioning, providing insights into how it is changing, how companies compete with each other, and how relationships between these companies and suppliers and buyers are formed. Examining the stages of internationalisation and globalisation of the industry sheds light on its operation in both the traditional model and the digital revolution era, while historically highlighting significant elements that have driven changes throughout its existence.

Chapter 2 presents the characteristics of the phonographic industry in the pre-digital era. The chosen model to determine its functioning from its inception to the mid-1990s is Porter's five forces model. This model is one of the classical approaches to sectoral analysis in economics at the meso level. It will best highlight the changes that occurred in the recording industry during the digital and ICT revolution, particularly the shift in power dynamics between consumers of recorded music, music producers (record labels), and artists. The backdrop for the analysis using Porter's five forces is the concept of oligonomy proposed by Hannaford (2007).

Chapter 3 analyses the changes that have taken place in the phonographic industry with the advent of the digital and ICT revolution, starting from the mid-1990s. This period marked significant transformations in the industry, primarily characterised by a decline in physical record sales, revenue for record companies, and the development of new forms of music distribution and promotion. The main drivers of these changes were technological factors (such as the widespread adoption of personal computers and the development of the global network) coupled with the digitisation of content. These elements, working in synergy, not only influenced the way music is consumed but also led to changes in the product itself – its quality, physical format, and the nature of its value – consequently altering the power dynamics in the phonographic industry.

The first part of Chapter 4 presents legal solutions and regulations related to copyright and funding for culture (including music) that have been implemented or planned to address the crisis in the phonographic industry arising from the informal circulation of culture and new models of digital music distribution. Although these phenomena have been regulated to some extent in the context of both copyright law and business practices, they have yet to provide satisfactory solutions for all industry stakeholders, particularly creators and consumers. It becomes evident that new intermediaries capture a significant portion of the value created. The second part of the chapter discusses blockchain, a technological innovation that appears to offer new possibilities for the development of the phonographic industry, this time providing specific solutions for creators.

The conclusion reflects on the value of recorded music in the context of the transformations examined in the book, both before and under the influence of the digital/ICT revolution.

Bibliography

Bauman, Z., 2000. *Ponowoczesność jako źródło cierpień*. Wydawnictwo Sic!, Warszawa.

Bille, T., Mignosa, A., Towse, R., 2020. *Teaching Cultural Economics*. Edward Elgar Publishing, Cheltenham.

Filiciak, M., Hofmokl, J., Tarkowski, A., 2012. The Circulations of Culture-On Social Distribution of Content [WWW Document]. URL https://ssrn.com/abstract=2246508, http://dx.doi.org/10.2139/ssrn.2246508 (accessed 3.04.21).

Gov.UK, 2001. Creative Industries Mapping Documents 2001 [WWW Document]. GOV.UK. URL https://www.gov.uk/government/publications/creative-industries-mapping-documents-2001 (accessed 6.13.21).

Hannaford, S. G., 2007. *Market Domination! The Impact of Industry Consolidation on Competition Innovation and Consumer Choice*. Bloomsbury Publishing USA, New York.

IFPI, 2023. *Global Music Report* [WWW Document]. IFPI. URL https://ifpi-website-cms.s3.eu-west-2.amazonaws.com/GMR_2023_State_of_the_Industry_ee2ea600e2.pdf (accessed 6.09.2023).

Rifkin, J., 2015. *The Zero Marginal Cost Society: The Internet of Things, the Collaborative Commons, and the Eclipse of Capitalism*. St. Martin's Press, New York.

Shy, O., 2004. *The Economics of Network Industries*. Cambridge University Press, Cambridge.

Stachowiak, K., 2017. *Gospodarka kreatywna i mechanizmy jej funkcjonowania: perspektywa geograficzno-ekonomiczna*. Wydawnictwo Naukowe Uniwersytetu im. Adama Mickiewicza, Poznań.

Toffler, A., 1980. *The Third Wave*. William Morrow, New York.

Towse, R., Hernández, T.N., 2020. *Handbook of Cultural Economics*. Edward Elgar Publishing, Cheltenham.

UNCTAD, 2018. *Creative Economy Outlook. Trends in International Trade in Creative Industries*. United Nations, UNCTAD, Geneva.

1 The recording industry and its environment

1.1 The recording industry: its scope within the economy

1.1.1 Constitutive elements of the recording industry

When analysing the recording industry, it is important to start by defining its scope within the economy. An industry can be described as a group of companies that produce substitute goods and services (Porter, 1980; Stonehouse, 2000) that are manufactured for the same market (Faulkner and Bowman, 1995). The three key constitutive elements of an industry are products (goods and services), companies, and markets.

A product is considered to be a commodity, service, or information consisting of a bundle of tangible and intangible attributes (features) that satisfy consumer needs and are exchanged for money or other units of value (Romanowska and Cylwik, 2004). Companies constitute the supply side of the industry. They can be categorised into leading firms and other firms, which most often imitate the strategies pursued by leading firms (Bieliński, 2006). Among the supply-side factors that determine the industry, one can mention the number of firms, their production capacity, exports, nature of competition, as well as horizontal and vertical linkages (Bieliński, 2006, p. 26).

As for the market, from the management science perspective, it is defined as a set of all potential customers who have specific needs or desires and who, seeking to satisfy those needs or desires, are willing and able to trade (Kotler, 2007). The market thus constitutes the demand side of the economic system of exchange (Stonehouse, 2000).

As the needs of customers evolve due to either changes in the industry environment or deliberate company actions, the boundaries of the market are fluid, and all these changes are also accompanied by the evolution of products. Industries evolve over time.

1.1.2 How and why industries evolve?

Industries evolve due to changes affecting their constitutive elements: products, companies, and the market. New products are introduced while

DOI: 10.4324/9781003414605-2

outdated ones are phased out. New entrants join the industry, and existing players adjust their strategies.

The factors influencing industry evolution can be categorised as either the company's controllable closer environment or the uncontrollable distant environment. The distant environment is often analysed using the PEST method (Aguilar, 1967), which considers political, economic, social, and technological factors. Political factors include, for example, the World Trade Organisation activities and international trade regulations, while economic factors encompass economic cycles and GDP trends. Social factors involve demographic shifts and consumer lifestyles, while technological factors pertain to innovation and technology transfer (Romanowska and Cylwik, 2004, p. 25). Additionally, legal and environmental factors (Porter, 1980) impact industry changes, although environmental factors have played a minor role in the recording industry's evolution.

The closer environment factors can be examined using Porter's five forces model. This model considers supplier power, buyer power, competitive rivalry, the threat of new entrants, and the threat of substitution (Porter, 1980). Factors such as concentration levels, vertical integration potential, entry barriers, economies of scale, and distribution channel access shape these forces and determine industry structure.

The international context is another significant aspect of analysing the recording industry. Like other industries, it is influenced by globalisation driven by market dynamics, cost factors, government regulations, and competition. Variables such as consumer behaviour and lifestyle evolution; distribution channel structures and marketing characteristics; economies of scale and technological advancements; trade or legal barriers; exports, imports, and global competitors shape the industry (Porter, 1980; Yip, 1995). The revolution in information and communication technology (ICT) and the globalisation of financial markets are additional influential factors.

1.2 Recording industry as part of the cultural industries

1.2.1 What is the recording industry?

The literature offers various definitions of the *recording industry*, highlighting its diverse range of music-related activities. Throsby argues that no single classification can encompass the entire scope of artistic and commercial music activities (Throsby, 2002, p. 2). Malm and Wallis refer to the *music industry* as a *complex animal*, comparable to the biological complexity of living organisms (Malm and Wallis, 1992).

The International Federation of the Phonographic Industry (IFPI)[1] often uses the terms *music industry* and *recording industry* interchangeably, covering live performances, online and physical retailers, ringtone vendors, audio equipment manufacturers, radio advertising revenues, performing rights revenues, music magazine revenues, radio subscriptions, digital player manufacturers and music publishing revenues. This reflects a particularly broad perspective.[2]

Scholars such as Longhurst and Bogdanovic, McCourt and Rothenbuhler, Negus, Frith, Shuker, Williamson and Cloonan discuss the *music industry* or *popular music* to understand the economics and politics surrounding music (Frith, 2004; Longhurst and Bogdanovic, 2014; McCourt and Rothenbuhler, 1997; Negus, 2001, 2012; Shuker, 2017; Williamson and Cloonan, 2007). They argue that the singular term *music industry* is inadequate and propose using the plural form *music industries* to capture its various sectors. The paper of Williamson and Cloonan provides examples of various music industry classifications that exist in official reports. For example, the Welsh Music Foundation distinguishes as many as 14 industries within the music industry (Williamson and Cloonan, 2007).

Hesmondhalgh divides the music industries into music recording, music publishing, and live performance (Hesmondhalgh, 1996, 2013). A similar approach is taken by Hull who suggests dividing the industry into three revenue streams, while Meisel and Sullivan distinguish between buying recordings, mass distribution, and live performances (Hull, 2004; Meisel and Sullivan, 2002, p. 17). Laing adopts a narrower definition that includes production activities, dissemination of compositions, recordings, and performances (Laing, 2009). Sun takes a different approach, using the term *music industry* for non-business aspects and *music business* specifically for the business side (Sun, 2019, p. 5).

For this book, the adopted framework is the tripartite division proposed by Hull and Hesmondhalgh, considering the recording industry as part of the broader music industry involved in phonogram production and distribution (Figure 1.1).

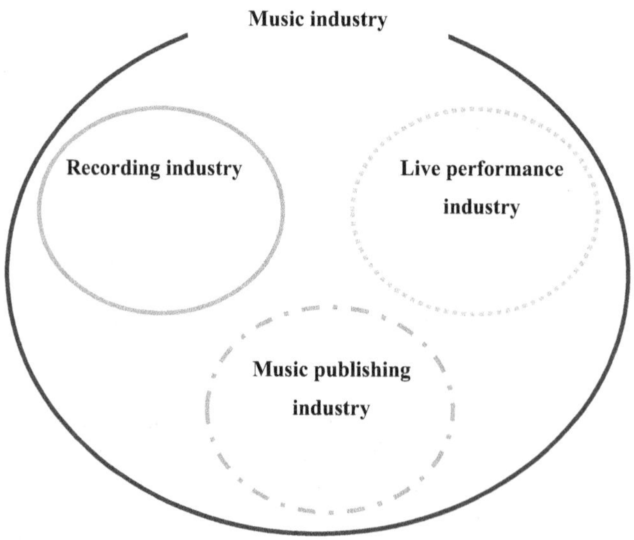

Figure 1.1 Structure of the music industry. Drawing by the author.

1.2.2 *Specific characteristics of the cultural industries*

The recording industry is part of the broader cultural industries/sectors, which share common characteristics influencing their structure and evolution (Askerud and Engelhardt, 2007; KEA, 2021; Marcus, 2009; Throsby, 2002; UNCTAD, 2010). These characteristics are summarised in Table 1.1.

Throsby (1998) notes that one feature of cultural products, including music products, is some form of intellectual property, which explains the World Intellectual Property Organisation's use of the term *copyright-based industries* (Chantepie and Le Diberder, 2010, p. 6). Wikström (2013) adopts a similar approach, arguing that it is copyright that allows for the commodification of a musical work. Intellectual property rights, along with trade, serve as the main revenue sources in the cultural and creative sectors (UNCTAD, 2008, p. 13).

The recording industry is often classified as an entertainment or leisure industry, offering personalised and accessible forms of entertainment (Hull et al., 2011; Vogel, 2011). It is also considered part of the media industries due to its integration into everyday activities, akin to reading newspapers or listening to the radio (Alexander et al., 2015, p. 44; Gronow, 1983).

These characteristics highlight the specific nature of cultural products, including recorded music. They encompass the distinction between content and carrier, especially relevant in the digital era with dematerialised carriers. Music creation is subject to intellectual property rights, and each musical product, whether a single work or an album, is a prototype with high initial costs and market risk (Curien and Moreau, 2010, p. 25) due to unpredictable consumer tastes referred to as 'nobody knows' principle (Caves, 2000, p. 3).

Table 1.1 Features of the cultural industries, based on Segers and Huijgh (2006)

	Features
1	They contain all organisations that are profit oriented or not, whose core activities are centralised around the symbolic meanings of their products (goods, services, experiences, and hybrids) that are capitalised through intellectual property rights
2	The process of (re)production, distribution, and consumption can be mediated or live, large or small scale, time and space attached, or free in different combinations
3	The cultural industries are associated with, or part of, global conglomerates
4	They are characterised by their cultural and economic ambivalences, a high capital intensity, and a strong risk factor
5	These characteristics are on the one hand consequences of the unpredictable taste of the diversified consumer (mass, niche, global, local)
6	On the other hand, they are the effect of both the uncertain outcome of the complex and intensive organisation and division of labour, that is structured around the work of relatively autonomous creative workers and of the contingency of income from the specific rewarding system, namely intellectual property rights

1.3 What is the product of the recording industry?

1.3.1 Terms used

The recording industry produces recordings, also known as *phonograms*,[3] which involve capturing music on a tangible carrier. Throughout its history, due to the technological changes, music has been recorded on various mediums, such as shellac discs, vinyl discs, cassettes, CDs, and, more recently, digital files. It is important to note that while these carriers play a role, the music itself is the essential component of a music product.

To avoid confusion, the terms *record*, *recording*, *phonogram*, *music product*, or *recorded music* will be used interchangeably in this book. Specific names of music carriers, such as *compact disc* (CD), *long-playing disc* (vinyl record or LP), *single*, *mp3*, as well as terms like *album*, *track*, or *digital file*, will also be used.

1.3.2 Recording as a subject of copyright and related rights

Recorded music is protected by intellectual property law, specifically copyright law (Lévêque and Ménière, 2003, p. 7).

Copyright law

Copyright law can be categorised into two main systems: the Anglo-Saxon system, known as copyright, and the European system derived from French *droit d'auteur*. European copyright is divided into moral rights and property rights. Moral rights pertain to authorship and decisions regarding the work's distribution and are non-transferable. Property rights, on the other hand, are transferable and limited in time. Under the Anglo-Saxon system, copyright may be granted to producers or publishers, while in the European system, it is granted to individuals.

Based on Benhamou and Farchy (2014).

The Berne Convention, the first international agreement on the protection of literary and artistic works, states that works must be fixed in a material form to be protected (WIPO, 1928, art.2 pt 2). The protection is for the benefit of the author and their successors (WIPO, 1928, art.2 pt 6). Following the provisions of the convention:

> the author shall have the right to claim authorship of the work and to object to any distortion, mutilation or other modification of, or other derogatory action in relation to, the said work, which would be prejudicial to his honour or reputation.
>
> (WIPO, 1928, art.6 bis pt 1)

Authors also have the exclusive right, i.e., monopoly, to dispose of their work, such as transferring economic copyright, licensing its use, and exploiting it in various fields (Benhamou and Farchy, 2014, pp. 23–24; WIPO, 1928, art. 10–12).

In the recording industry, authors and performers typically enter into contracts with phonogram producers or music publishing companies, in which they transfer the economic copyright of their works. This grants the producer or music publishing company the exclusive right to dispose of the work and receive remuneration for its use. Copyright protection is limited in time, expiring 70 years after the author's death in the European Union (EU, 2011), after which the work enters the public domain.

Related rights protect artistic performances, phonograms, and broadcasts. They also cover phonogram producers (music labels) and broadcasters (radio and television stations). The phonogram itself, containing the musical work and its fixation, is considered a protected form of sound recording (Piesiewicz, 2009, p. 61).

Copyright and related rights holders are entitled to remuneration when their works are used in various fields of exploitation. This includes reproduction, marketing, lending or renting the original copies, public performance, exhibition, broadcasting, and making the work available to the public. Remuneration (royalties) due to rights holders are divided into performance royalties, synchronisation royalties, and mechanical royalties (Wikström, 2013, p. 57).

Collecting societies play a vital role in the collection and distribution of fees and remuneration to rights holders. They handle the complex task of collecting payments and ensuring fair distribution to a large number of artists, reducing transaction costs associated with individual licensing (Wikström, 2013, p. 57).

1.3.3 Phonogram as an experience good

Phonograms, as products of the recording industry, fall under the category of experience goods (Byun, 2016, p. 23; Nelson, 1970), which are goods that consumers evaluate only after consuming them. This implies that consumers are more inclined to purchase recordings they are already familiar with in order to minimise the risk of dissatisfaction. They may become acquainted with the product through media exposure or by relying on the reputation of successful artists. This characteristic has significant implications for the marketing strategies employed by recording companies and the emergence of new business models in the digital era.

Experience good

The concept of experience goods was introduced by economist Nelson (1970), and today, there are various interpretations of this notion (Towse, 2019, p. 151). Nelson identified the inability to assess the quality of experience goods prior to purchase as a fundamental characteristic. He distinguished experience goods from search goods and emphasised the role of information in the decision-making process. Search goods are tangible goods for which consumers can gather information or rely on previous experience (Andersson and Andersson, 2006, p. 83). However, cultural goods, including musical works, differ from one another, making it challenging for consumers to rely solely on experience or provided information. Taste and preferences play a significant role in the consumption of experience goods, and measuring music consumption becomes complex due to the multidimensional and subjective nature of utility.

Based on Frej (2014).

1.3.4 Costs associated with the production of a recording

When discussing recordings, it is important to consider the costs involved in their production. In the case of music content, there are significant fixed costs that are considered sunk costs (Vogel, 2011, p. 10). These fixed costs constitute approximately 75% of the total costs, mainly because music products are prototype goods. The majority of expenses are incurred in producing the first copy, while reproduction on carriers becomes relatively inexpensive (Curien and Moreau, 2010, p. 25; Shy, 2004). These costs are sunk because there is a high risk associated with the market success of these products (Caves, 2000, p. 3). In the recording industry, only one in ten records released achieve commercial success, making financing the production a challenging endeavour.

As for the carrier, it has undergone significant evolution over the recording industry's history, transitioning from shellac records to compact discs. With the advent of the digital revolution, the carrier has 'dematerialised,' resulting in a minimisation of the use of tangible mediums to store information.

1.3.5 Categorisation of music products

Music products can be categorised based on the carrier used to record the sound (Table 1.2).

These products can be seen as imperfect substitutes since they involve different recording technologies, whether analogue or digital and utilise different carriers. Despite this, they fulfil a common consumer need – the desire to listen to music – while also catering to individual needs such as mobility or improved sound quality.

Another approach to understanding the product in the recording industry is to consider the artist as the product or brand. In this perspective, the

Table 1.2 Categorisation of music products according to medium

Product type	*Features*
Shellac disc, 78 rpm disc	It was invented by E. Berliner at the end of the 19th century; the first discs were made from various materials, but shellac was the one that remained in use for the longest time; however, these discs were very fragile and could only hold five minutes of music, so longer pieces had to be split up into several discs, which were called an album, a name that is still used in the industry today, although it refers to a set of pieces of music on a single carrier (physical or digital).
Vinyl disc, analogue record, LP, 33 1/3 rpm disc	It was introduced to the market in the late 1940s and early 1950s; sales of vinyl records fell sharply from 1.2 billion units to just 128 million between 1981 and 1992, when they almost ceased to be produced; they were replaced by the compact disc; today, the LP is enjoying a renaissance, as some popular novelties as well as classics of various musical genres (e.g., jazz, rock classics or simply classical music) are released on vinyl.
Single disc, 45 rpm disc	It was introduced alongside a LP; popular until albums began to be released as an elaborate whole; the seminal album that blew the popularity of singles was *Sgt. Pepper's Lonely Hearts Club Band* by The Beatles, was released in 1967; from then on, 45 rpm records were used exclusively to promote LPs, which was particularly noticeable in the United States; as early as 1975, singles' share of sales had fallen below 8%.
Cassette	It was introduced on the market in 1964; the number of recorded cassettes produced each year in the United States between 1970 and 1980 is estimated to have been the same as LPs; in 1992, cassette sales reached 1.551 billion units; today it is a medium that is almost no longer used.
Compact disc, CD	It was marketed in 1982; by 1986, 50 million were already sold; by 1992, sales reached 1.152 billion units and the value of almost $30 billion (Anderton et al., 2013, p. 29); at the turn of the 20th century, CD sales began to drop sharply when the digital music files arrived.
Digital formats, e.g., mp3	It appeared on the market in 1990; the carrier here can be easily separated from the content, although it is needed to store it; a more detailed description of these formats is provided in the following chapters.

Based on Anderton et al. (2013), Burnett (2010), Ferstler (2005), Janowska (2008), Kominek (1986), Tournès (2012).

product becomes a complex entity comprised of various works by the artist that contribute to their overall value. This concept forms the basis of the star system model predominantly employed by major recording companies. Further discussion on this topic will be presented later in the book.

1.3.6 Quality of the music product

The quality of a music product encompasses various aspects. Firstly, the quality of the carrier and recording itself can be objectively measured and assessed by informed consumers. Some audiophiles may prioritise these technical aspects and base their choices on the reputation of the recording company.[4] Others may consider factors such as ease of use, mobility, or personalisation when selecting among different carriers. However, for many casual consumers, technical issues are of little importance and their choices are guided by other criteria.

On the other hand, the quality of the music itself is a subjective matter that is challenging to quantify. Comparing diverse genres or objectively measuring artists' talent is difficult due to the absence of objective tools (Curien and Moreau, 2010, p. 56; Fort, 2000; Hamlen, 1994, 1991; Krueger, 2005; Rosen, 1981). Therefore, music quality is often perceived as the match between consumer tastes and the genre of music offered, referred to as *matching*. The industry aims to achieve the best possible match, ensuring that the music generates significant interest from the audience. However, this task is challenging since consumer tastes evolve over time. The UK Monopolies and Mergers Commission acknowledges:

> [...] record sales can be defined as a fad industry, where styles are constantly changing. When music catches the taste of a large audience, sales increase [...] but when consumers get bored with a genre, sales decline until a new genre catches their interest. There are, however, musical categories (e.g., classical music and mainstream rock) for which demand is relatively stable.
>
> (MMC, 1994, p. 77)

1.4 Companies in the recording industry

1.4.1 Between a label and a major

Apart from the product, another constitutive element of the recording industry is the companies that produce phonograms, commonly known as *labels*. These labels can be referred to by various terms in the literature, such as *record company* (Huygens et al., 2001, p. 25; Wikström, 2013), *phonogram company* (Burnett, 2010, p. 18), *majors* (Strasser, 2010, p. 84; Vogel, 2011, p. 230), *independent record company* (Mol et al., 2005), or *independent label* (Burnett, 2010, p. 59; Vogel, 2011, p. 230).

According to the *Encyclopedia of Recorded Sound*, the term *label* is used to describe a recording company or a part of it (Hoffmann, 2005, p. 593). Gałuszka (2009, pp. 50–54) suggests using the term *recording company* for large and medium-sized companies, while *label* can be used for very small entities. The definition provided by Curien and Moreau

(2010, p. 15) distinguishes a *label* as a brand used to commercialise artistically homogeneous products, while a *major* refers to a large, transnational recording company that often controls the entire production and distribution cycle. This description highlights the nature of labels, which corresponds to both historical and contemporary perspectives on these companies. In the early days of the recording industry, labels primarily focused on specific genres of music. For example, Blue Note was known for producing jazz music, Capitol Records for country and blues music, and Motown Records for soul music (Coleman, 2005).

The status of recording companies operating in the market varies in importance. Curien and Moreau (2010) differentiate among *majors*, *integrated/dependent labels* owned by large record companies, *labels under license* owned by independent producers with licensing agreements, *labels in distribution* that have signed distribution agreements, and *independent labels*, often referred to as *indies*, which have no affiliation with major companies. Passman (2015) and Gałuszka (2009) propose a similar classification, while Anderton et al. (2013) add *pseudo-independent labels* created by majors but distributed by independent distributors, *microlabels* established by artists with support from fan networks, and *online labels* exclusively releasing and distributing music online. Additionally, there are *netlabels* (Gałuszka, 2012a) that offer music for free download with the option to support the artists.

1.4.2 *Structure and ways of operating of the large recording companies (majors)*

The large recording companies, known as *majors*, currently consist of three transnational companies: Warner Music Group, Sony Music Entertainment, and Universal Music Group.

EMI

In 2012, the recording industry consisted of four major companies: Universal Music Group, Sony Music, Warner Music Group, and EMI. However, EMI was later acquired by Universal.

EMI was established in 1931 through the merger of Gramophone Co. and Columbia Gramophone Co., Ltd. This merger created the largest recording company at the time, with control over 50 factories in 19 countries. The merger was a response to the significant losses the industry had suffered during the Great Depression. One of EMI's early initiatives was the establishment of The Abbey Road studio, where iconic albums by The Beatles were recorded. EMI also obtained patents for stereo recording.

Based on Hoffmann and Ferstler (2005).

A major record company is a comprehensive entity that controls the manufacturing, marketing, and distribution of products, as well as artist signings and recording production (Laing, 2009, p. 23). These companies have subsidiaries in key markets, possess an international distribution network, and are part of broader structures involved in music publishing, film, radio and television networks, and audio/video electronic equipment production. They also oversee groups of subsidiary labels and provide services to independent labels. The basic structure is presented in the Figure 1.2.

Majors are part of larger structures, such as media conglomerates, within the macro-environment of the recording industry. They occupy the top position in the hierarchy. For instance, Universal Music Group is part of the holding company Vivendi ("Nos activités. Musique," 2020), which also owns TV stations, film studios, publishing houses, and has ties to the video game sector. Sony Music Entertainment, previously known as Sony BMG Music Entertainment, is a subsidiary of the multinational Sony ("Corporate History," 2020), renowned for its consumer electronics production and ownership of film and television studios, as well as involvement in consumer electronics manufacturing and video game consoles. Warner Music Group, formerly under Time Warner Inc., is now part of the conglomerate Warner Bros. Discovery, which encompasses television stations, film studios, and video game production, among other ventures ("Our Brands," 2022).

A music group primarily consists of a music publishing company, which manages the rights to the musical works it owns, and a recording company (referred to as the record group in the figure). The recording company owns various labels or groups of labels, often specialising in specific musical genres. For instance, Deutsche Grammophon, owned by Universal Music Group, is a renowned producer of classical music.

The most significant departments within a recording company are the artists & repertoire department (A&R) and the marketing department (Hull et al., 2011). The A&R department traditionally handles talent scouting, supervises the recording process, and negotiates contracts with artists (Burnett, 2010, p. 74). Scouting involves actively observing the music scene (concerts) and passively reviewing demo recordings, which labels receive in large quantities on a weekly basis. The department assists artists in selecting their repertoire and organises the recording process. Independent producers often collaborate with artists, fulfilling similar functions to the A&R department at recording companies, including assisting in repertoire and style selection, overseeing the budget for rehearsal, recording, mixing, and album production (Vogel, 2011, p. 242). They may also be involved in album cover preparation.

The marketing department is typically the largest unit within a recording company and is responsible for delivering phonograms to consumers through wholesalers and retailers, as well as attracting consumer attention to the label's products. This is achieved through promoting recordings for radio and television broadcast, launching advertising campaigns in press and retail outlets, and securing appearances of promoted artists on television

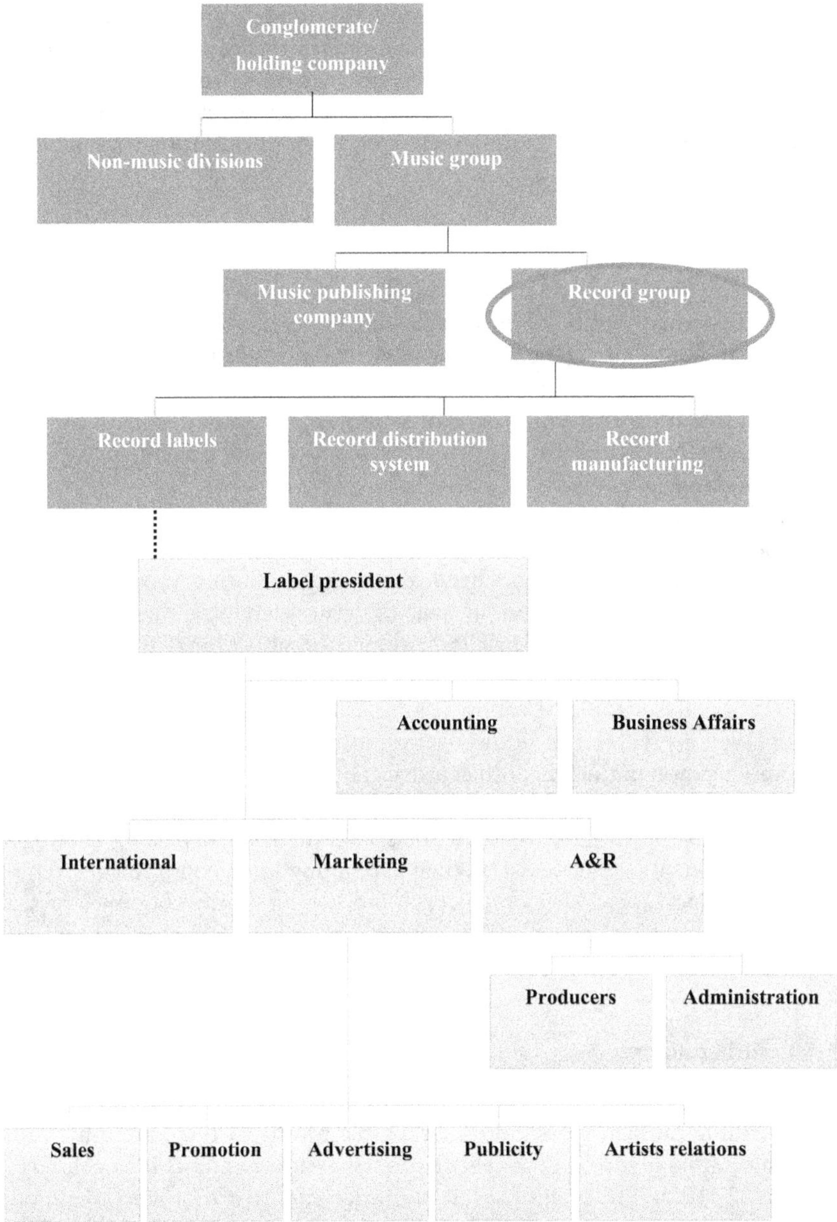

Figure 1.2 Typical structure of a large recording company. Based on Hull (2004, pp. 131–132).

and radio programs. The publicity department prepares press releases, artist information kits (including biographies and photographs), and ensures that promoted artists are invited to participate in television and radio programs. Some of these responsibilities may be delegated to artists' managers.

The artist relations department supervises the artists' career progression and coordinates the work of other units. Personnel in this department closely collaborate with managers, ensuring the coherence of artists' image and label's marketing activities. Additionally, in certain contracts, the department may handle live performances as they serve as a form of promotion for recorded music.

1.4.3 Specificities of small labels

Although the organisational structure described above primarily applies to large labels, small entities follow a similar pattern, with individuals taking on specific functions. Depending on their relations with the majors, small labels retain some autonomy in different areas, e.g., talent scouting, recording production, distribution, or promotion (Laing, 2009, p. 23). Whether independent or owned by majors, labels possess several advantages that majors leverage.

Firstly, their proximity to the market allows them to understand and respond to changing consumer tastes. Majors often acquire small labels to enter specific market segments rather than exploring unknown niches. Secondly, their specialisation in specific genres enables them to identify promising artists. Thirdly, their streamlined organisational structure facilitates swift decision-making processes. These characteristics position small labels as catalysts for innovation (Laing, 2009, p. 22). Independent labels have played a pivotal role in discovering talents like Elvis Presley, rock and roll, and hip-hop in the late 20th century. They serve as the A&R department for majors, scouting and testing new talent while shouldering the risks and costs of investing in new trends. Labels also manage their song catalogues and the careers of signed artists. When expanding into geographically remote markets to increase chances of success and benefit from economies of scale (Henriksson and Janowska, 2023), labels often outsource physical and digital distribution to majors (Curien and Moreau, 2010, p. 20).

1.5 Other actors

Alongside the recording companies mentioned earlier, which play a role in transforming musical works into marketable products, there are other indispensable actors involved in the entire process (Hull et al., 2011; Vogel, 2011). Burnett (2010, p. 70) categorises industry actors into artists who create popular cultural artefacts and others who develop these artefacts into marketable items. Similarly, Power and Hallencreutz (2007) distinguish between the aesthetic and industrial aspects of production. The industrial part includes session musicians who record music in studios, sound engineers who control the recording process, record producers who finalise the product, distribution agents involved in digital distribution, and media programmers who promote songs through various channels (Hull et al., 2011). Parikh (1999) presents an organisational diagram of the recording industry, illustrating the positions of

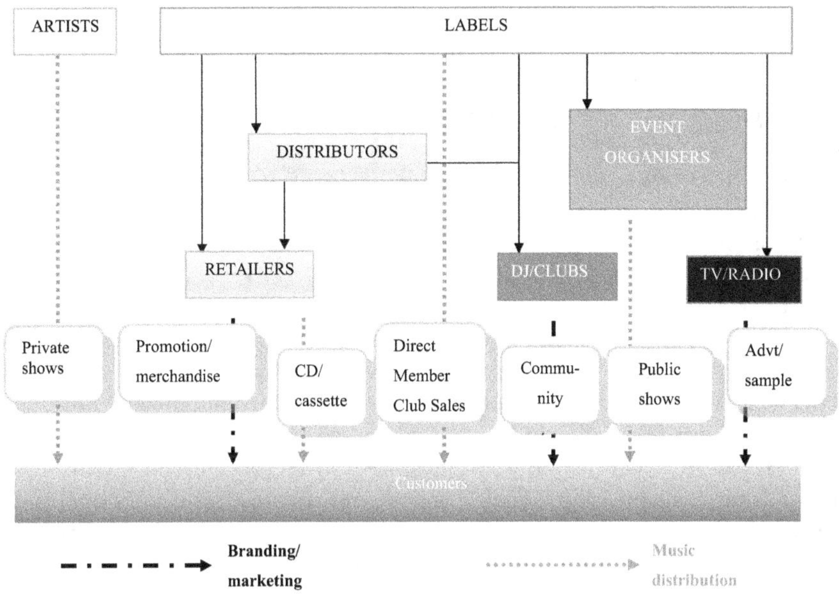

Figure 1.3 Structure of the recording industry in the pre-digital shape. Based on Parikh (1999).

various actors, their functions, and the relationships between them, which is shown in Figure 1.3.

The diagram illustrates the movement of music from artists to consumers in a traditional, non-digital system. It highlights the involvement of recording labels, distributors, retailers, DJs in clubs, and media programmers (referring to radio and television) as intermediaries responsible for distribution and promotion within the system. In the digital environment, new intermediaries such as global platforms have emerged, facilitating the distribution of music in digital form. Consumers, particularly prosumers, also play a role in the system by engaging in music reviews and recommendations to enhance the value of the final product.

1.6 Consumers of recorded music

The demand side of the phonographic market consists of individual music consumers and entities that utilise music for their own products, such as radio stations and music television acting to some extent as gatekeepers (Burnett, 2010, p. 81).

1.6.1 Who consumes music and in what ways?

Individual music consumers are diverse in terms of their tastes, behaviours, and resources allocated to purchasing phonograms. Nielsen conducted a study in 2013 among consumers in the United States, categorising them into different groups based on their music consumption patterns (Nielsen, 2013). These groups include *aficionado fans* who discover new artists and genres, buy music in various formats, including physical ones and act as trendsetters; *digital fans* who rely on online platforms and social media for music discovery, preferring to follow popular choices rather than discovering new music on their own; *big box fans* who consume popular genres known from advertising, video games, and films and for whom price is important in their choices; *occasional concert consumers* who listen to music outside their homes and enjoy live performances; *ambivalent consumers* who have limited interest in music and listen to music principally on free online stations but may pay for unique content; and *background music consumers* who casually listen to free content without actively seeking out music sources. Aficionado fans tend to be the highest spenders, while background music consumers spend the least.

In addition to individual attributes, several factors influence consumers' purchasing decisions. Household income, product price, product quality are the basic determinants shaping demand. Prices of substitute and complementary goods and the demographic structure of buyers also play important roles.

Regarding the income elasticity and the concept of Maslow's needs hierarchy, it is worth noting that music is considered a high-level need in the pyramid. Therefore, during unfavourable economic climates and declining household incomes, sales of recorded music also tend to decrease (Passman, 2015, pp. 105–106). This effect is evident in the sales of cultural products during the Great Depression in the 1930s (Seaman, 2006). Research conducted in the UK also suggests that the impact of income on music purchases is more significant compared to current consumption (MMC, 1994).

The consumer response to changes in prices of recorded music is multifaceted. Firstly, studies indicate that demand for recordings with the same content, such as the same title by the same artist, is typically inelastic (Hull et al., 2011; Seaman, 2006). However, one effective strategy employed by record labels to combat record piracy has been to lower album prices (Curien and Moreau, 2010, p. 49).

Secondly, the price can be a significant factor for different carriers. For certain consumers, the recording quality and additional features like mobility, comfort of use, and durability may be irrelevant. In such cases, CDs, vinyl, and cassettes are considered perfect substitutes, and price becomes a more important criterion for choice. However, for other consumers, these features may hold more importance than price, leading them to opt for higher quality and more expensive products.

Price elasticity is influenced by various product characteristics, including the artist's status and the release date. These factors are reflected in three price categories for music products (Gałuszka, 2009, p. 171):

- standard price (full price) applies to new releases and popular records;
- mid-price, set at around 60%–70% of the standard price, is used for older or less popular recordings;

- budget price, approximately 50% of the standard price, is assigned to products with lower potential, such as compilations or older recordings, including classical music.

The majority of sales are generated by albums sold at the standard price. The price category serves as an indicator to consumers of the product's newness and popularity. Therefore, labels do not engage in price competition with each other, as it may have a negative impact on sales (Boorstin, 2004, p. 20; MMC, 1994, p. 26).

Furthermore, demand tends to be inelastic when it comes to recordings by different artists. Typically, consumers seeking an album by a specific artist will not substitute it with a cheaper album by another artist (Gałuszka, 2009, p. 162). However, for some consumers, the genre rather than the specific artist is the determining factor, making albums imperfect substitutes and demand more elastic. A similar phenomenon can be observed in the context of classical music, where consumers often prioritise the name of the composer over the performer. Some labels, like Naxos, leverage this effect by releasing recordings by lesser-known conductors and orchestras at lower prices (Bernstein et al., 2007, p. 12).

The price of complementary goods also influences consumer choices and sales volume. In the case of recorded music, CDs and CD players serve as complementary goods, and their pricing can impact consumers' willingness to purchase music in those formats. For example, in 1983, a year after the introduction of CDs, the price of CD players in Japan dropped to $500, resulting in increased consumer interest in CDs (Kominek, 1986, pp. 215–216). Sony, in an effort to boost CD sales, launched portable CD players (Discmans) in 1984, priced at around $200. This move led to a surge in CD sales, prompting other CD player manufacturers to lower their prices. Consequently, sales of CD players increased, the number of CD titles available expanded, and the recording industry as a whole began to recover from a previous decline.

Another factor that influences the demand for recorded music is the evolution of complementary goods due to technological advancements (Throsby, 2002, p. 9). Portable cassette and CD players, such as Walkmans and Discmans, allowed individuals to listen to music while engaging in outdoor activities like walking, running, or traveling. The portability of these devices increased the amount of time people could spend listening to music, leading to a growth in demand. According to IFPI report (2019), up to 70% of surveyed consumers reported listening to music in their cars.

The demographic structure of phonogram buyers also plays a role in music consumption patterns. Boorstin (2004, p. 27) reports that, in terms of physical formats, young people between 15 and 24 years old tend to purchase the most records, while those aged over 45 purchase the least. Vogel (2011, p. 13) similarly highlights that teenagers are significant purchasers of recorded music. In the realm of digital music consumption, the demographic pattern differs slightly. The largest consumer group consists of individuals aged 31–40, followed by those aged 41–50, with the group of users aged

16–30 trailing behind. The other age groups exhibit lower levels of digital music consumption (Aguiar and Martens, 2016).

Taste is another influential factor in the consumer's decision to purchase music (Hull et al., 2011, pp. 178–180). McCain (2003) asserts that subjective feelings impact consumer preferences for specific goods, and these preferences vary among individuals. The exposure to an artist through media presence and concert attendance, as well as the artist's prior album success, also play a role. Elements that shape taste include the consumer's investment in developing their musical preferences, the social context, and trends (Caves, 2000, p. 173). Hennion (2005, p. 9) argues that taste is not inherent but rather constructed through experiences and interactions, stating that it is formed, not given, it is an endeavour, it is constructed from what happens, it is not an assertion of external reality.

The consumption of creative goods is also influenced by the effect of experience and learning by consuming, namely cultural consumption capital (Caves, 2000, p. 176), also known as cultural capital (Bourdieu, 1979). This cultural capital enables consumers to make more informed decisions and maximise their utility (Towse, 2019). Consumers build their cultural capital through factors such as the time spent listening to music, education, and interactions with others who possess knowledge and appreciation for music. The role of recognised experts in a particular field is significant, as their expertise and experience can ensure the quality of the creative goods purchased. However, Holbrook (2005, p. 76) argues that, at the moment of choice, the influence of *herd effect* and preferences for less valuable products often prevail.

Cultural (consumption) capital is closely related to the concept of *rational addiction*, as proposed by Becker et al. (1991), Becker and Murphy (1988), and Castiglione and Infante (2016). This theory suggests that the more pleasure a consumer has derived from using a product in the past, the more inclined they will be to continue using it in the future. Therefore creative goods, including music, do not adhere to the law of diminishing marginal utility commonly observed in most goods.

Contrary to the theory presented by Stigler and Becker in their article *De Gustibus Non Est Disputandum* (1977), the preferences for cultural goods are not static over time. Levy-Garboua and Montmarquette (2011) have shown that taste for experience goods, including music, is influenced by various factors, such as the amount of time dedicated to consuming these goods.

Caves (2000, p. 175) argues that "creative goods are consumed in a social context, not by isolated hermits." Consumer decisions are significantly influenced by what others are buying, leading to phenomena like the *bandwagon effect* (Leibenstein, 1950), *herd effect*, mimeticism, or fads. Consumers often choose certain music based on brand associations and lifestyle considerations (Frith, 2017). This phenomenon is also known as *ostentatious consumption* (Towse, 2019; Veblen, 2016), wherein consumers listen to specific music due to social norms. The impact of social influence on consumption can either reinforce or inhibit consumption, depending on whether individual preferences align with the norm (Andersson and Andersson, 2006).

As music is an experience good, consumers often rely on the herd effect to reduce the costs associated with searching for information and minimise the risk of dissatisfaction. Sampling plays a crucial role in this context, allowing consumers to listen to a piece of music before making a purchase, which is called *sampling effect* (Liebowitz, 1985) or *consumer exposure to music effect* (Hull et al., 2011). Media platforms serve also as experts or advisors (Benhamou, 2008, p. 18), as it is commonly believed that only works deserving of attention are broadcasted and promoted. Hence, objective information from the media and experts resolves consumers' information problem and provides more reliable references than direct product advertising from producers. In the digital era, recommendation systems and consumer opinions about the product play a vital role (to be discussed further in Chapter 3).

A similar effect is observed with respect to the artist's status or brand, which serves as a guarantee of quality. It is evident that if previous works have gained recognition, the subsequent ones are likely to be of interest. Artist status operates in conjunction with the mechanisms described above.

These elements are directly related to the characteristics of the consumer, particularly whether they are fans or casual consumers (Gans, 2011). Fans form a devoted *tribe* around their favourite artist (Maffesoli, 2019; Owsinski, 2014) and invest more time and resources into building higher cultural capital. Casual consumers have lower cultural capital as they have dedicated fewer resources to its development. Casual consumers' capital is lower, they seek direct satisfaction from experiencing cultural goods, displaying less emotional involvement in the product and the circumstances surrounding its consumption. They pay less attention to quality and novelty, with the exception of young people who tend to be particularly sensitive to new products (Caves, 2000, p. 185).

1.6.2 Consumers – programmers

For the recording industry, radio and television play a crucial role as programmers. Radio stations rely on recordings to fill their airtime, which is a cost-effective solution compared to producing other programs (Burnett, 2010, p. 81). The significance of music for radio is evident in the fact that the nature of a radio station is defined by the music it broadcasts, known as the radio format. In many radio stations, music accounts for more than 80% of their broadcast time (Kowalski, 2006, pp. 179–199). The attractiveness of the programming, primarily music, determines the size of a radio station's audience and its ability to attract advertisers to finance its activities. The audience size is a crucial factor that influences potential advertisers' expenditure on media advertising.

As a result, radio stations carefully select the music they include in their playlists. The selection process is based on four approaches within the radio format (Ahlkvist and Faulkner, 2002):

- subjective approach: programmers choose new and interesting artists based on their own taste and experience;
- objective approach: station managers rely on research about the preferences of their target audience, resulting in fewer new artists being featured on the radio;
- populist approach: programmers empathise with the tastes of their audience and select songs that align with their preferences; this decision is not supported by market research but is based on the proximity between the program authors and the audience;
- synergy method: radio stations collaborate with record companies in selecting the repertoire, benefiting both parties.[5]

Producers are eager to have their music played on radio and television because increased airtime increases the likelihood of listeners purchasing the recordings (Frith, 2017, p. 202). Media platforms, therefore, act as gatekeepers, determining which products are admitted for promotion.

The same applies to the use of recordings in other cultural or creative products such as films, TV series, video games, or advertisements. Placing songs by well-known artists in these products boosts the sales of recorded music. For example, the soundtrack of the James Bond film *Skyfall* by Adele contributed to the song entering Billboard's top 10 chart and receiving an Oscar nomination (Szalai, 2013). Another older example is the global success of the song *Lambada* by the French band Kaoma, which gained popularity worldwide, in part due to a video clip created to promote the Orangina brand (García, 2006). Statistics indicate that revenue from music publishing, which manages the rights to songs for use in other cultural and creative products, is on an upward trend (Statista, 2020; Towse, 2017).

1.7 Macro-environment factors and the evolution of the recording industry

The macro-environment of the recording industry is influenced by various economic, social, political, legal, and technological factors, all of which have played a significant role in its evolution, from its inception to the digital and ICT breakthroughs. While technology is often viewed as the primary driver of change, these other factors have also had a substantial impact.

In terms of economic factors, two significant crises affected the global economy in the 20th century. The first was the Great Depression of the 1930s and the second was the crisis of the late 1970s, which resulted in a decline in household purchasing power. These economic downturns led to a decrease in phonogram sales and the closure of many smaller record companies.

Political factors have also influenced the industry, including two world wars and the establishment of the GATT, which later led to the formation of the WTO. These events have particularly strengthened the position of the US recording industry and increased the share of American music in global recording sales. They also brought about a new paradigm for the industry.

Social factors have played a role as well, including demographic changes and shifts in people's lifestyles due to economic and political transformations.

Legal developments have been crucial, especially in the realm of intellectual property law, particularly copyright, which serves as the foundation for all cultural industries (Benhamou and Farchy, 2014; Hartley et al., 2013; Throsby, 1998).

1.7.1 The recording industry in the context of economic changes

The evolution of the recording industry has been influenced by various economic factors, including global crises and periods of economic prosperity. Janowska (2011) highlights the impact of these global crises on the industry, while Vogel (2011) points out the cyclical fluctuations in demand for recorded music, which align with general economic trends. During recessions, the growth in the industry tends to be lower compared to the overall trend, whereas consumer spending on music is typically highest at the peak of economic activity or shortly thereafter. This pattern results in the lowest values occurring a few months later, after the general minimum period.

During the Great Depression, the recording industry faced its first major crisis. The crash of the US stock market in 1929 had a significant impact on industrialised countries like the United States and Germany. Jachowicz (2009, p. 11) states that the GDP of these countries fell by 25%–30% between 1928 and 1932. Industrial production also declined, by 40% in the United States and 11% in England. This economic downturn led to bankruptcies and increased unemployment, causing a sharp decline in record sales due to reduced household purchasing power. In the United States, record sales plummeted to 6 million records and 40,000 gramophones in 1932, a significant drop compared to sales in 1927. In the British market, which was the largest in Europe at that time, sales of the two main companies, Gramophone Co. and Columbia Graphophone Co., declined from £1.5 million to £160,000 between 1928 and 1930 (Kominek, 1986).

The crisis had a particularly detrimental effect on small recording companies, which specialised exclusively in recording music. These companies, with limited financial resources, had to outsource pressing to larger companies that also produced recording equipment and mass-market disc-playing devices. The decline in household purchasing power made it impossible for these small companies to recover from the slump, as they had no alternative revenue source (Gronow, 1983, p. 62). In response, major record labels implemented strategies to cope with the crisis, which was concentration. This led to the formation of the first 'empires of sound' (Bishop,

2005) resulting in the oligopoly structure that persists in the industry today. Major companies started merging, such as the merger of British companies Gramophone – His Master's Voice and Columbia, which gave rise to the major label EMI. They also acquired other important European companies like Lindström and Pathé, as well as smaller independent companies. Additionally, large companies from unrelated industries entered the recording industry, such as the radio network RCA purchasing the Victor label and the US part of Columbia being owned by CBS, who needed music for their radio programs (Frith, 2017).

Another response to the decline in record sales was a reduction in prices, leading to a price war. However, this strategy did not yield the expected increase in sales. Decca, a new player in the recording market, proposed a different approach by employing aggressive press and billboard advertising (Frith, 2017). They capitalised on the cost breakdown of record production, focusing on a small number of projects performed by renowned artists and extensively promoting them to maximise sales. This strategy aimed to maximise sales rather than profit, concentrating on economies of scale and intense marketing, which gave large companies a competitive advantage. Radio networks played a crucial role in directing public attention towards selected artists.

In the 1950s and 1960s, developed countries experienced a significant economic boom. The United States had an average growth rate of 3.7%, Germany had 5.9%, and England lagged behind with 2.8% annual growth (Jachowicz, 2009, p. 18). This economic prosperity, coupled with technological advancements and social changes, propelled the vinyl record to become a mass-produced and widely purchased product in industrialised nations. Sales growth rates reached up to 20% annually, with approximately 1.5 billion records sold worldwide in 1975 (Tournès, 2012, p. 76). The higher price of the product contributed to increased sales revenue and improved profit margins.

Another crisis struck the recording industry in the late 1970s, attributed to factors such as the oil crisis and declining household purchasing power (Tschmuck, 2014). The emergence of alternative entertainment options like video games and videotapes further contributed to the decline in music sales. To combat the recession, the industry adopted a strategy similar to the previous crisis, focusing on heavy marketing of a select few stars through radio, MTV, and films. This resulted in a decrease in the diversity of music offerings, with significantly fewer new albums released annually. During the 1970s, approximately 4,000–5,000 new albums were released each year, but by the 1980s, this number had dropped to around 2,000 (Frith, 2017). The industry's recovery began in 1982, and by 1984, record sales started to gradually rebound. A peak in the industry was reached in 1988, with record sales in the United States and Canada reaching their highest levels ever.

Economic factors play a significant role in the development of the recording industry, particularly during periods of economic downturn when household purchasing power diminishes. Record companies actively seek solutions to recover lost revenue by turning to technological innovations to reduce production costs. They also employ strategies to outpace competitors, such as horizontal concentration to strengthen their market share and the introduction of new business models that leverage alternative distribution channels and more effective promotional methods. These actions lead to substantial changes in both the operations of recording companies and the overall structure of the industry.

1.7.2 Politics and the recording industry

The world wars had a significant impact on the development of the recording industry, influencing it politically, economically, and technologically. During the First World War, European recording companies shifted their production to support the war effort, leading to a decline in the number of phonograms released. However, music records played a crucial role as a propaganda tool, with thousands of songs conveying patriotic messages being recorded and distributed, both to soldiers on the front lines and to civilians (Watkins, 2003).

The war had a particularly profound effect on European recording companies, paving the way for the rise of American dominance in the industry. European record factories and equipment were destroyed, and the absence of potential consumers on the front lines further hindered sales. Meanwhile, the United States witnessed the emergence of numerous new record producers, with around 200 companies publishing approximately 2 million records annually by the war's end (Tournès, 2012, p. 40). The flourishing American recording industry can be attributed not only to the weakened European phonography but also to the trade blockade between the continents. This forced US companies to focus on local artists who catered to diverse racial and national audiences, representing a substantial portion of the population and a promising new market segment.

The Second World War had a significant impact on the European recording industry, leading to reduced production and various challenges. Firstly, recordings were used as propaganda tools, both displeasing and exploited by the occupiers. For example, the Polish Syrena Record[6] label, owned by Jewish entrepreneurs, was closed down by the German occupier (Lerski, 2004).

Secondly, there was a shortage of raw materials for record production, particularly shellac, which was imported from Asia. The war disrupted the supply chain, and existing shellac reserves were mostly seized for military purposes. As a result, smaller shellac records with a short duration of only four minutes were produced, but they were too fragile and eventually replaced by vinyl records.

Meanwhile, in the United States, the recording industry was recovering from the Great Depression. By 1940, record sales reached 100 million in the United States (Huygens et al., 2001, p. 22). The industry's growth was supported by initiatives to boost the morale of the US military deployed worldwide. Special songs were recorded and distributed to the armed forces, broadcasted through the American Forces Network in conflict zones (Tournès, 2012, p. 68). It was during this time that American dominance in the music industry was solidified.

Another significant political factor that shaped the cultural and recording industries was the General Agreement on Tariffs and Trade (GATT) and its Final Act, signed during the Uruguay Round. This led to the establishment of the World Trade Organization (WTO) and the signing of the Agreement on Trade-Related Aspects of Intellectual Property Rights (TRIPs) (Gagné, 2011; Throsby, 2010, p. 10). The GATT aimed to eliminate barriers to international trade, but it did not provide an exception for cultural production (Janowska, 2012; Strasser, 2010, p. 74), which conflicted with the principles of European cultural policy. European cultural policy recognised the need for special treatment of cultural industry products. Restrictions on the free circulation of national artistic or archaeological assets were already introduced in Article 36 of the Treaty of Rome (Gierat-Bieroń, 2018). The 1992 Maastricht Treaty further reinforced this approach in Article 128 stating: "The Community shall contribute to the flowering of the cultures of the Member States, while respecting their national and regional diversity and at the same time bringing the common cultural heritage to the fore" (EU, 1997).

During the Uruguay Round negotiations, France strongly opposed the treatment of cultural products as mere commodities, advocating for measures to protect European culture from Americanisation. France proposed a quota system to ensure a proportion of local and EU-origin productions in media broadcasts (Benghozi, 2017). Similar quota systems have been implemented in Poland and Québec, with the aim of supporting the development of local music (Gałuszka, 2012b).

The protectionist measures implemented by certain countries aim to promote domestic artists and enhance their efficiency in creative and production processes. Local independent labels, primarily focusing on domestic artists, have a higher chance of obtaining a return on their investments as their music receives airplay on radio stations, leading to increased recognition among listeners and potentially higher sales. This policy can also incentivise major record labels, which have a presence in most national markets, to invest in local music. The requirement to broadcast local music on radio stations helps to lower entry barriers in terms of promotion, with radio being an influential channel. Consequently, protectionism can contribute to greater music diversity in local markets.

1.7.3 *Social and demographic factors shaping the transformation in recording industry*

The social and demographic factors play a significant role in shaping the transformation of the recording industry. Consumer lifestyles and preferences are crucial in determining the type and format of music consumed, which directly influences the industry's operations and product offerings. Consumer needs encompass not only the desire to listen to music but also factors such as quality, context, and the ability to share music with others.

Demographic factors, particularly age, are vital considerations in music consumer segmentation. Younger consumers are more inclined towards technological innovations and portable music players, while older, more established consumers with specific tastes and consumption habits may show interest in technically sophisticated or collector's editions that are usually more expensive.

To fully comprehend the impact of social and demographic factors on the recording industry's evolution in the 20th century, it is essential to trace back to its inception during the turn of the previous century. The inventions of Thomas Edison's phonograph and Emile Berliner's gramophone, pivotal technological advancements in the recording industry, coincided with the surge in home music listening. This was influenced by societal changes such as rapid urbanisation, the growth of working and middle classes, and the formation of new identities. Urban expansion posed challenges in accessing theatres and concert halls, leading to a higher demand for music consumption at home (Tournès, 2012, p. 27).

Berliner, the pioneer of recording and reproducing music on discs, envisioned their potential as a music carrier and a convenient medium for duplication, labelling, transportation, and storage. He also foresaw the gramophone becoming a central element of home entertainment (Kominek, 1986, p. 46). Consumers embraced his invention, resulting in a significant surge in record demand. By 1900, the Berliner Gramophone Company's catalogue already included 5,000 record titles (Kominek, 1986, p. 49). The popularity of home playing equipment also grew, with approximately 16% of American households equipped with a gramophone by 1920. The middle-class households became the mass consumers of music in the early 20th century (Frith, 2017, p. 99). The timing of this invention coincided with a favourable socioeconomic environment, allowing it to establish itself in the market.

Moreover, the migration of African-American populations from the southern to northern regions of the United States during and after the First World War played a crucial role in the dissemination of black music. These new consumers could now afford turntables and records. Initially, small labels owned by black individuals recorded music for these audiences. However, when major producers like Columbia recognised the revenue potential of African-American music, they began investing in genres such as blues and jazz. The support of white publishers (Kenney, 2003, p. 111) who lent credibility to this music among white listeners was instrumental in its popularity. These recordings, initially known as race records and later as rhythm and blues, gained wider appeal with the backing of leading market companies. The acquisition of small labels by larger companies provided international distribution networks and promoted the music beyond the United States (Tournès, 2012, p. 42). The growth of this genre was also facilitated by radio stations initially neglecting to broadcast this repertoire, necessitating its spread primarily through recordings (Frith, 2017, p. 100). These factors contributed to increased record sales prior to the Great Depression.

Once the major recording labels were the only ones left in the market after the economic crash in the late 1920s, it became apparent that entertainment habits among audiences were changing. Radio and sound films emerged as substitute products, replacing records as the primary form of entertainment (Tournès, 2012, p. 42). Consequently, sales of records declined as households had to allocate their lower budgets to various goods. To adapt, the industry focused on generating revenue through music distribution in these new media. Music publishing became a significant source of income, prompting Warner film studios to enter the music market by acquiring a music publishing company, Tin Pan Alley (Frith, 2017, p. 100). This move diversified revenues and reduced transaction costs by eliminating the need to pay external companies for music rights in films. Following the Second World War, Warner Corporation became one of the major players in the recording industry.

Social factors had a notable impact on the industry's development in the post-war period. The European population experienced a baby boom between 1945 and 1975, increasing from 360 million to 460 million (Tournès, 2012, p. 88). This baby boom generation became the audience for rock and roll, English pop music, and major music festivals. It marked a moral revolution that coincided with broader societal changes, including a shift in social values, rejection of authority figures like school and family, and the emergence of new ideologies and social movements. Industrialisation improved living conditions of the inhabitants of Western European society, leading to increased consumerism and a greater emphasis on material wealth. Entertainment spending in America reached approximately one-seventh of GDP (Boyer et al., 2018). The younger generation, growing up in prosperity and unaware of war hardships, rebelled against their parents' values, prompting a shift towards stress-free parenting models and changes in women's rights, including voting and access to contraception (Escoffier, 2003).

The baby boom not only spurred manufacturing and technological advancements but also gave rise to an industry catering to teenagers, who sought enjoyment and entertainment more than the previous wartime generation. With the means to buy records and attend concerts and discos, young people gained autonomy in choosing the music they wanted to listen to.

The recording industry capitalised on these changes, particularly the growing popularity of rock and roll, which had its roots in black rhythm and blues. Rock and roll became a musical and social phenomenon, representing youthful rebellion against parental rules (D'Anjou, 2003). The genre's appeal, as well as the charismatic personality of Elvis Presley, resonated with the post-war teenage generation's tastes and desires.

Meanwhile, major recording labels in the late 1940s and early 1950s focused on releasing commercially successful music, deeming emerging genres like rock and roll unprofitable. This created an opportunity for small independent labels to thrive. Labels such as Atlantic Records, Imperial, Dot, Sun, and Chess emerged, collaborating with local radio stations and specialising in niche genres (Huygens et al., 2001, p. 23). These labels recognised the demand for diverse music styles among new consumers in the market.

Local radio stations, initially popular among African-Americans, soon attracted young white listeners as well. Around 700 local radio stations (Coleman, 2005, p. 77) played a vital role, with estimates suggesting that 20%–30% of their listeners were white in the early 1950s (Clarke, 1996). This synergy between local radio stations and small record producers fostered the development of rock and roll. By the late 1950s, small independent labels had gained a significant share of the market. In 1955, the market was valued at $277 million, with 75% controlled by major recording companies. However, by 1959, the share of major labels had dropped to 34% while the overall market value reached $603 million (Huygens et al., 2001, p. 24).

The success of rock and roll was paralleled by the phenomenon of Beatlemania, which swept across the UK, Europe, and eventually the world. The popularity of The Beatles, along with other pop groups like The Rolling Stones, propelled major record companies to regain their market dominance. These companies held the rights to blockbuster releases by these artists, and their international distribution ensured the widespread popularity of these new stars (Tournès, 2012, p. 110). This marked the end of industry deconcentration and the emergence of a new oligopoly. Between 1973 and 1978, global sales surged from $4.75 billion to $7 billion (Burnett, 2010, pp. 44–45), with six conglomerates, including CBS, Warner, RCA, EMI, PolyGram, and MCA, dominating the market (Bishop, 2005, p. 448).

Favourable social and demographic conditions, accompanied by the increasing demand for music, provided recording companies with opportunities for expansion. They invested in new technologies to enhance recording quality, reduce costs, and develop more efficient business models. These conditions also attracted new entrants to the industry, particularly after the Second World War. The growing number of potential music consumers, coupled with a favourable economic climate and technological innovations, shaped the operating model of the recording industry, which remained largely unchanged until the advent of the digital revolution.

1.7.4 Recording industry and law

Music is governed by intellectual property laws, including copyright (author's right) and related rights (Bernstein et al., 2007; Curien and Moreau, 2010; Wikström, 2013). This justifies the World Intellectual Property Organization's (WIPO) use of the term *copyright-based industries* to describe the recording industry.

Patents also played a crucial role as legal factors influencing the industry. In the early days, companies in the recording industry secured patents for recording technology and playback devices, granting them control over related markets. Subsequently, patents primarily focused on the production of mediums such as vinyl records, cassette tapes, and CDs. Ownership of these technologies provided companies with a competitive advantage, allowing them to prioritise the marketing of products developed using the patented technology and generate additional revenue through licensing.

While record companies began specialising in recording production from the 1930s onwards, they became part of conglomerates involved in other sectors of the economy, such as media (e.g., CBS in radio and television, Warner in film) and playback equipment manufacturing (e.g., Sony, Philips). As a result, even though recording technologies were not developed within the recording companies themselves, they were owned by the conglomerates, and the benefits derived from their use were directly transferred to the recording companies.

At the beginning of the 20th century, the significance of patents diminished while the importance of copyright, which forms the basis of the traditional model of the recording industry, grew. The industry's historical structure aimed to ensure fair compensation for authors, composers, publishers, and performers for their creative work (Vogel, 2011, p. 232). In the continental (European) legal system, this compensation is guaranteed through authors' rights and related rights, with the former covering remuneration for authors and the latter for performers, producers, and broadcasters. Within the recording industry, economic copyrights, which are exclusive, time limited, and transferable, play a crucial role (Benhamou and Farchy, 2014, p. 16; Hull et al., 2011). Producers of recordings become owners of the works and have the exclusive rights to make copies (such as pressing records), broadcast the works in various media and public places, and utilise them in films or advertisements (Hull et al., 2011; Tschmuck, 2009).

However, the right of ownership is limited in time. The Berne Convention for the Protection of Literary and Artistic Works, the first international copyright convention between sovereign states (Strasser, 2010, p. 19), establishes a term of protection of 50 years. Signatory states have the option to extend this period, as demonstrated in the directives of the European Parliament and the Council. Council Directive 93/98/EEC sets the term of copyright protection at 70 years after the author's death or 70 years after the work is lawfully made available to the public, and related rights are protected for 50 years from the relevant event[7] (Directive 93/98/EEC). In the United States, the Copyright Act of 1976 established a protection period of 50 years after the author's death for individuals and 75 years for corporations. After the expiration of the statutory time, the work enters the public domain and can be freely used.

Copyright law plays a crucial role in granting rights owners a monopoly over the control and revenue derived from their works. Recording companies, with their extensive catalogues, strive to extend the term of protection for as long as possible. An example of the influence of media and entertainment corporations on legislation is the Sonny Bono Copyright Term Extension

Act, enacted in the United States in 1998. This law extended the term of protection to 70 years for individuals and from 95 to 120 years for corporations. Its timing coincided with the imminent entry of the character Mickey Mouse, owned by Disney, into the public domain, leading to its pejorative nickname, the Mickey Mouse Protection Act (Latrive, 2007; Lessig, 2004).

Similar lobbying efforts can be observed in the European Union, where directives to harmonise copyright and related rights are being developed. An instance of this is the push by the UK Committee for Culture, Media and Sport to extend the term of protection for producers of works from 50 to 70 years (Helberger et al., 2008, p. 174). This push occurred when the early works of C. Richard and The Beatles were approaching the public domain. The recent Directive of the European Parliament and the Council on copyright and related rights, effective since April 2019, generated substantial public consultation and excitement among stakeholders operating in the digital market for cultural content (Misiewicz, 2019; Senftleben et al., 2018).

Another legal factor that impacted the recording industry was the process of media deregulation in the 1980s, a time when recording companies had a global presence (Herman and McChesney, 2014, pp. 26, 38). The emergence of new cable and satellite television networks led to an increased demand for music, as it became an essential element of newly launched programs. This shift contributed to the growth of music publishing, as recording companies increasingly sold rights to recordings and charged royalties for their use. According to the National Music Publishers' Association (NMPA), global revenues from music publishing grew at a rate of 10% per year since 1982, reaching $3.5 million by 1990 (with the United States accounting for 20% of that total) (Huygens et al., 2001, p. 21).

Television played a significant role in the recording industry, not only as a source of revenue but also as a platform for promotion. The launch of the first music channel, MTV, in 1981 revolutionised the industry by broadcasting music videos to promote recordings. As MTV expanded globally in 1984, its influence as a distribution platform had a profound impact on the recording industry.

The close relationship between television and music was facilitated by the shared interests of both industries and their affiliation with multinational conglomerates. This allowed companies to diversify their revenue streams and act as gatekeepers, selecting and promoting songs or artists for which they owned the rights. This increased barriers to entry in terms of promotion and limited the exposure of competing labels' products. Intra-corporate trade, particularly in music exploitation rights, grew from 20% in the 1970s to over 30% in the 1990s (Herman and McChesney, 2014, p. 27).

Television and the recording industry also employed a synergy strategy, engaging in intra-corporate commerce. Music programs like Star Academy or Idol served as platforms where aspiring artists competed for the chance to record an album. By promoting these artists on television and involving audiences in the selection process, the risk of failure in the recording market was significantly reduced. The artist already gained recognition through the TV show, and their subsequent album, derived from the TV program, didn't carry the status of a debut release. In this case, the TV program, apart from being a revenue source for the TV station, became a significant revenue generator for the music label.

1.7.5 Technology as driving force of the recording industry

1.7.5.1 Pre-digital changes

According to Gierszewska and Romanowska (2017, p. 30), technological change can result in a very rapid decline of certain industries and the emergence of new ones. The evolution of the recording industry seems to confirm this hypothesis. In fact, its origins can be traced back to a technological invention – the phonograph by T. Edison and later the gramophone by E. Berliner. This technology, combined with other factors, primarily social and economic, led to the emergence of a new sector in the economy. The creators' patented technologies gave them control of the recorded music market right from the beginning.

The role of patents is emphasised by Bishop (2005), who notes that control over technology meant, and still means, control over associated markets. Therefore, patents were among the most valuable assets of the early recording companies. On the other hand, Frith (1986, p. 116) points out that technological innovations that decentralised the production and consumption of music, at least in the short term, were the ones that became popular and influenced the development of the recording industry. Both arguments find support in the industry's historical development.

A rapid development of the recording industry, characterised by the emergence of new entrants and a partial loss of market control by leading companies,[8] occurred after 1914 when patents for recording technology and disc-playing equipment expired. Devices manufactured by an increasing number of competitors began to enter the market, not only in the United States but also in other markets (Huygens et al., 2001, p. 21). Within a few years, the number of American record labels grew from a dozen to around 200. The increasing popularity of these devices was followed by an explosion in demand for records: in 1929, 150 million records were sold, 50% more than in 1921 (Huygens et al., 2001, p. 21).

A slightly different situation, also related to patent issues and their expiration, occurred after the Second World War. At that time, the shellac disc, on which music had been recorded and sold, needed to be replaced by a new medium. However, the rights to the new invention, the 33 rpm vinyl record (longplay), belonged to the CBS label. Another major American company, RCA, owned a competing technology, the 45 rpm vinyl record (single). It was then that CBS decided to license its technology to new companies emerging in the US market. As a result, the 33 rpm disc gained popularity, leading to a deconcentration or decentralisation of production in the recording industry (Frith, 2017). The number of small labels increased from 11 in 1949 to over 200 in 1954 (Kominek, 1986, p. 102). Subsequently, other large companies adopted this technology, making it the standard carrier for music until the early 1980s.

CBS's decision to free the patent for the 33 rpm disc, despite facing competition from the more cost-effective 45 rpm carrier, was driven by the need for widespread market adoption. Leveraging their ownership of radio stations and the Columbia label, acquired in 1938, CBS promoted their products through radio promotion and harnessed the innovative power of smaller companies. The extensive promotion aimed to make Columbia's (CBS) music more popular and desired by the public. On the other hand, small labels, operating locally and thus closely connected to new music genres, performers, and audiences, provided bottom-up support while popularising longplays.

Independently released singles continued alongside the dominance of longplays, creating new distribution channels beyond music shops. Singles, being cheaper to produce and transport, led to the emergence of distribution companies that made recordings from small labels available in various locations such as department stores, supermarkets, drugstores, and petrol stations (Kominek, 1986, p. 110).

The introduction and popularisation of LPs helped classical music gain a stronger presence in the market. Long compositions could now be recorded on a single disc without the need to split them into four-minute parts to fit on the old shellac discs. Decca, with a catalogue that already numbered 3,500 discs by around 1969, was the first European company to adopt longplays, gaining dominance in the UK market and solidifying its position through a partnership with RCA-Victor. Meanwhile, Europe's largest recording company, EMI, delayed its decision to adopt LPs until 1952. EMI was concerned about the potential loss of profits from its catalogue recorded on the old 78 rpm shellac discs (Kominek, 1986, p. 101). This industry shift, driven by new carriers, echoes the recurring phenomenon in today's digital formats.

An invention that had a significant impact on the recording industry was radio. Initially seen as competition for recorded music, the decline in record sales seemed to confirm this. However, it soon became clear that radio and the recording industry could mutually benefit each other's growth by working together. The emergence of radio as a new promotional channel for recorded music brought about significant changes in the industry's structure.

Before the advent of radio, stars were primarily promoted through live performances in theatres, opera houses, and philharmonic halls. Their popularity would then be solidified through record sales. However, with the rise of radio, alliances between recording companies and strong radio networks began to form, leading to the establishment of the star system. The merging of local radio stations into networks enabled the offering of similar programs and music to residents across different regions. This led to a certain homogenisation of music offerings nationwide and increased the reach of popular stars. Recording companies embraced this trend and developed a new strategy focused on promoting a select few stars and maximising album sales.

The advent of radio also had a profound impact on music consumption and diversity. The popularity of radio sets in households broadened the audience for music, resulting in massive music consumption as highlighted by Alexander et al. (2015, p. 228). Simultaneously, radio played a crucial role in increasing musical diversity. Albums by artists promoted through radio networks fuelled the search for new talent and genres. On-air promotion reduced the risk of newly released albums going unnoticed, which could result in artistic failure and financial losses for labels.

The introduction of radio broadcasting of records had a transformative effect on the recording industry. Lerski (2004, p. 101) states that since the radio started broadcasting records, the demand for records in general has tremendously increased. Far from killing the phonographic industry, radio contributed to its development. Companies lending records to radio stations experienced a flood of inquiries about records heard on air. Overall, radio played a vital role in reshaping the recording industry, establishing the star system, expanding music consumption, and driving album sales.

Magnetic tape, introduced into recording studios after the Second World War, played a crucial role in the development of the recording industry. Deutsche Grammophon Ges was one of the first companies to adopt this technology in Germany in 1946, followed by EMI in England in 1948. Subsequently, all record companies abandoned the old method of recording on discs in favour of magnetic tape.

The advent of magnetic tape brought significant advantages to the recording process. Firstly, the tape allowed for easy editing, making recording process more efficient and shorter.[9] Secondly, portable tape recorders could be installed in concert halls, enabling live recordings as an additional product within a single artistic project.[10] This expansion broadened the potential customer base, attracting new segments of music consumers.

The reduced production costs associated with magnetic tape technology facilitated the entry of new players into the market. Small local labels, at relatively low costs, established their own recording studios (Gronow, 1983, p. 70). This shift in the industry's landscape altered the balance of power and marked a new phase of intensive development.

Another outcome of the cost reduction in recording was the increased variety of music available. On one hand, new small labels had the opportunity to offer niche, locally focused repertoire. On the other hand, larger recording companies sought to expand their portfolios and began recording genres that were previously underrepresented, such as baroque works and early music (Tournès, 2012, p. 84). Consequently, an additional segment of music consumers emerged, providing access to their favourite genres beyond local radio stations or live concerts.

Following the introduction of magnetic tape, the next breakthrough came with the cassette tape, developed by Philips Phonographische Industries. Philips licensed the technology to interested parties, leading to its rapid global adoption. It is estimated that between 1970 and 1980, the annual production of recorded cassettes in the United States equalled that of long-playing records (Ferstler, 2005, p. 171).

Record labels capitalised on the cassette's popularity by releasing albums simultaneously on both vinyl records and cassettes. This approach allowed them to reach a broader audience and increase revenues. Consumers were segmented based on their ability to afford more expensive vinyl record equipment, valuing music quality and the associated listening ritual. Meanwhile, younger individuals with limited financial resources could only afford portable cassette players. They were more inclined to personalise their music consumption and preferred the mobility that the new medium provided. Cassettes offered longer soundtracks (up to 120 minutes) and enabled listeners to create their own musical compilations. Initially integrated into cars, cassette players later found their way into portable transistor radios and eventually became a staple feature of walkmans, offering a mobile form of music consumption.

However, the cassette tape also had a negative impact on the recording industry. It became associated with a crisis characterised by a significant decline in phonogram sales. The affordability of sound recording through cassettes led to their widespread use in the mass production of illegal copies (Figure 1.4).

Home taping is killing music

It was the title of a campaign conducted by record companies in the 1980s through their respective organisations, namely the Recording Industry Association of America (RIAA) in the United States and the British Phonographic Industry (BPI) in the UK. Its objective was to discourage consumers from making copies of cassettes at home and to advocate for a change in the existing law that permitted private copying.

It also illustrates how the major recording companies utilised their influence in the market through the organisations representing them.

Based on Bottomley (2015).

The advent of music *piracy*, including the copying of music for personal use, marked a significant phenomenon. It is estimated that between 1980 and 1984, home copying in the United States alone increased by 24%, while record production experienced a decline of 16% during the same period.

Television emerged as the next major invention with substantial implications for the recording industry, particularly in terms of artist promotion. Its

Figure 1.4 "Home taping is killing music." From https://en.wikipedia.org/wiki/Home_Taping_Is_Killing_Music#/media/File:Home_taping_is_killing_music.png.

significance grew with the process of media deregulation, which led to the launch of the music station MTV in August 1981 (Shuker, 2017). Music videos became a vital component of MTV's programming, selected based on the songs' popularity in the US charts. Managing artists' image became integral to marketing activities and an essential aspect of the music product. Creating music videos and broadcasting them on music and general stations became crucial.

The impact of music videos on album sales and artist stardom became evident. A notable example is Michael Jackson's album "Thriller," which achieved 30 times platinum status and sold over 100 million copies worldwide. It is considered the bestselling album of all time (Hoffmann and Ferstler, 2005a; RIAA, 2015), with its success attributed, in part, to the high-budget music videos accompanying its tracks. Another example is the hit song *Lambada*, which gained widespread exposure through its use in a commercial for Orangina. The frequent airing of the song's video on television contributed to its sales of 10 million copies worldwide within a year (Tournès, 2012, p. 129).

MTV gradually expanded its repertoire to include new music genres and emerging performers, leading music videos to evolve into artistic productions with increasingly higher budgets. As a globally broadcast station, MTV played a significant role in the creation of global music stars (Shuker, 2017) and further solidified the star system. During its peak, MTV potentially reached an audience of 400 million viewers across 166 countries (Kowalski, 2006, p. 209). The extensive coverage provided by MTV strengthened the market position of major recording companies, which held the rights to release works by artists promoted on television. Through global television and the associated global promotion, these companies could enhance their sales maximisation strategies and leverage economies of scale.

1.7.5.2 The impact of the digital turn on the recording industry

Scientific literature discusses various phenomena that have influenced the recording industry's evolution. These include the information revolution, telecommunications revolution (Huberman, 2003, p. 11; Rieffel, 2014), digital revolution (Alexander et al., 2015; Chantepie and Le Diberder, 2010; Hamel and Prahalad, 2010), and the ICT revolution (Jorgenson and Khuong, 2016). These terms encompass the emergence and development of personal computers, computer chips, digital switches, the Internet, and mobile telephony. The digitisation of content is also a significant factor (Friedman, 2005, p. 11; Rieffel, 2014). These technological advancements represent sources of fundamental changes that have impacted the economy since the late 20th century.

Beyond the purely technological aspects, additional changes have shaped the recording industry (Toffler, 2006). Key developments at the end of the 20th century include:

- the rise of network industries and the network effect,[11] which have played a crucial role in new forms of music distribution such as file-sharing networks, social media, and music ranking and recommendation systems;
- the recognition of the non-rivalrous and inexhaustible nature of knowledge products, attributing them characteristics of public goods; this change has significant implications for music production funding and has influenced the emergence of new business models for distribution, as well as approaches to the protection of music as intellectual property;
- the de-massification and increasing individualisation of products; this shift is evident in the transformation of the product itself, as consumers now create personalised playlists of their favourite songs rather than relying solely on predefined albums; this change also reflects evolving consumer expectations regarding the variety and diversity of available music offerings, as explored by Anderson (2006) through the *long-tail* theory;
- the effects of global capital mobility, leading to the global reach of recording companies; this phenomenon has been observed previously in the formation of *global empires of sound* within the recording industry (Bishop, 2005).

The *long-tail* theory

Popularised by Chris Anderson, it traces its origins back to J. Bezos, the founder of Amazon, who developed the idea in 1994. Anderson introduced the term in a presentation slide in 2004 and later published an article titled *The Long Tail* in Wired magazine in October of the same year. This article quickly became the most extensively referenced text in the magazine's history. In 2006, Anderson expanded on the concept in his book *The Long Tail: Why the Future of Business Is Selling Less of More.*

The core premise of the theory is the transformation of the mass market into a niche market composed of mini and microstars. While not intending to entirely supplant the traditional blockbuster market, this niche market competes with it on equal terms. It unveils the previously unseen market segment where songs bypassed by record companies' selection systems for mass distribution and promotion can now be discovered by consumers. Similarly, independent productions have gained widespread visibility as information about them has become readily accessible.

Based on Anderson (2006).

1.7.5.2.1 CONTENT DIGITISATION INVENTIONS THAT HAVE INFLUENCED THE DEVELOPMENT OF THE RECORDING INDUSTRY

Digitisation of content has significantly impacted the recording industry. This process, driven by advancements in electronics and digital communication, aimed to enhance the technical quality of recordings, streamline the recording process, and reduce costs. It unfolded in three stages: digital sound recording in studios, recording on compact discs (CDs), and the detachment of digitised music from physical carriers, enabling compression, copying, and long-distance transmission. This digital revolution, coupled with other elements of the ICT revolution, sparked a transformation within the industry.

In 1979, Nippon Columbia (Denon) introduced the first *digital records* (Kominek, 1986, p. 193), marking a shift in sound quality. The success of digitally recorded discs prompted wider adoption of digital technology, leading to price reductions and lowering barriers to entry for new music recording businesses, such as independent studios and production companies.

Concurrently, research focused on improving the compact disc as the carrier medium. The CD was launched in Japan in 1982 and witnessed rapid sales growth. The year 1988 was the first year that more CDs than LP were sold and by 1992, CDs sales accounted for over 1.152 billion (Burnett, 2010, p. 45). Sales of vinyl records fell dramatically from 1.2 billion to just 128 million units between 1981 and 1992, when they almost disappeared from the market. Researchers acknowledge that the invention of the CD revitalised the recording industry, rescuing it from a decline experienced in the late 1970s. Sales continued to rise between 1981 and 1992, contributing to an increase in the total value of music sales from $12 billion to $29 billion (Burnett, 2010, p. 45).

The popularity of CDs can be attributed to their superior quality compared to vinyl records, enticing music enthusiasts to replace their collections. Labels took advantage of this trend, reissuing their catalogues on the improved medium. Compilation albums and re-releases became prevalent, with catalogue stock accounting for a significant portion of total sales, reaching up to 40%. The higher quality of the carrier also justified higher prices, although production costs had decreased. Revenues from the use of catalogue albums played a substantial role, potentially constituting half of major labels' total revenues and up to three-quarters of their profits (Vogel, 2011, p. 253). Additionally, the lower costs of transporting and storing CDs contributed to increased income.

When Sony and Philips collaborated to establish a standardised CD format, they garnered support from companies like Matsushita and Nippon Columbia (Denon), known for their expertise in consumer electronics. Alongside hardware production, Sony, Philips, Nippon Columbia, and later Matsushita (which acquired MCA in 1990) also released CDs. The promotion of the CD standard proved beneficial for both CDs and CD players, which were complementary goods, leading to increased sales and revenue diversification.

Frith (1986, p. 116) states that the recording industry is inherently conservative, using new inventions to do old things more efficiently or more cheaply, rather than to do new things. The focus of these inventions was primarily on reducing manufacturing and distribution costs rather than improving sound quality or user experience. However, the process of digitisation brought about unexpected changes, leading to a crisis. Frith (1986, p. 117) further notes the slow response and apparent ignorance of recording company owners regarding the effects of their own inventions.

In the late 1980s, the Fraunhofer Institute in Germany initiated research on audio data compression to maintain optimal sound quality while reducing file size. This led to the development of the mp3 format in the 1990s (Denegri-Knott and Tadajewski, 2010; Tschmuck, 2014, p. 184). Sound compression had two significant effects on the music product: it detached music from physical carriers, leading to a kind of dematerialisation, and it reduced storage space requirements. These changes had a profound impact on the distribution cost and accessibility of music.

1.7.5.2.2 ICT INVENTIONS THAT IMPACTED ON THE DEVELOPMENT OF THE RECORDING INDUSTRY

In addition to the aforementioned changes, the recording industry was significantly impacted by the emergence of various ICT inventions. This includes the widespread use of personal computers, the development of the Internet, the rise of mobile telephony, and the popularity of digital music players. The convergence of these elements created a favourable environment for rapid transformations that ultimately led to an industry crisis.

The 1970s witnessed the introduction of microcomputers, particularly affordable personal computers, which enabled both artists and consumers to create and listen to music (Allan, 2004, p. 3/8; Eskelsen et al., 2010). In 1992, the global expansion of the Internet commenced, offering a cost-effective platform for music dissemination, promotion, and information retrieval (Castells, 2002, p. 42; Rifkin, 2015).

Furthermore, portable digital music devices gained popularity in the early 21st century, with Apple's iPod leading the way and quickly becoming a cult gadget, especially among young people. However, it was soon overshadowed by the mobile phone and its subsequent evolution into the smartphone, transforming into a portable personal entertainment centre for users. Apple's iPhone, launched in 2007, marked the beginning of smartphones (Rudnicki and Pisarski, 2019). Mobile networks evolved into new music distribution channels, encompassing various formats such as ringtones, music ringtones, and streaming technology for free access to music catalogues.

These technological advancements directly influenced the costs of production, distribution, promotion, and availability of phonograms. Industry players were able to leverage these elements to gain market share. On one hand, the proliferation of technology reduced barriers to entry for new producers in terms of production and sometimes distribution. On the other hand, the integration of emerging media platforms empowered large recording companies, solidified the star system, and further concentrated and integrated the industry, a trend that persists to this day.

1.8 Internationalisation of the recording industry

According to international business theory (Dunning, 2013, p. 111), the expansion of companies into foreign markets can be achieved through exports, cooperative agreements, and foreign direct investment. In the recording industry, exports initially involved the sale of music equipment and discs to foreign markets. Due to the high distribution costs, the local pressing plants started to produce copies from the exported *master records*. This unique form of export was primarily focused on copyright buying and selling, where local subsidiaries paid the foreign artists through the mother company.

Over time, this export approach evolved into cooperative agreements. Local pressing plants started working directly for major foreign labels, their subsidiaries, and independent companies, manufacturing CDs under licence from multinational corporations. Cooperative agreements also included access to distribution channels, particularly for independent labels that utilised international distribution channels owned by major record companies. In this process, foreign companies ordered copies of albums to be pressed in a specific market using masters provided to them and then distributed the albums themselves.

Foreign direct investment in the recording industry involves different aspects of the value creation chain, such as creation, production, distribution, and promotion, with a focus on the latter two stages. Large corporations establish their own pressing plants, create distribution networks, and open subsidiary offices to produce local artists and promote and distribute international stars. This often involves acquiring independent local labels and integrating them into the structures of major companies, enabling them to quickly gain control of local markets, access song and performer catalogues, and leverage the expertise of local companies.

Gronow (1983) distinguishes three periods of international expansion of the industry:

- up to the First World War;
- up to the Great Depression;
- from the early 1950s to the late 1970s.

However, Gronow's article was written in 1983, so it does not cover the period of intense international expansion from the late 1970s to the mid-1990s, nor the subsequent information revolution, which will be discussed later in this chapter.

1.8.1 The first period of international expansion up to the First World War

Music, being easily transportable across borders (Burnett, 2010, p. 10), led to the early international activities of the recording industry. During the competition between Thomas Edison and Emile Berliner, their inventions, the phonograph, and gramophone, respectively, gained interest in foreign markets. Alexander Graham Bell also tried to compete in the market with his graphophone, eventually focusing on the manufacture of Edison's wax cylinders and Berliner's gramophone records.

By the 1880s, phonographs were demonstrated in several countries, including England, France, Germany, Russia, India, Egypt, and Japan (Gronow, 1983, p. 55). These devices and pre-recorded music were imported from the United States. The gramophone was patented by Berliner in the United States in 1887, however, initially, the equipment was manufactured in Germany, where Berliner partnered with a toy company (Kominek, 1986, p. 46). In 1895, he established the Berliner Gramophone Company in the United States, followed by subsidiaries in Germany (Berliner Grammophon), the UK (Berliner Gramophone Company of London), and France (Compagnie française du gramophone) (Tournès, 2012, p. 24). The German subsidiary became the first record pressing plant, which later evolved into the renowned Deutsche Grammophon label. Berliner's company also expanded to Russia and Montreal.

In the early 20th century, the Victor Talking Machine Co. succeeded Berliner's American company, and together with Gramophone Co. (in which Victor had a 50% share), they became the dominant recording companies globally. Victor focused on the United States, South America, and the Far East, while Gramophone covered the rest of the world. Production was primarily concentrated in the United States, and overseas factories in China and South America were established after the First World War. Recordings were made in each country, but processing and pressing exclusively took place in the United States before being shipped to respective markets (Gronow, 1983, p. 56).

Gramophone Company adopted a decentralised approach to its operations. In larger and promising markets, it established record pressing factories alongside branches. Factories were set up in various countries, including the UK, Germany, Austria-Hungary, Spain, Russia, India, France, and Italy, managed by local subsidiaries. Smaller markets relied on local agents who served as talent scouts and importers of records and equipment (Huygens et al., 2001, p. 20).

Other companies followed a similar approach to the British Gramophone Company. One notable example was the largest German label, Carl Lindström AG, establishing factories in European countries, Argentina, Brazil, and eventually, in 1910, in the United States (Gronow, 1983, p. 56). During that time, its market share in the British recording market, which is now the largest European market, reached a significant 30%, with the UK importing over 4 million recordings in 1913 (Martland, 2008). Another portion of the market was divided among the Gramophone Company, Columbia, Edison Bell, and smaller exporters like the French Pathé. The latter also established its manufacturing plants in Belgium, Austria-Hungary, Russia, and the United States. Edison, on the other hand, focused on production in the United States but developed a highly efficient distribution network in Europe.

As European production patents for equipment and phonograms expired, local recording companies emerged in England, Germany, Russia, Italy and later in Turkey, Egypt, and Japan. Due to high costs, these companies often commissioned major labels for recordings and pressing of discs, which were then distributed locally under their own label brands.

Japan, now one of the world's largest recording markets, initially experienced significant expansion with the establishment of branches by English and American companies. While the first phonographs and recordings were imported from the United States, two Japanese companies were established by 1909 (Tournès, 2012, p. 29). The Far East, largely under the British Empire, played a crucial role in the industry's early internationalisation. Although the primary audience for recordings in these markets consisted of white colonisers, there was also a demand from the local middle class. Thus, alongside the export of Western music, local music was also produced in these regions.

Before the First World War, the recording industry had already become a truly international business on multiple levels. Firstly, playback devices and phonographs were exported from the United States to various countries, either directly or through company branches. Secondly, American companies formed partnerships with local companies in specific markets, granting them licences to produce devices and recordings. Lastly, foreign subsidiaries were established to import, export, and produce recordings locally. The Polish market serves as a notable example, where imported phonographs, devices assembled from imported parts, or unauthorised (without patent holders' consent) locally manufactured devices were sold (Janczewska-Sołomko, 2002). While a significant portion of recordings were imported, a substantial number were also recorded locally, either by major company branches or by independent record companies like Syrena Records.

Information on the size of the world's main markets during that time is limited. According to some sources, annual record sales in the United States were estimated to be at least 30 million around 1910, with 20 million in Russia in 1915, 18 million in Germany in 1907, and 10 million each in

France and the UK. The size of markets where records were not pressed can be inferred from the volume of imports. For instance, Argentina imported nearly 2 million records around 1910, while India imported 600,000 (Gronow, 1983, p. 60).

1.8.2 The second period of internationalisation – the years of interwar crisis

The First World War brought significant changes to the international recording market. European record companies shifted their focus towards producing for the army, while the demand for discs declined due to the wartime circumstances. Meanwhile, the American recording industry flourished. The freeing up of patents and the emphasis on American local music, such as jazz and blues, propelled its success. Small labels initially recorded these genres and were later acquired by major companies. For instance, Columbia purchased the label that released recordings by Louis Armstrong and promoted him globally through its international network of subsidiaries.

The adoption of electric sound recording by major American companies, namely the Victor Talking Machine Company and Columbia, further solidified their competitive advantage after the war. This technology revitalised and expanded their repertoire. They also gained an edge in Europe by sharing the technology with British companies like His Master's Voice and British Columbia, which were connected to the American majors through licensing agreements and financial shares. The technology was later transferred to subsidiaries in various national markets. The growing demand for discs prompted renowned artists, who had previously prioritised live performances, to recognise the importance of recording their work. The distribution networks established by American companies facilitated the global reach of these recordings.

While turntables and discs were affordable for average users in industrialised countries, developing countries had lower average incomes. Nonetheless, annual sales of 1–2 million encouraged recording companies to release recordings in these markets and even establish local production (Gronow, 1983, p. 64).

The 1920s and 1930s brought significant challenges to the recording industry. The American industry nearly disappeared by the early 1930s (Kominek, 1986, p. 71), with the two largest companies being taken over by radio networks and forming RCA-Victor and Columbia-CBS. The crisis also impacted Europe, causing small companies to go bankrupt or be acquired by major labels. Sales of recordings from British companies, Gramophone Co. and Columbia saw a sharp decline. In 1931, the two rival companies merged to create EMI – Electric and Musical Industries Ltd., becoming the world's largest recording company at the time (Hoffmann and Ferstler, 2005b, p. 374). EMI gained control over the majority of the recording industry in Europe as Columbia controlled the Carl Lindström Company (Germany) and

Pathé Frères (France) and remained the strongest European company until the 1970s. Its main competitor was Deutsche Grammophon, while Decca emerged as a new player in the market in 1929, establishing a branch in the United States in 1934 and becoming the second largest in the UK market by 1939 (Tournès, 2012, p. 58).

During the interwar period, the recording industry continued to be dominated by a few multinational corporations. Foreign subsidiaries of American and British companies expanded as major branches, and some gained shares in local markets through label acquisitions, especially in Europe. In certain markets like Scandinavia and South America, imported recordings dominated, although local production had started to emerge before the Second World War. In Japan, the branches of major companies became independent and were nationalised, alongside a few local labels, resulting in the production of approximately 15 million phonograms annually in the 1930s. The recording industry was also nationalised in the Soviet Union, where an estimated 55 million records were issued by the late 1930s (Gronow, 1983, pp. 64–65).

1.8.3 Progressive internationalisation by the mid-1980s

After the Second World War, major recording corporations such as CBS, RCA, Capitol, and Decca dominated the recording market in the United States. These companies formed licensing agreements with European counterparts, enabling them to distribute each other's productions in both the United States and Europe (Tournès, 2012, p. 77). The United States began to promote a free market and free flow of information in Europe, implementing a global media system similar to its own (Herman and McChesney, 2014, p. 17). They exported a large number of records to Europe, allowing consumers to re-engage with American music. The expansion of major recording companies outside the United States led to the next era of concentration of power in the media and entertainment industries.

In the post-war years, the recording industry witnessed a battle for market dominance between proponents of the 33 rpm long-playing records and those of the 45 rpm singles referred to as battle for standards. The industry landscape was further transformed by new inventions, the emergence of independent companies, and the rise of rock and roll. While the European recording industry slowly recovered, it took until the late 1950s to reach sales levels comparable to those of 1929. European companies such as EMI and Philips started to establish themselves in the US market through strategic acquisitions, including EMI's purchase of Capitol Records in 1955 and Philips' deal with CBS and acquisition of Mercury Records in 1961. In Louviers, France, Philips built the then most modern record factory (Encyclopédisque, no date). However, American Decca and RCA-Victor experienced a decline in market share due to the expansion of rival European labels and the increasing strength of independent American labels. In the British market, EMI and Decca emerged as the two major labels, bolstering their international standing, in part thanks to the success of The Beatles and The Rolling Stones.

During this time, the recording industry witnessed a concentration of power, with the top ten multinational corporations producing approximately half of all recordings worldwide. These companies shifted their focus to mass-market popular music and divested from gramophone production, focusing exclusively on music-related activities (Gronow, 1983, p. 65). As they became part of larger media and entertainment corporations, they employed synergy strategies to generate revenue from various sources.

Starting from the early 1960s, the recording industry experienced intense consolidation as companies aimed to develop international distribution networks and reduce fixed costs. This involved gaining a larger market share by acquiring local labels and forming federations of labels similar to Warner Records. By the 1970s, five major multinationals – CBS, Warner, RCA, EMI, and PolyGram – controlled approximately 50% of the world market share (Herman and McChesney, 2014, p. 20).

1.8.4 International development of the industry after 1980

From the mid-1980s onward, album sales experienced a gradual increase, growing at an average rate of 7% annually between 1986 and 1996 (Throsby, 2002, p. 3). In the mid-1990s, sales reached record highs, reaching around $40 billion. However, sales revenue started to decline in the late 1990s, primarily due to technological factors.

The international trade in music products is often based on the exchange of mother (master) discs, from which local copies are manufactured. In the UK market, for example, the export of finished products accounted for a small percentage of total wholesale sales for major companies such as BMG, PolyGram, Sony, and EMI (MMC, 1994, p. 165).

In terms of market size, Europe held the top position, but its market was diverse due to linguistic and cultural differences. The North American market, predominantly the United States, remained the largest domestic recording market globally, while Canada had a relatively smaller share of global record sales (3%). In Asia, Japan held the largest market share, accounting for 15.2% in 1992 (Throsby, 2002, p. 5). Among the national European markets, Germany, the UK, and France had significant shares, with the UK market boasting a unique characteristic: despite its modest size, up to 18% of global music sales came from British artists, largely attributed to the dominance of the English language in popular music (Burnett, 2010, p. 48; MMC, 1994, p. 44).

Despite the internationalisation of the music market and its homogenisation due to the influence by American and British stars, the importance of local production in national markets should not be overlooked. In the United States, indigenous production accounted for 92% of all music sold, which is not surprising considering the dominance of global stars from the country. Similarly, other countries also had significant shares of national production, such as Brazil (75%), Mexico (46%), China (47%), Turkey (94%), Latvia (66%), Czech Republic (61%), and Greece (57%) (Bernstein et al., 2007; Throsby, 2002, p. 5).

There are several reasons for the increase in the share of national repertoire in total sales. Firstly, music is closely tied to the territory and nationality of its creators, carrying cultural values and serving as a means of communication and social commentary (Throsby, 2002, p. 19). This reflects the embeddedness of music within geographic, social, and cultural contexts (Coe, 2015, 2018). Secondly, the enjoyment of music is enhanced when consumed together with members of one's social groups, particularly at concerts where the majority of performances are by national artists (Laing, 2009, p. 20). Thirdly, some countries, like Poland and France, employ protectionist measures in media broadcasting, including music compositions, through broadcasting quotas. These policies result in a greater presence of indigenous songs on radio and television, leading to higher sales (Benghozi, 2017; CSA, n.d; Gałuszka, 2012b; 'German quota' on the radio. The Endless Debate, 2016).

Lastly, the sale of recorded music is a high-risk endeavour, and major labels often enter national markets by acquiring local labels, thereby obtaining market shares and catalogues featuring projects by local artists. Consequently, a significant portion of recorded music sold in many national markets consists of local repertoire.

1.9 Globalisation of the recording industry

According to Yip (1995, p. 40), globalisation of industries is influenced by market, cost, government, and competition factors, which are further shaped by variables like consumer behaviour and evolution of lifestyles, distribution channel structures, economies of scale, trade barriers, technological advancements, existence of tariff (or legal) barriers, information revolution, and global financial markets. Globalisation is considered a more advanced stage in the internationalisation of economic activity (Zorska, 2002, p. 14).

The recording industry has been subject to globalisation since its inception in the early 20th century. Before the digital revolution, recording companies operated in major local markets, creating global stars through their international distribution networks. Media outlets such as press, radio, and television, owned by multinational media companies such as NBC Universal, Warner Media, or Viacom CBS, played a significant role in promoting and broadcasting music globally. This led to the homogenisation of music tastes and lifestyles (Solomon et al., 2019, p. 43). MTV, for instance, started broadcasting local music in individual markets only in the late 1990s (Herman and McChesney, 2014, p. 42).

P2P (peer-to-peer)

They are file-sharing networks on the Internet that function as decentralised storage and sharing systems. Originally designed to harness the collective computing power of networked computers and used in projects such as SETI@Home, they promote principles of sharing, collaboration, and communication. One notable example is Napster, developed by S. Fanning, which allowed unauthorised file sharing over the Internet. Napster operated by using a central server as a search engine for files stored on users' hard drives, enabling music file downloads. Due to copyright infringement concerns, Napster was shut down in 2001. However, it was soon succeeded by other P2P systems such as KaZaA, Morpheus, Audiogalaxy, eMule, and BitTorrent.

Based on Benkler (2006), Coleman (2005), Janowska (2008).

The Internet and web distribution have expanded access to music content previously targeted at specific national markets. This was facilitated by the emergence of global online sales networks like Amazon.com, as well as peer-to-peer (P2P) networks and social media platforms, initially enabling unrestricted music sharing.

When it comes to legal digital music services like iTunes, Spotify, or Tidal, their distribution reflects more of a *myth of ubiquity* (Kowalski, 2006). Despite having a global presence, these platforms operate within local contexts. When entering new markets, each music platform needs to negotiate distribution terms with local labels, as there is no international, cross-border copyright law. Apple's case exemplifies this issue, as iTunes became available in Central and Eastern European markets later than in Western Europe. In response to allegations of discrimination, Apple explained that obtaining rights and complying with local laws in each EU country was necessary and they had to evaluate the costs and profits associated with content distribution (Niklewicz, 2009).

Copyright regulation issues remain significant barriers to e-commerce, as highlighted in a 2009 European Commission report (EC, 2009). Major music labels, who are the copyright owners, determine the territories and conditions for music distribution. This has resulted in restrictions on the presence of legal services in specific markets. The adoption of Directive (EU) 2019/790 of the European Parliament and of the Council aimed to regulate international e-commerce, including music trade, within the EU. However, its implementation remains controversial (Association, 2019; Misiewicz, 2019).

In the realm of music accessible through mobile networks, the myth of ubiquity persists. Despite significant consolidation among major telecom companies since the late 1990s (Herman and McChesney, 2014, p. 113), the music services offered by these companies remain confined to local markets, aligning with the overall scope of services available in each specific market. Once again, the primary obstacle lies in the differing legal regulations that exist across individual local markets.

Notes

1 The International Federation of the Phonographic Industry represents the interests of its approximately 8,000 members worldwide, such as major and independent recording companies (IFPI, n.d.).

2 Williamson and Cloonan (2007) criticise the approach of the IFPI and its member organisations with regard to the use of terms such as *music industry* instead of *recording industry*, which is a substantive error. They argue that these institutions, which only represent the recording industry, deliberately confuse the terms in order to give the impression that they represent the entire music industry, which would serve their vital interests (e.g., in the fight against so-called internet piracy).

3 Despite the various definitions of the term, it should be assumed that what is meant here is the content, i.e., the music recorded on some carrier, regardless of the nature of the latter (Burnett, 2010, p. 2; EU, 2011; McQuail, 2005; Mirski, 1998; "WIPO Lex," n.d.)

4 Some labels are particularly famous for the high technical quality of their recordings, e.g., Verve, ECM, JVC. There are also labels for audiophiles on the market, such as Alfa, Musical Fidelity, and Reference Recording. Japanese releases are also very much appreciated by enthusiasts of good sound.

5 This category includes the formerly used *payola* mechanism, which will be discussed in more detail in later chapters.

6 Compare Lerski (2004, p. 76). Syrena Record was founded in 1904 (according to some sources it was 1908) by J. Feigenbaum, i.e., when the Societa Italiana di Fonotipia was founded, considered the first fully European record label. Syrena Record produced turntables, recorded music and also pressed records. It is noteworthy that its recordings were of a very high technical quality, often even higher than those of the best English or German labels, with prices lower than those of imported records. Syrena Record was also the first label in Europe to introduce a photograph of the performer on the record label (in 1913).

7 Following EU directives: Council Directive 93/98/EEC of 29 October 1993 on the harmonisation of the term of protection of copyright and certain related rights; Directive 2006/116/EC of the European Parliament and of the Council of 12 December 2006 on the term of protection of copyright and certain related rights; Directive 2011/77/EU of the European Parliament and of the Council of 27 September 2011 concerning the amendment of Directive 2006/116/EC on the term of protection of copyright and certain related rights; Directive (EU) 2019/790 of the European Parliament and of the Council of 17 April 2019 on copyright and related rights in the digital single market and amending Directives 96/9/EC and 2001/29/EC.

8 The big three companies at the time were: Edison, Columbia and Victor (Bishop, 2005).

9 During the era of recording music onto discs in the studio, the process of cutting the sound track into the recording matrix was costly and time consuming. If a recording failed, the entire piece had to be re-recorded on a new disc. This technology required multiple recordings on separate carriers, resulting in higher expenses and an extended recording period. The discs themselves and the sound recording equipment were also relatively costly. In contrast, the advent of magnetic tape recorders and magnetic tapes offered greater convenience. Compositions could be recorded in parts, and once recorded, the tape could be reused for subsequent recordings.

10 The primary product of the recording industry was the studio album, which was later promoted through live performances of the recorded tracks. Concert releases, recorded on professional multitrack tape recorders, served as additional products. They catered to consumers who were unable to attend the live events, and also served as souvenirs for those who did participate.

11 The network effect is a phenomenon where the value of a product or service grows as more individuals join and utilize the network. The concept was introduced by B. Metcalfe, the creator of the Ethernet standard and founder of 3Com Corporation. The network effect is often known as Metcalfe's law, as coined by B. Metcalfe himself (Hagstrom, 2007, p. 226).

Bibliography

Aguiar, L., Martens, B., 2016. Digital Music Consumption on the Internet: Evidence from Clickstream Data. *Information Economics and Policy* 34, 27–43.

Aguilar, F.J., 1967. *Scanning the Business Environment*. Macmillan, New York.

Ahlkvist, J.A., Faulkner, R., 2002. Will This Record Work for Us? Managing Music Formats in Commercial Radio. *Qualitative Sociology* 25, 189–215.

Alexander, A., Owers, J., Carveth, R., Hollifield, C.A., Greco, A.N., 2015. *Media Economics: Theory and Practice*. Routledge, Abingdon.

Allan, R.A., 2004. *A History of the Personal Computer: The People and the Technology*. Allan Publishing, London.

Anderson, C., 2006. *The Long Tail: How Endless Choice Is Creating Unlimited Demand*. Business Books, London.

Andersson, Å.E., Andersson, D.E., 2006. *The Economics of Experiences, the Arts and Entertainment*. Edward Elgar, Cheltenham.

Anderton, C., Dubber, A., James, M., 2013. *Understanding the Music Industries*. Sage, Los Angeles, CA, Londyn.

Askerud, P., Engelhardt, R.A., 2007. Statistics on Cultural Industries: Framework for the Elaboration of National Data Capacity Building Projects (No. 9292231316 9789292231316). UNESCO Asia and Pacific Regional Bureau for Education, Bangkok.

Association, C., 2019. Our Guidelines for the Implementation of the DSM Directive. International Communia Association. URL https://www.communia-association.org/2019/12/02/guidelines-implementation-dsm-directive/ (accessed 4.15.21).

Baldwin, R.E., Martin, P., 1999. Two Waves of Globalisation: Superficial Similarities, Fundamental Differences (No. w6904). National Bureau of Economic Research. https://doi.org/10.3386/w6904

Bazen, S., Bouvard, L., Zimmermann, J.-B., 2014. Jamendo et les Artistes: Un Nouveau Modèle pour l'Industrie Musicale ? Doctoral dissertation, Propice, projet ANR. URL https://halshs.archives-ouvertes.fr/halshs-00989740 (accessed 3.4.21).

Becker, G.S., Grossman, M., Murphy, K., 1991. Rational Addiction and the Effect of Price on Consumption. *The American Economic Review* 81, 237–241.

Becker, G.S., Murphy, K., 1988. A Theory of Rational Addiction. *The Journal of Political Economy* 96, 675–700.

Benghozi, P.-J., 2017. What Efficiency and What Future for the Cultural Quotas in the Digital Age? *DigiWorld Economic Journal* 107, 139–162.

Benhamou, F., 2008. L'économie de la culture. La Découverte, Paris.

Benhamou, F., Farchy, J., 2014. *Droit d'auteur et copyright*. La Découverte, Paris.

Benkler, Y., 2006. *The Wealth of Networks: How Social Production Transforms Markets and Freedom*. Yale University Press, New Haven.

Bernstein, A., Sekine, N., Weissman, D., 2007. *The Global Music Industry. Three Perspectives*. Routledge, New York, London.

Bieliński, J., 2006. *Rozwój sektorów we współczesnej gospodarce*. Wydawnictwo Uniwersytetu Gdańskiego, Gdańsk.

Bishop, J., 2005. Building International Empires of Sound: Concentrations of Power and Property in the "Global" Music Market. *Popular Music and Society* 28, 443–471.
Boorstin, E., 2004. *Music Sales in the Age of File Sharing*. Senior thesis. Department of Economics. Princeton University, Princeton, NJ.
Bottomley, A.J., 2015. 'Home Taping Is Killing Music': The Recording Industries' 1980s Anti-Home Taping Campaigns and Struggles Over Production, Labor and Creativity. *Creative Industries Journal* 8, 123–145.
Bourdieu, P., 1979. *La Distinction. Critique Sociale du Jugement*. Minuit, Paris.
Boyer, P.S., Clark, C.E., Rieser, A., Halttunen, K., Kett, J.F., Salisbury, N., Sitkoff, H., Woloch, N., 2018. *The Enduring Vision: A History of American People*. Cengage Learning, Boston, MA.
Brochand, C., 1994. *Histoire générale de la radio et de la télévision en France*. La documentation française, Paris.
Burnett, R., 2010. *The Global Jukebox: The International Music Industry*. Routledge, London.
Byun, C.H.C., 2016. The Economics of the Popular Music Industry [WWW Document]. URL https://doi.org/10.1057/9781137467058
Castells, M., 2002. *The Internet Galaxy: Reflections on the Internet, Business and Society*. Oxford University Press, Oxford.
Castiglione, C., Infante, D., 2016. Rational Addiction and Cultural Goods: The Case of the Italian Theatregoer. *Journal of Cultural Economics* 40, 163–190. https://doi.org/10.1007/s10824-015-9247-4
Caves, R.E., 2000. *Creative Industries: Contracts between Art and Commerce*. Harvard University Press, Cambridge, MA, London.
CC, n.d. About CC Licenses [WWW Document]. URL https://creativecommons.org/about/cclicenses/ (accessed 9.18.20).
Chantepie, P., Le Diberder, A., 2010. *Révolution numérique et industries culturelles*. La Découverte, Paris.
Clarke, D., 1996. *The Rise and Fall of Popular Music*. St. Martin's Griffin, New York.
Coe, N.M., 2018. Global Production Networks. *Routl Companions* 147–160. https://doi.org/10.4324/9781315667379
Coe, N.M., 2015. Global Production Networks in the Creative Industries, in: Jones, C., Lorenzen, M., Sapsed, J. (Eds.), *The Oxford Handbook of Creative Industries*. Oxford University Press, Oxford, pp. 486–501.
Coleman, M., 2005. *Playback: From the Victrola to MP3, 100 Years of Music, Machines, and Money*. Da Capo Press, Cambridge, MA.
Corporate History [WWW Document], 2020. Sony. URL https://www.sony.net/SonyInfo/CorporateInfo/History/company/ (accessed 10.28.20).
CSA, n.d. Les quotas de chansons à la radio [WWW Document]. Conseil Supérieur de l'Audiovisuel. URL https://www.csa.fr/Reguler/Promotion-de-la-production-audiovisuelle/Les-quotas-de-chansons-a-la-radio (accessed 8.3.21).
Curien, N., Moreau, F., 2010. *L'industrie du disque*. La Découverte, Paris.
D'Anjou, L.J.M., 2003. The Riddles of Rock and Roll. *Soundscapes Online Journal on Media Culture* 6. URL http://hdl.handle.net/1765/886 (accessed 3.5.21).
Denegri-Knott, J., Tadajewski, M., 2010. The Emergence of MP3 Technology. *Journal of Historical Research in Marketing* 2, 397–425.
Dunning, J.H., 2013. *International Production and the Multinational Enterprise*. Routledge, London, New York.
EC, 2009. Communication from the Commission to The European Parliament, The Council, The European Economic and Social Committee and The Committee of

The Regions on Cross-Border Business to Consumer e-Commerce in the EU. Commission of the European Communities, Brussels.

EEC, 1993. Council Directive 93/98/EEC of 29 October 1993 harmonizing the term of protection of copyright and certain related rights, OJ L.

Encyclopédisque, n.d. Louviers, capitale du microsillon. Encyclopédisque. URL http://www.encyclopedisque.fr/disque/32379.html (accessed 3.23.21).

Escoffier, J., 2003. *Sexual Revolution*. Thunder Mouth Press, New York.

Eskelsen, G., Marcus, A., Ferree, W.K., 2010. Digital Economy Fact Book (No. 10). The Progress and Freedom Foundation. URL www.pff.org/digital-economy-fact-book/ (accessed 3.23.21).

EU, 2011. Directive 2011/77/EU of the European Parliament and of the Council of 27 September 2011 amending Directive 2006/116/EC on the term of protection of copyright and certain related rights, EU, Publications Office of the EU.

EU, 1997. Treaty establishing the European Community, 11997E151. Official Journal C 340. URL https://eur-lex.europa.eu/legal-content/EN/TXT/HTML/?uri=CELEX%3A11997E151 (accessed 4.29.23).

Faulkner, D., Bowman, C., 1995. *The Essence of Competitive Strategy, the Essence of Management Series*. Prentice Hall, New York.

Ferstler, H., 2005. Cassette, in: Ferstler, H. (Ed.), *Encyclopedia of Recorded Sound*. Routledge, New York.

Filiciak, M., Hofmokl, J., Tarkowski, A., 2012. The Circulations of Culture-On Social Distribution of Content [WWW Document]. URL https://ssrn.com/abstract=2246508, http://dx.doi.org/10.2139/ssrn.2246508 (accessed 3.04.21).

Font, F., Brookes, T., Fazekas, G., Guerber, M., La, A., Plans, D., Plumbley, M.D., Shaashua, M., Wang, W., Serra, X., 2016. Audio Commons: bringing Creative Commons audio content to the creative industries. Presented at the Audio Engineering Society Conference: 61st International Conference: Audio for Games, Audio Engineering Society, p. 8.

Fort, M.-L., 2000. Signaux qualitatifs et phénomène de star. Document de travail – Economie (1991-2003) 2000-13, LATEC, Laboratoire d'Analyse et des Techniques Economiques, CNRS UMR 5118, Université de Bourgogne. URL https://ideas.repec.org/p/lat/lateco/2000-13.html (accessed 3.4.2021).

Frej, J., 2014. Ewolucja konsumpcji muzyki w kontekście przełomu technologicznego. MA thesis, SGH Warsaw School of Economics, Warszawa.

Friedman, T.L., 2005. *The World Is Flat: A Brief History of the Twenty-first Century*, 1st ed. Farrar, Straus and Giroux, New York.

Frith, S., 2017. *Taking Popular Music Seriously: Selected Essays*. Routledge, London, New York.

Frith, S., 2004. *Popular Music*. Routledge, London, New York.

Frith, S., 1986. Art Versus Technology: The Strange Case of Popular Music. *Media, Culture & Society* 8, 263–279.

Gagné, G., 2011. Free Trade and Cultural Policies: Evidence from Three US Agreements. *Journal of World Trade* 45, 1267–1284.

Gałuszka, P., 2012a. Netlabel: Independent Non-Profit Micro-Enterprise or Just another Player in the Music Industry?, in: Nawojczyk, M. (Ed.), *Economy in Changing Society: Consumptions, Markets, Organizations and Social Policies*. Cambridge Scholars Publishing, Newcastle, pp. 173–190.

Gałuszka, P., 2012b. Economic Analysis of the Language Quotas for Polish Songs on the Radio. *Polish Yearbook of Law and Economics* 2, 29–48.

Gałuszka, P., 2009. *Biznes muzyczny*. Placet, Warszawa.

Gans, H.J., 2011. *Popular Culture and High Culture: An Analysis and Evaluation of Taste*. Basic Books, New York.
García, L., 2006. Le phénomène « Lambada » : globalisation et identité. Nuevo Mundo Mundos Nuevos. Nouveaux mondes mondes nouveaux – Novo Mundo Mundos Novos – New world New worlds. https://doi.org/10.4000/nuevomundo.2181 (accessed 5.23.23).
"German quota" on the radio. The Endless Debate [WWW Document], 2016. URL https://www.goethe.de/en/kul/med/20867119.html (accessed 7.20.20).
Gierat-Bieroń, B., 2018. *Polityka kulturalna Unii Europejskiej*. Wydawnictwo Uniwersytetu Jagiellońskiego, Kraków.
Gierszewska, G., Romanowska, M., 2017. *Analiza strategiczna przedsiębiorstwa*. Polskie Wydawnictwo Ekonomiczne, Warszawa.
Gronow, P., 1983. The Record Industry: The Growth of a Mass Medium. *Popular Music* 3, 53–75.
Hagstrom, R.G., 2007. *Essential Buffett: Timeless Principles for the New Economy*. John Wiley & Sons, New York.
Hamel, G., Prahalad, C.K., 2010. *Competing for the Future*. Harvard Business School Press, Boston, MA.
Hamlen, W.A., 1994. Variety and Superstardom in Popular Music. *Economic Inquiry* 32, 395–406.
Hamlen, W.A., 1991. Superstardom in Popular Music: Empirical Evidence. *The Review of Economics and Statistics* 73, 729–733.
Hartley, J., Potts, J., Cunningham, S., Flew, T., Keane, M., Banks, J., 2013. *Key Concepts in Creative Industries*. SAGE, Los Angeles, CA.
Helberger, N., Dufft, N., Van Gompel, S., Hugenholtz, B., 2008. Never forever: Why Extending the Term of Protection for Sound Recordings Is a Bad Idea. *European Intellectual Property Review* 30, 174–181.
Hennion, A., 2005. Pour une pragmatique du goût. CSI Working Papers Series No 001. URL https://shs.hal.science/halshs-00087895/document (accessed 3.4.2021).
Henriksson, T., Janowska, A.A., 2023. Production Networks in the Cultural and Creative Sector: Case Studies from the European Music Industry. CICERONE Horizon 2020. URL https://zenodo.org/record/6885744#.ZEqwrHbP1PY (accessed 6.30.23).
Herman, E.S., McChesney, R.W., 2014. *The Global Media. The New Missionaries of Global Capitalism*. Bloomsbury Academic, London.
Hesmondhalgh, D., 2013. *The Cultural Industries*, 3rd ed. SAGE, Los Ángeles, CA, London, New Delhi, Singapore, Washington, DC.
Hesmondhalgh, D., 1996. Flexibility, Post-Fordism and the Music Industries. *Media, Culture & Society* 18, 469–488.
Hoffmann, F.W., Ferstler, H., 2005a. EMI Group Ltd, in: Ferstler, H. (Ed.), *Encyclopedia of Recorded Sound*. Routledge, New York.
Hoffmann, F.W., Ferstler, H., 2005b. Disc, in: Ferstler, H. (Ed.), *Encyclopedia of Recorded Sound*. Routledge, New York.
Holbrook, M.B., 2005. The Role of Ordinary Evaluations in the Market for Popular Culture: Do Consumers Have "Good Taste"? *Marketing Letters* 16, 75–86.
Huberman, B.A., 2003. *The Laws of the Web*. The MIT Press, Cambridge, London.
Hull, G.P., 2004. *The Recording Industry*. Routledge, New York.
Hull, G.P., Hutchison, T.W., Strasser, R., 2011. *The Music Business and Recording Industry: Delivering Music in the 21st Century*. Taylor & Francis, New York, London.

Huygens, M., Van Den Bosch, F.A.J., Volberda, H.W., Baden-Fuller, C., 2001. Co-Evolution of Firm Capabilities and Industry Competition: Investigating the Music Industry, 1877–1997. *Organization Studies* 22, 971–1011.

IFPI, 2019. Music Listening. IFPI. URL https://www.ifpi.org/wp-content/uploads/2020/07/Music-Listening-2019-1.pdf (accessed 4.29.21).

IFPI, n.d. What We Do [WWW Document]. IFPI. URL https://www.ifpi.org/about-us/what-we-do/ (accessed 5.11.21).

Jachowicz, P., 2009. Wielki Kryzys, szoki naftowe i obecny kryzys finansowy: próba analizy porównawczej, in: Osiński, J., Sztaba, S. (Eds.), *Nauki Społeczne Wobec Kryzysu Na Rynkach Finansowych*. Oficyna Wydawnicza SGH, Warszawa, pp. 11–31.

Janczewska-Sołomko, K., 2002. The Contribution of Polish Phonography in the Early Period Development of This Discipline, in:*Dyskopedia poloników do roku 1918*. Biblioteka Narodowa, Warszawa, pp. 1–3. URL http://conf.evarussia.ru/upload/echolot2005/reports/dokla-dEn_762.doc (accessed 3.24.21).

Janowska, A.A., 2012. Problem globalnej ochrony własności intelektualnej, in: Molendowski, E. (Ed.), *Globalizacja i regionalizacja we współczesnym świecie*. Uniwersytet Ekonomiczny w Krakowie, Kraków, pp. 351–360.

Janowska, A.A., 2011. Kryzysy a rozwój branży fonograficznej w XX i XXI wieku. *Prace i Materiały Instytutu Studiów Międzynarodowych Szkoła Główna Handlowa* 40, 75–108.

Janowska, A.A., 2009. Polityka audiowizualna Unii Europejskiej, in: Bonikowska, M. (Ed.), *Media a Wyzwania XXI Wieku*. Wydawnictwo Trio, Warszawa, pp. 313–325.

Janowska, A.A., 2008. Ewolucja konsumpcji muzyki – tendencja antropotropiczna. *Studia i Prace Kolegium Ekonomiczno-Społecznego SGH Zeszyt Naukowy* 15, 191–208.

Jorgenson, D.W., Khuong, M.V., 2016. The ICT Revolution, World Economic Growth, and Policy Issues. *Telecommunication Policy* 40, 383–397.

KEA, E.A., 2021. *Market Analysis of the Cultural and Creative Sectors in Europe*. EIF, Brussels.

Kenney, W.H., 2003. *Recorded Music in American Life: The Phonograph and Popular Memory, 1890–1945*. Oxford University Press, New York.

Kominek, M., 1986. *Zaczęło się od fonografu*. Polskie Wydawnictwa Muczyzne, Kraków.

Kotler, P., 2007. *Marketing Management: Analysis, Planning Implementation and Control*, 2nd ed. Prentice Hall of India, New Delhi.

Kowalski, T., 2006. *Media na rynku: wprowadzenie do ekonomiki mediów, Edukacja Medialna: podręcznik akademicki*. Wydawnictwa Akademickie i Profesjonalne. GrupaKapitałowa WSiP, Warszawa.

Krueger, A.B., 2005. The Economics of Real Superstars: The Market for Rock Concerts in the Material World. *Journal of Labor Economics* 23, 1–30.

Laing, D., 2009. World Music and the Global Music Industry: Flows, Corporations and Networks, in: Tuulikki, P. (Ed.), *World Music: Roots and Routes*. Studies across Disciplines in the Humanities and Social Sciences 6. Collegium for Advanced Studies, Helsinki, pp. 14–33.

Latrive, F., 2007. *Du bon usage de la piraterie*. Découverte, Paris.

Leibenstein, H., 1950. Bandwagon, Snob, and Veblen Effects in the Theory of Consumers' Demand. *The Quarterly Journal of Economics* 64, 183–207.

Lerski, T., 2004. *Syrena Record. Pierwsza polska wytwórnia fonograficzna. 1904–1939*. Karin, Warszawa.

Lessig, L., 2004. Free Culture: How Big Media Uses Technology and the Law to Lock Down Culture and Control Creativity [WWW Document]. URL http://www.free-culture.cc/freeculture.pdf

Lévêque, F., Ménière, Y., 2003. *Economie de la propriété intellectuelle*. La Découverte, Paris.

Levy-Garboua, L., Montmarquette, C., 2011. Demand, in: Towse, R. (Ed.), *A Handbook of Cultural Economics*. Cheltenham, Northampton, MA, pp. 177–187.

Liebowitz, S.J., 1985. Copying and Indirect Appropriability: Photocopying of Journals. *Journal of Political Economy* 93, 945–957.

Longhurst, B., Bogdanovic, D., 2014. *Popular Music and Society*. Polity, Cambridge.

Maffesoli, M., 2019. *Le temps des tribus: le déclin de l'individualisme dans les sociétés postmodernes*, 4e éd. Petite vermillon (Paris). La Table ronde, Paris.

Malm, K., Wallis, R., 1992. *Media Policy and Music Activity*. Routledge, London.

Marcus, C., 2009. *Future of Creative Industries*. Implications for Research Policy. Publications Office of the EU, EU.

Martland, P., 2008. The Failed 1912 Merger between Carl Lindström AG, the Gramophone Company Ltd and the Victor Talking Machine Co Inc. Presented at the Carl Lindsröm AG conference, Carl Lindsröm AG conference, Budapest.

McCain, R.A., 2003. Taste Formation, in: Towse, R. (Ed.), *A Handbook of Cultural Economics*. Edward Elgar Publishing Inc., Northampton, MA, pp. 445–450.

McCourt, T., Rothenbuhler, E., 1997. SoundScan and the Consolidation of Control in the Popular Music Industry. *Media, Culture & Society* 19, 201–218.

McQuail, D., 2005. *Mass Communication Theory*. Sage, London.

Meisel, J.B., Sullivan, T.S., 2002. The Impact of the Internet on the Law and Economics of the Music Industry. *INFO* 4, 16–22.

Mirski, J.-Y., 1998. L'industrie phonographique française dans le contexte mondial. Presented at the Les enjeux du multimédia pour la production musicale, M & M conseil, Paris.

Misiewicz, A., 2019. Dyrektywa o prawie autorskim na jednolitym rynku cyfrowym. ZAiKS. URL https://zaiks.org.pl/1707,0,dyrektywa_o_prawie_autorskim_na_jednolitym_rynku_cyfrowym (accessed 8.3.21).

MMC, 1994. *The Supply of Recorded Music*. Monopolies and Mergers Commission, London.

Mol, J.M., Wijnberg, N.M., Carroll, C., 2005. Value Chain Envy: Explaining New Entry and Vertical Integration in Popular Music. *Journal of Management Studies* 42, 251–276.

Negus, K., 2012. *Popular Music in Theory: An Introduction*. Polity, Cambridge.

Negus, K., 2001. *Producing Pop: Culture and Conflict in the Popular Music Industry*. Arnold, London.

Nelson, P., 1970. Information and Consumer Behavior. *The Journal of Political Economy* 78, 311–329.

Nielsen, 2013. Turn it Up: Music Fans Could Spend Up To $2.6B More Annually [WWW Document]. URL https://www.nielsen.com/us/en/insights/article/2013/turn-it-up--music-fans-could-spend-up-to–2-6b-more-annually/ (accessed 7.11.20).

Niklewicz, K., 2009. Tu nie gra muzyka [WWW Document]. wyborcza.pl. URL https://wyborcza.pl/1,155287,6358020,Tu_nie_gra_muzyka.html?disableRedirects=true (accessed 4.15.21).

Nos activités. Musique [WWW Document], 2020. Vivendi. URL https://www.vivendi.com/nos-activites/musique/ (accessed 10.28.20).

Our Brands [WWW Document], 2022. Warner Bros. Discovery. URL https://wbd.com/our-brands/ (accessed 5.25.23).

Owsinski, B., 2014. *Music 3.0: A Survival Guide for Making Music in the Internet Age*. Hal Leonard Books, Milwaukee.

Parikh, M., 1999. *The Music Industry in the Digital World: Waves of Changes*. Polytechnic University, Singapore.

Passman, D.S., 2015. *All You Nneed to Know about the Music Business*. Simon&Schoster, New York.

Piesiewicz, P.F., 2009. *Utwór muzyczny i jego twórca*. Wolters Kluwer Polska, Warszawa.

Porter, M.E., 1980. *Competitive Strategy*. The Free Press, New York.

Power, D., Hallencreutz, D., 2007. Competitiveness, Local Production Systems and Global Commodity Chains in the Music Industry: Entering the US Market. *Regional studies: Journal of the Regional Studies Association* 41, 377–390.

RIAA, 2015. Michael Jackson's "Thriller" First Ever 30X Multi-Platinum RIAA Certification. Gold&Platinum. URL https://www.riaa.com/michael-jacksons-thriller-first-ever-30x-multi-platinum-riaa-certification/ (accessed 4.3.21).

Rieffel, R., 2014. *Révolution numérique, révolution culturelle*. Gallimard, Paris.

Rifkin, J., 2015. *The Zero Marginal Cost Society: The Internet of Things, the Collaborative Commons, and the Eclipse of Capitalism*. St. Martin's Press, New York.

Robertson, R., 2003. *The Three Waves of Globalization: A History of a Developing Global Consciousness*. Zed Books, Nova Scotia, New York.

Romanowska, M., Cylwik, A., 2004. *Leksykon zarzadzania*. Difin, Warszawa.

Rosen, S., 1981. The Economics of Superstars. *The American Economic Review* 71 (5), 845–858.

Rudnicki, R., Pisarski, M., 2019. Historia pierwszego iPhone'a od Apple. Telefon, który zmienił wszystko [WWW Document]. Komputer Świat. URL https://www.komputerswiat.pl/artykuly/redakcyjne/iphone-historia-jak-powstawal-pierwszy-iphone-od-apple/90ln46b (accessed 3.23.21).

Seaman, B.A., 2006. Empirical Studies of Demand for the Performing Arts, in: Ginsburgh, V.A., Throsby, D. (Eds.), *Handbook of the Economics of Art and Culture*. Elsevier, Amsterdam, pp. 415–471.

Segers, K., Huijgh, E., 2006. Clarifying the Complexity and Ambivalence of the Cultural Industries, Working Papers 8. CeMeSo Centre for Media Sociology, Brussels.

Senftleben, M., Angelopoulos, C., Frosio, G., Moscon, V., Peguera, M., Rognstad, O.A., 2018. The Recommendation on Measures to Safeguard Fundamental Rights and the Open Internet in the Framework of the EU Copyright Reform. *European Intellectual Property Review* 40, 149–163.

Shuker, R., 2017. *Popular Music: The Key Concepts*. Routledge, London, New York.

Shy, O., 2004. *The Economics of Network Industries*. Cambridge University Press, Cambridge.

Solomon, M.R., Askegaard, S., Hogg, M.K., 2019. *Consumer Behaviour: A European Perspective*. Pearson Education, Harlow.

Statista, 2020. Music publishing revenue worldwide 2020 [WWW Document]. Statista. URL https://www.statista.com/statistics/1264901/music-publishing-revenue-worldwide/ (accessed 5.23.23).

Stigler, G.J., Becker, G.S., 1977. De Gustibus Non Est Disputandum. *The American Economic Review* 67, 76–90.

Stonehouse, G., 2000. *Global and Transnational Business: Strategy and Management*. John Wiley and Sons, Chichester.

Strasser, R., 2010. *Music Business: The Key Concepts*. Routledge, London, New York.
Sun, H., 2019. *Digital Revolution Tamed: The Case of the Recording Industry*. Palgrave Macmillan, Cham.
Szalai, G., 2013. Adele to Perform 'Skyfall' at the Oscars. Billboard. URL https://www.billboard.com/music/music-news/adele-to-perform-skyfall-at-the-oscars-1526275/ (accessed 5.23.23).
Throsby, D., 2010. *The Economics of Cultural Policy*. Cambridge University Press, Cambridge, New York, Melbourne, Madrid, Cape Town, Singapore, Sao Paulo, Delhi, Dubai, Tokyo.
Throsby, D., 2002. *The Music Industry in the New Millennium: Global and Local Perspectives*. UNESCO, Paris.
Throsby, D., 1998. *Economics and Culture*. Cambridge University Press, Cambridge.
Toffler, A., 2006. *Revolutionary Wealth*, 1st ed. Knopf, New York.
Tournès, L., 2012. *Du phonographe au MP3: une histoire de la musique enregistrée: XIXe-XXIe siècle*. Éditions Autrement, Paris.
Towse, R., 2019. *A Textbook of Cultural Economics*, 2nd ed. Cambridge University Press, Cambridge.
Towse, R., 2017. Economics of Music Publishing: Copyright and the Market. *Journal of Cultural Economics* 41, 403–420. https://doi.org/10.1007/s10824-016-9268-7
Tschmuck, P., 2014. *Creativity and Innovation in the Music Industry*. Springer Berlin, Berlin.
Tschmuck, P., 2009. Copyright, Contracts and Music Production. *Information, Communication and Society* 12, 251–266.
UNCTAD, 2010. *Creative Economy. A Feasible Development Option*. UNCTAD, United Nations, Geneva.
UNCTAD, 2008. *Creative Economy: Report 2008*. United Nations, Geneva, New York.
Veblen, T., 2016. *The Theory of the Leisure Class*. Perennial Press. URL https://www.scribd.com/read/375413331/The-Theory-of-the-Leisure-Class.
Vogel, H.L., 2011. *Entertainment Industry Economics: A Guide for Financial Analysis*. Cambridge University Press, Cambridge, New York, Melbourne, Madrid, Cape Town, Singapore, Sao Paulo, Delhi, Dubai, Tokyo, Mexico City.
Watkins, G., 2003. *Proof through the Night: Music and the Great War*. University of California Press, Los Angeles, CA, London.
Wikström, P., 2013. *The Music Industry: Music in the Cloud*. Polity, Cambridge, MA.
Williamson, J., Cloonan, M., 2007. Rethinking the Music Industry. *Popular Music* 26 (2), 305–322.
WIPO, 1928. Berne Convention for the Protection of Literary and Artistic Works, WIPO. WIPO.
WIPO Lex [WWW Document], n.d. URL https://www.wipo.int/wipolex/en/text/295578 (accessed 5.24.23).
Yip, G.S., 1995. *Total Global Strategy II*, 2nd. ed. Prentice-Hall Inc, Upper Saddle River, NJ.
Zorska, Anna., 2002. Ku globalizacji?: przemiany w korporacjach transnarodowych i w gospodarce światowej. Wydaw. Naukowe PWN, Warszawa.

2 Power structure before the digital revolution

2.1 Recording industry as oligonomy

The recording industry is traditionally seen as an oligopoly, with several sellers offering similar products that are close substitutes and their pricing decisions affecting each other (Curien and Moreau, 2010; Vogel, 2011). This structure exhibits characteristics such as vertical integration, horizontal concentration, transnational structures, pseudo-diversity, and acquiring innovative firms (Bishop, 2005; Curien and Moreau, 2010; Hannaford, 2007; Hull, 2004; Wikström, 2020). Collusion among companies, known as *friendly enemies*, is also common in oligopolies (Williamson and Cloonan, 2007).[1]

Hannaford (2007) adds the concept of an oligopsony, where there are few buyers and many sellers in the industry, to the description of the recording industry's characteristics. In the recording industry, both oligopoly and oligopsony exist, forming an oligonomy. Companies act as an oligopoly for one part of the sector and as an oligopsony for another. See Figure 2.1 for an illustration of these relationships.

The recording industry exhibits the characteristics of an oligonomy, where major recording labels act as buyers in their interactions with artists, while individual consumers make up a large group of buyers on the other side. The major recording companies leverage their position on both the supply and demand sides of the market, aiming to acquire content at low costs and sell it to a wide audience at high prices.

Researchers hold different views on the impact of this configuration on musicians' opportunities and consumer offerings. Some argue that large companies in an oligonomy foster innovation by bearing its costs and passing on the benefits to consumers. Others believe that powerful actors in the oligonomy lack incentives to explore innovative solutions (Shuker, 2017, p. 172). This perspective finds support in the emergence of certain musical genres like rock and roll and hip-hop, which initially thrived under smaller labels before being marketed globally by majors. On the other hand, when it comes to technological advancements, major players have historically led the way, such as with the introduction of long-playing disc (LP) or compact disc (CD)

DOI: 10.4324/9781003414605-3

Figure 2.1 Oligonomy in the recording industry. Author's draft based on Bishop (2005, pp. 443–471).

standards. However, the majors initially underestimated the impact of the digital revolution, resulting in serious consequences for them (Arditi, 2015).

The relationship among these market players is analysed in detail using Porter's five forces model.

2.2 Porter's five forces model – theoretical background

According to Williamson and Cloonan (2007, p. 28), the history of popular music is a history of conflict, both between artists and recording companies and among the recording companies themselves. This conflict also extends to distributors, retailers, and the media. Consumers also have divergent interests from the other actors involved.

These conflicts form the basis of Porter's five forces model (2008) applied to the analysis (Figure 2.2), which includes the following forces:

- the threat of new entrants; they enter the industry with the intention of seizing some market share; they try to exert pressure on established companies through prices, costs and the level of investment required to compete; new entrants to the recording industry are mainly not only new recording companies but also new music distributors;

- the bargaining power of suppliers and their ability to exert pressure on companies in the industry; powerful suppliers can keep some of the value from the whole chain for themselves by lowering the quality of service, imposing higher prices or higher switching costs that companies should have to bear; in the recording industry songwriters, composers (authors) and performers are the suppliers; in some genres, authors and performers are the same people; for recording companies, it is the performers who are most important, giving shape to the intangible part of the industry's product;
- the bargaining power of buyers and their ability to exert pressure on the companies in the industry; strong buyers may require a reduction in prices, an increase in the quality of the products offered, they may also take actions that increase the rivalry between individual companies in the industry, which affects its overall revenues; the main group of buyers in the analysed area are individual consumers as well as entities that use music to create their own products; the most important of the latter are media (programmers) (Curien and Moreau, 2010), as well as, e.g., film studios or video game producers;
- the threat of substitutes; substitutes fulfil the same or similar function as products existing in the market; if the threat of substitutes is high, all companies may be affected in terms of revenue; therefore they should take measures, for example, to increase the efficiency of their products (their potential usefulness to buyers) or to improve their marketing; a substitute product in the recording industry may be either a recording format (e.g., analogue or digital) or an artist or an individual piece of music;
- the industry rivalry; it usually consists of lowering prices, introducing new products, using advertising campaigns and improving the quality of the products; if competition in the industry is high, revenues of the whole industry decrease, because there is competition by price; if, however, competition is based not on price, but rather on product features, delivery time or brand image, the profitability of the industry does not decrease, because the value of the product increases, allowing companies to maintain higher prices; if, however, every company targets a different segment of consumers with different prices, products, services or brands, the result may be a positive-sum rivalry, meaning a higher average profit for the whole industry.

The forces mentioned above are influenced by various factors, as stated by Gierszewska and Romanowska (2017, p. 75). These factors include the degree of concentration, the possibility of vertical integration, the height of barriers to entry, economies of scale, and access to distribution channels. In the recording industry, access to promotion channels is also crucial.

The power dynamics within the recording industry are greatly impacted by its unique characteristics. These include the nature of the product as an experience good, consumer tastes driving demand, high uncertainty regarding the success of the product, a cost structure with high fixed costs and low marginal production costs. Consequently, companies adopt a strategy focused on maximising sales rather than maximising profit, aiming to achieve economies of scale. As Frith (1988) highlighted, recording companies prefer to sell 500,000 copies of one album rather than 50,000 copies of ten different albums.

The strategy of maximising sales in the recording industry involves implementing various measures, including:

- diversifying the product offering through overproduction: recording companies produce a large number of projects to minimise the risk of failure; by catering to different tastes and interests, they expect that some projects will resonate with a significant consumer base, generating revenue that can offset the costs of less popular ones;
- developing the star system: the focus is on creating and promoting star brands to reduce the risk of consumer dissatisfaction with their purchases; by associating their products with popular and well-established artists, recording companies aim to enhance consumer appeal and increase sales;
- expanding the distribution network: the goal is to maximise the benefits derived from economies of scale and eliminate competitors; recording companies strive to establish a robust and extensive distribution network that ensures broad market reach and efficient delivery of their products;
- intensifying promotional activities: promotional efforts are intensified to support the star system and enable consumers to become familiar with the product before making a purchase; through marketing campaigns, advertising, and other promotional tactics, recording companies aim to create awareness, generate interest, and drive sales.

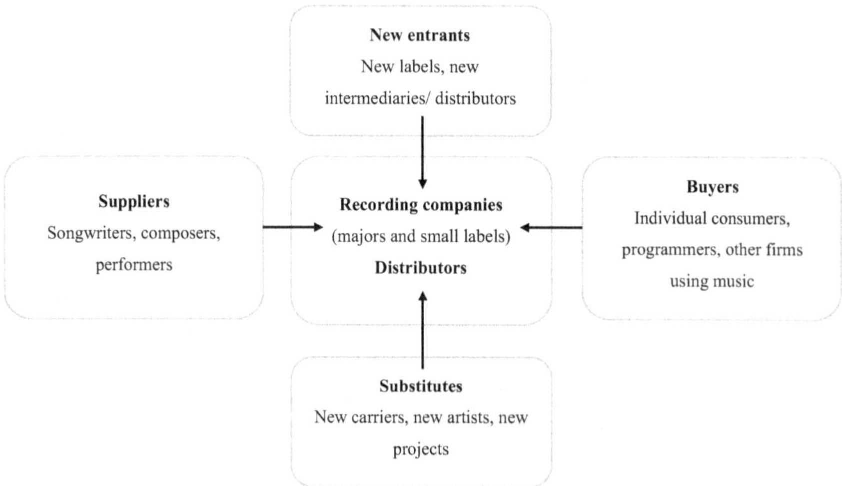

Figure 2.2 Porter's five forces diagram for the recording industry.

2.2.1 *The threat of new entrants*

The entry of new producers into the recording industry depends on the height of the entry barriers at the production level, which primarily involves the expenses associated with developing this aspect of the business. Moreover, access to the right input, i.e., authors and performers, is also important. Another significant element is access to distribution and promotion channels.

In the history of the recording industry, there were a few periods in which new music producers entered the field. The first of these occurred after 1914, when patents to produce recorded music and playback equipment expired (Alexander, 1994; Bishop, 2005).[2] With patent expiry, the principal barrier to entry for new businesses lowered, so their number grew annually, until 1923 by about 20% and until 1929 by about 11% (Alexander, 1994). It resulted in higher competition and consequently lower prices for reproduction equipment. Furthermore, as companies were improving technology of both recordings and turntable manufacturing, the cost of producing and reproducing phonograms declined, facilitating the entry of more players into the industry. The ongoing development of the mass market was an additional factor favouring the evolution of the industry and the emergence of new manufacturers. It resulted in a separation of functions: some companies began to specialise in recording production, while others continued to produce and sell phonographs.

Recording companies, as they wanted to gain more market share, began to develop and diversify their products dividing them into different music genres. They also started to release more artists which made the sales of phonograms increase. However, this prevented them from achieving the economies of scale and increasing revenues. Decca, a new entrant to the market, adopted an innovative strategy. It focused on releasing a small number of titles in high volumes, inviting the greatest stars of the time to collaborate, running aggressive advertising and also reducing album prices by almost half. At the same time, it was concerned with the high technical quality of the recordings (Frith, 2017). That is how Decca quickly attained a very strong position in the market. Already in 1938, together with RCA-Victor, they produced 75% of all records released in the United States (Kominek, 1986, p. 74). The success of the companies in the industry came to be determined by access to promotional channels, especially the promotion of recordings on radio networks.

The post-war years were another significant period in history when numerous new companies entered the industry. Technological innovations allowed for a large reduction in production costs, and social changes led to an increased demand for music. Small, dynamic players emerged on the market with lower operating expenses, faster information circulation, a willingness to take risks, and close cooperation with local radio stations for music promotion. While the majors' market share in 1948 was around 75%, it decreased to 48% in 1956 and 25% in 1962 (Alexander, 1994). Independent labels held the majority of the market at that time.

This marked the last period when small companies had such a large market share in the industry. The majors gradually regained their position through strategic activities in three areas: diversifying the genres of music to capture various market segments, developing an international distribution network, and intensifying marketing activities. These endeavours required substantial financial investments that only large companies could afford, enabling them to take control of the market and expand internationally. Small labels were relegated to local roles, as noted by Hannaford (2007) in his concept of oligonomy in the recording industry.

The threat of new entrants primarily came from big players who extended their activities into the recording industry, having previously operated in other areas. In the early 1960s, Warner Bros (previously active in the cinema industry) entered the scene by launching Warner Records. Other companies such as Bertelsmann, Sony, Matsushita, and Seagram's also joined the field by acquiring existing major record labels. Matsushita acquired MCA and Seagram's purchased 80% of it later on. Additionally, Seagram's acquired PolyGram and merged it with MCA to form Universal Music Group. Bertelsmann acquired RCA and renamed it BMG. Sony, in its pursuit of building a multimedia empire, also purchased CBS Records. At this stage, the majors were no longer competing primarily in terms of production but focused on distribution and promotion of music.

2.2.2 *The bargaining power of suppliers*

The suppliers in the recording industry, including artists and producers, share two common goals. The short-term goal is to release recordings and generate profits from their sales, while the long-term goal is to develop the artist's career and establish a sustainable source of revenue. However, conflicts arise when it comes to certain details, such as artistic vision, creative freedom, quality, originality, and novelty. Artists are deeply connected to their own ideas and seek recognition from both the audience and the creative community. They often explore new sounds and artistic visions. On the other hand, recording companies are primarily concerned with maximising album sales and appealing to the widest possible audience. Originality and innovation may not only be viewed as undesirable but may also be perceived as posing a risk to the project's success. This is due to the fact that a significant portion of the audience prefers familiar music, either out of fear of disappointment or because of a tendency to conform to popular trends. This fundamental divergence lies at the core of the conflict between creators and recording companies. The aim of the recording companies is succinctly captured in the statement: "[...] a musician is a product, not a buddy, you grab a trendy model, squeeze out as much as you can, and that's it" (Janowska, 2016; Vinyl [TV series], 2023). This statement reflects the power dynamics between artists and recording companies.

Another source of conflict between artists and labels arises from the limited number of labels compared to the large pool of artists seeking representation.

Labels receive hundreds of demo recordings each week from aspiring artists eager to secure a contract (Caves, 2000, p. 61). As major labels offer greater revenue and popularity opportunities, they become the primary target for emerging artists. Consequently, the relationship between suppliers and producers exhibits characteristics of an oligopsony, where labels dictate terms to less established and debut artists. In contrast, established stars and megastars who have achieved success can negotiate more favourable terms of cooperation.

The industry's high concentration creates significant barriers to entry for newcomers. For example, in the UK, at the beginning of 1993, major labels had contracts with only 513 performers (MMC, 1994). As noted by Hannaford (2007), musicians aspiring to gain popularity must capture the interest of the *big six*[3] labels, as they wield considerable influence in determining which music gets recorded, distributed, promoted, and ultimately listened to. Consequently, these labels serve as gatekeepers in the music industry.

Being gatekeepers, labels play a crucial role in selecting projects that have the potential for future success. They employ four primary strategies to achieve this (Burnett, 2010, p. 73). Firstly, they engage in overproduction, releasing a large number of records in the hopes that one of them will become successful. Secondly, they diversify their album releases across different genres to cater to a wide range of consumers and capture market shares in various segments. Thirdly, they promote albums and artists who sound similar to established and popular stars, positioning them as almost perfect substitutes. Lastly, they take risks by releasing completely unknown projects, aiming to foster trends and attract consumers.

The selection process involves several stages. Upon receiving numerous proposals from aspiring artists, labels rely on demos as the initial basis for selection. The producer's decision is often influenced more by the reputation of the artist's manager or independent producer rather than the quality or appeal of the work itself. The collaboration between the artist and the independent agent, along with the aforementioned strategies, shape the nature of the future project. Once selected, the project moves into production. The label enters into a comprehensive contract with the artist, covering aspects such as recording, pressing, promotion, distribution, and subsequent exploitation of the album. Among these contracts, the most significant one for a recording company is the performance contract, signed with the performer who ultimately gives the final artistic form to the musical work. Rights related to music and lyrics are typically handled by music publishing companies, although sometimes labels directly purchase songs (handled by the artists & repertoire department) and then find performers to record them. This occurs when the performer is not the author of the songs they are recording.

Performers enter into exclusive contracts with recording companies to produce a series of albums. Table 2.1 provides an overview of the types of contracts prevalent in the industry.

Table 2.1 Types of contracts in the recording industry. Based on Gałuszka (2009), Curien and Moreau (2010), Hull et al. (2011), Arditi (2015).

Type of contract	*Characteristics*
A 360° contract	In this type of contract, the label retains control over various aspects of the artist's career, including recording, live performances, music publishing revenues, and the use of the artist's brand; by assuming control over these activities, the label minimises its risk by ensuring involvement in all revenue streams; additionally, the label has influence over the artist's repertoire selection, aiming to reduce the risk of project failure by programming music with the highest chance of success; this type of contract is commonly signed with performers catering to a mass audience.
A standard contract	Under this contract, the label agrees to finance the production, distribution, and promotion of the music in exchange for royalties paid to the performer; the label holds the rights to the recording, and the performer receives compensation based on the agreed-upon royalty rate.
A licensing contract	Similar to the standard contract, the artist signs a licence contract for a fixed period of time, granting the label permission to use the recording while retaining certain rights; this type of contract is typically signed with established artists when it is mutually beneficial for both the artist and the label.
A profit-sharing contract	In this deal, the record company takes on the responsibility of promoting and distributing the music without financing the recording itself; the artist retains the economic rights to the work, and profits from the sale of the recordings are shared according to the terms outlined in the agreement.
Pressing and distribution contract	In this arrangement, the artist or a small label commissions a larger label to press and distribute the records, and in return, the larger label receives a contractually defined commission.

Once a record has been made, authors of musical works receive remuneration for the mechanical reproduction of their works, which refers to their fixation on a carrier. On average, they receive 8%–9% of the wholesale net price of the recording. However, this amount is subject to deductions, such as those for returned copies (Curien and Moreau, 2010).

For performers, there are two types of income from recording activities. Firstly, they receive royalties from the sale of their albums, and secondly, they receive remuneration from related rights. Additional sources of income may include earnings from performances and merchandising. The specific remuneration for the artist is outlined in the contract they sign with the label. As noted by Gałuszka (2009, p. 76), the contracts between artists and recording companies serve to reduce risk for the labels. This means that if a project is successful, the artist will continue recording further albums for the same label. This helps recoup the initial risky investment and lowers the risk of failure, as the artist's brand created with the first product and ongoing promotion are at play.

The remuneration in the form of royalties typically amounts to around 7% of the catalogue price of an album (Hoffmann and Ferstler, 2005, p. 952), but it is reduced to cover various costs, including promotion, album edition (graphics), and touring. Royalties can reach up to 15% or even 20% of the album price (Curien and Moreau, 2010, p. 14; Vogel, 2011, p. 243). In some cases, superstar rates can be even higher, such as M. Jackson's royalties reaching 41% of the net wholesale price of the album (Caves, 2000, p. 382).

The royalty structure is complex (Strasser, 2010, p. 134), consisting of a royalty advance (a fixed part that serves as a loan from the recording company) and potentially additional royalties. The advance provides financial support to the artist from the start of the creative process until the beginning of sales. The specific amount of the advance depends on the contract and the artist's status. Emerging artists may receive a few thousand euros, reflecting the high uncertainty of success based solely on their talent and time. In contrast, established stars command significantly higher value and face a lower risk of failure. Consequently, their bargaining power in relation to the recording company is substantial, enabling them to negotiate large recording advances and secure a significant share of sales revenue. For example, the group Aerosmith received a $13.5 million advance from Sony Music for their fourth album, with royalties set at 25% of the wholesale price (Burnett, 2010, p. 25).

Additional royalties are paid to artists when the label's revenue exceeds the amount advanced. However, if the revenue from record sales does not cover the costs, recording companies have the option to terminate the contract with the artist or offset the artist's royalties from future records (through a cross-collateralising system) (Caves, 2000, p. 63). According to Boorstin (2004), artists typically start earning when record sales reach at least 500,000 copies. It's important to note that despite the contracted amount of royalties, various deductions are applied by recording labels, such as packaging costs, promotional copies, and potential returns of discs (Shemel and Krasilovsky, 2007).

Considering the calculations above and assuming a record price of $15, the artist receives $0.45 per record sold. Since only a few projects achieve significant success, artists often earn an amount equivalent to the advance, and in some cases, they may have to repay a portion of the advance when recording the next album. Vogel (2011, p. 248) reports that a maximum of 10% of artists earn more from selling an album than the advance received from the label.

The second form of remuneration for performers is derived from what is known as related rights. These rights entail fees collected by collecting societies that represent performers, creators, and phonogram producers. These fees are obtained from various sources, including broadcasters such as radio and television stations, discotheques, pubs, supermarkets, and importers of devices and blank media used for personal copying (Golat, 2008, p. 72).

The collected fees are then distributed among the relevant parties involved in the creation and production of the music.

The oligopsony structure in the recording industry enables recording companies to establish high barriers to entry and dictate terms in their contracts with artists. This influence is also reflected in the selection of albums that receive promotion and distribution, which are the subsequent stages where labels act as gatekeepers. Such selection is necessary due to the significant costs involved in wide-scale promotion and distribution.

Alexander (1994) highlights that the production costs for albums by major labels can range from $100,000 to over $500,000. These costs are considered sunk costs, which makes recording labels cautious in their selection of projects for promotion and distribution. Established artists are generally easier to predict in terms of success. However, for emerging artists, predicting success is much more challenging, although producing their albums has one major advantage for labels. Once a project by an emerging artist becomes successful, the label's profit margin is very high, as the remuneration for these artists is typically modest.

However, not all new performers choose to work with major labels. One reason is the intense competition and multi-stage selection process described earlier. Another reason is the creative process itself, as major labels often have limitations on creative freedom that may not suit all artists. Major labels are known for their risk aversion, which can limit opportunities for innovative projects. Independent labels, on the other hand, provide a platform for artists to have more creative control and take risks.

Independent labels also serve as a stepping stone for artists to build their careers. The cost of recording an album under a small label is generally between $4,000 and $25,000 (Alexander, 1994), and promotion and distribution are often limited to local scales, which keeps the costs relatively low. In some cases, artists may even contribute to covering the costs or forego profits in order to release their first album and gain exposure in the market, increasing their chances of attracting interest from major labels.

In conclusion, the bargaining power of suppliers, particularly in relation to major labels, is generally low due to the concentration of demand and the abundance of supply. This leads to intense competition among suppliers. The situation is somewhat different with independent labels. Given their smaller size and greater number, performers have a relatively higher bargaining power when it comes to negotiating with independent labels compared to major labels.

2.2.3 *The bargaining power of buyers*

According to the basic principles of economics, when supply exceeds demand, the buyer generally has a stronger bargaining position. In the recording industry, overproduction is a risk-reduction strategy employed by major recording companies. One might assume that this gives consumers the power to exert pressure on companies. However, only a small percentage of music products gain recognition and achieve success in the market. Additionally, out of the numerous projects produced, only a small proportion are profitable. In general, products in the industry do not compete primarily on price, but rather on other factors such as quality. Caves (2000, p. 77) argues that talent, associated with quality, is not the sole determinant of success. Instead, other factors such as taste, fashion, and the herd effect play more significant roles.

Hendricks and Sorensen (2009) argue that the limited success of certain records is primarily due to a lack of information about them (information asymmetry), which negatively impacts consumer purchasing decisions. They argue that when consumers are poorly informed about most products, demand depends less on preference and more on knowledge – specifically, how consumers obtain that knowledge and the cost associated with acquiring it. This implies that consumers tend to buy products they have heard about, and they often hear about products that have been purchased by other consumers. As a result, the success of a particular record becomes self-perpetuating.

Hull et al. (2011, p. 136) provide data from the US market, indicating that in 2000, approximately 35,000 new albums were released, with 29,000 of them coming from independent labels. Despite the high number of releases from independent labels, their revenue accounted for only 16% of the industry's total. In fact, 85% of album releases sold fewer than 1,000 units per year. In the same year, there were 406 albums that sold more than 250,000 units, representing 44% of the total album sales revenue, and these were primarily released by major labels.

This situation occurs because labels focus their promotion efforts on a limited number of titles, not because buyers determine the success of these titles over others. By investing in the promotion and distribution of select projects, companies concentrate demand, resulting in higher revenue. The success of these projects then helps finance the remaining ones (Dantec and Levy, 2005). Therefore, the overproduction observed in the recording industry does not translate into an abundance of supply. In reality, consumers have a relatively small number of products to choose from because the cost of searching for less-promoted projects is high within the traditional model. The nature of the industry can thus be characterised as an oligopoly, with the producers of recorded music holding more power.

2.2.4 *The threat of substitutes*

It is assumed that different carriers of music, such as vinyl records, compact discs, and cassettes,[4] can be considered as substitutes. However, they are not perfect substitutes since they differ in terms of technical quality and convenience of use. These distinctions in characteristics are important to some consumers.

According to an analysis conducted by Vogel (2011, p. 243) on the sales of the three most popular physical carriers between 1975 and 2005 in the United

States, the process of replacing one carrier with another, and subsequently the products with their potential substitutes, took place over an extended period of time. Moreover, there was no clear and immediate link between the rise of one carrier and the decline of another at the same time. In fact, when cassette tapes were introduced, sales of vinyl records continued to grow for several years, alongside the increasing sales of cassettes (RIAA, 2022). These figures can be considered representative of the overall recording industry, given the prominence of the US market.

A similar pattern of simultaneous growth in sales of both the older and newer carriers was observed with cassette tapes and CDs, albeit over a longer period. The popularity of cassettes gradually declined in the late 1980s and early 1990s, which could potentially be attributed to the introduction of CD-R (recordable CDs) to the market, although empirical confirmation of this hypothesis is difficult. It is plausible that CD-Rs replaced blank cassette tapes, which were commonly used by consumers to record customised music compilations.

The different physical carriers were not highly substitutable; rather, they complemented each other. Cassettes were affordable, portable, and suitable for on-the-go listening on portable players. They also allowed for customisation. On the other hand, vinyl records offered superior sound quality and a certain ritualistic listening experience. These features catered to different consumer segments: younger, more mobile consumers preferred cassettes, while older, more mature individuals with sophisticated tastes gravitated towards vinyl records.

Blank carriers, such as cassettes and CD-Rs, provided consumers with the ability to copy music at home, which had a significant impact on the industry. According to estimates from the British Phonographic Industry, the recording industry experienced a loss of £200 million in 1980 due to home copying. In the United States, the cassette bootleg market was already valued at $100 million in 1971 (Hoffmann and Ferstler, 2005, p. 839). Ten years later, American music collectors produced the equivalent of 564 million LPs as tape copies for personal use, which exceeded the annual production of CDs in the United States in 1982 by 20%. While private copying increased by 24% in this market in 1980, CD production fell by 16% (Kominek, 1986, p. 140). Private copies became substitutes for purchased products.

Alongside copying for private use, the act of copying for commercial purposes thrived and became known as piracy, which refers to unauthorised reproduction or copying of original creations without the author's permission (Czetwertyński, 2019, p. 133). Southeast Asia, India, and Latin America were prominent global centres for such activities (Hoffmann and Ferstler, 2005, p. 840). Piracy proved to be profitable due to the extremely low marginal cost of producing copies. Additionally, pirates benefited from the costly advertising efforts of recording companies, which made their products popular. The distribution of pirated phonograms was local, and its associated costs were minimal, allowing the price of pirated products to be set below that of legal counterparts.

Illegal copies began to pose a serious competitive threat to legal products, primarily in terms of price. The quality of the recording in pirated copies was often comparable to that of the originals, making them nearly perfect substitutes. With the advent of digital media, particularly recordable CDs, piracy became an increasingly significant challenge for the recording industry. In 1999, the market for illegal copies was estimated at nearly 2 billion units (1.4 billion of which were cassettes), valued at $4.1 billion (IFPI, 2000). The IFPI also reported that pirated recordings accounted for approximately one-third of global music sales that year, identifying piracy as the most significant factor contributing to the decline in legal music sales.

When considering the content of music itself, the issue of substitutability becomes more complex. It largely depends on whether the consumer is a fan of a particular artist or performer or falls into the category of a background music consumer who is influenced by the environment and media. For a dedicated fan, an album by another artist or band may not be a substitute. However, for an uninvolved consumer, any new release in the market may potentially serve as a substitute for existing offerings.

Substitutability is a desired characteristic pursued by all phonogram producers. Despite employing different strategies, they share the common goal of making new projects appealing to consumers and ensuring their success. Consequently, the threat of substitutes remains an ever-present feature in the recording industry, particularly regarding the content of the music itself.

2.2.5 *The industry rivalry*

Rivalry is the last force in Porter's model that occurs among companies within the industry. In the recording industry, both major companies and small labels compete with each other in the market, employing various strategies to gain a competitive advantage. These strategies include horizontal concentration, vertical integration, lowering barriers to entry, achieving economies of scale, overproduction, and the star system (Noam, 2009, p. 35).

According to Doyle (2000), media companies can pursue three different paths to achieve market advantage:

- horizontal mergers: these mergers aim to expand market share, optimise resource utilisation, and achieve economies of scale;
- vertical mergers: such mergers are intended to reduce transaction costs and increase control over the company's activities by integrating different stages of the value chain;
- lateral mergers: this type of merger involves diversifying production and services by adding new products and services to the company's existing portfolio.

Horizontal mergers are also commonly referred to as horizontal concentration, while vertical mergers are known as vertical integration. The term *lateral mergers* implies a specific situation that falls under the *threat of new entrants* category in Porter's model. All three types of mergers are prevalent in the recording industry.

Bishop (2005, p. 447) emphasises that both horizontal concentration and vertical integration have played significant roles in the development of the recording industry. According to Laing (2009, p. 24), the tactics employed by companies are a result of the power dynamics within the oligopolistic structure of the industry.

2.2.5.1 The importance of horizontal concentration

Concentration in the recording industry can be defined as the dominance of one or more companies in the market, which can result from processes such as acquisitions, mergers, or the disappearance of competitors (Sánchez-Tabernero and Carvajal, 2002). One way to measure concentration is by comparing the market shares of the major players in the industry.[5] If the four largest firms occupy more than 50% of the market, or if the eight largest firms control more than 70%, this can indicate monopolistic or oligopolistic behaviour that can have negative effects on the market (Sánchez-Tabernero and Carvajal, 2002).

The recording industry has experienced significant concentration over the years. While the sector has always had a small number of companies, a strong trend towards concentration began in the early 1960s and has continued to the present day. This trend aligns with the broader pattern of acquisitions and mergers seen in the global economy since the 1980s (Coutinet et al., 2006; Noam, 2009). In 1979, six major labels, namely CBS, Capitol, MCA, PolyGram, RCA, and Warner, controlled 85% of the market (Coase, 1979, p. 317). Over the next decade, new players entered the market through acquisitions, such as Sony acquiring CBS and BMG buying out RCA. The growing revenues from recorded music, which increased by approximately 25% per year in 1994, attracted new entrants to the sector (Tschmuck, 2014).

At its peak before the digital revolution, around 90% of phonograms sold in the United States and 70%–80% sold worldwide were produced by the *big six* major labels (Burnett, 2010, p. 18). The remaining market share belonged to numerous small independent labels. Before the digital revolution, the *big five* major labels held about 80% of the market, while the remaining 20% was controlled by small independent labels. The important stages of concentration are illustrated in Figure 2.3.

The provided diagram represents a simplified depiction of the historical evolution of record labels. It also illustrates two types of mergers specific to the media and entertainment industries: horizontal and lateral mergers. For instance, when Seagram's acquired MCA and PolyGram, it merged them to form Universal Music Group. This merger involved a lateral component,

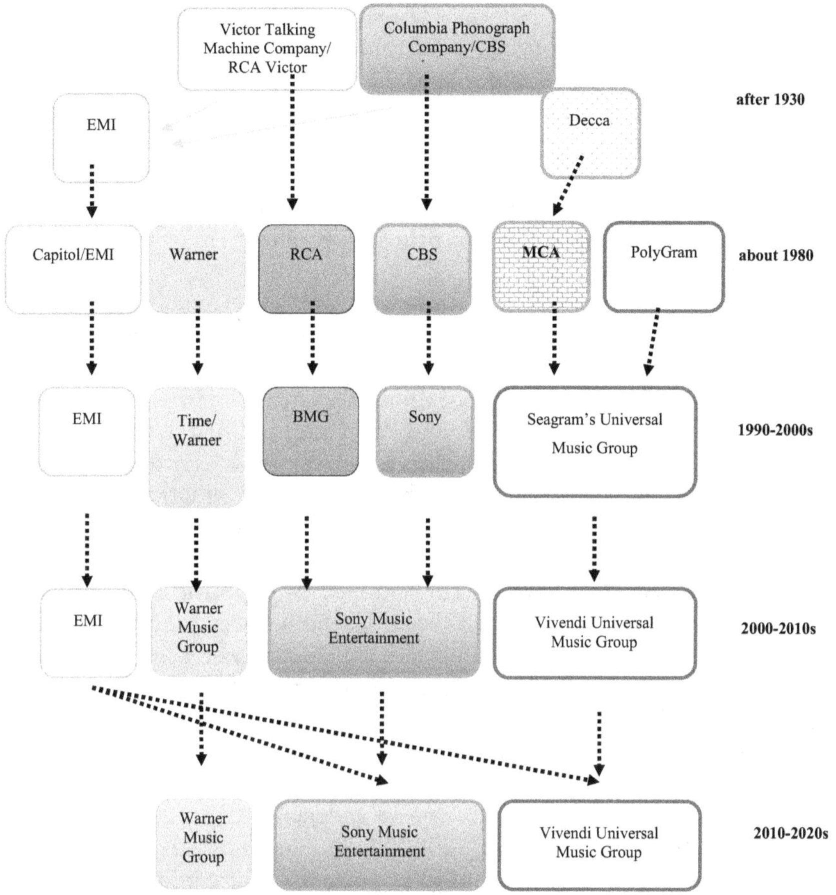

Figure 2.3 History of concentration in the recording industry (drawing by the author based on Coase, 1979; Alexander, 1994; Huygens et al., 2001; Bishop, 2005; Hull et al., 2011; Tschmuck, 2014; Passman, 2015; Shuker, 2017).

where a company previously active in a different industry entered the recording industry, followed by a horizontal merger of the two recording companies into one. The entry of large media companies like Sony, BMG, and Time/Warner into the recording industry is another example of lateral mergers.

Horizontal concentration in the recording industry can take three forms: mergers between major labels, acquisitions of independent producers by major labels, and catalogue buyouts (Curien and Moreau, 2010, p. 28). Alexander et al. (2015, p. 231) argue that horizontal concentration offers several key benefits to record companies:

- increased potential revenue streams: by owning the rights to various works, the record company can generate income from their exploitation, transforming the production cost into revenue;

- coordinated resource utilisation: the record company can coordinate and control the use of resources, adjusting activity schedules and product launches to maximise efficiency;
- organisational savings: centralising certain functions such as accounting and management allows the record company to achieve organisational cost savings;
- distribution advantage: by distributing different labels, the recording company gains an advantage over those without access to its distribution channels.

These benefits align with the three forms of horizontal concentration mentioned earlier.

As for the mergers of large corporations, they are primarily driven by strategic motives. The merger of MCA and PolyGram resulted in the creation of Universal Music Group holding the largest share of the recording market. In addition to the cost savings achieved through the consolidation of organisational functions, the advantage of such a move lies in the significant size and power of the new company, allowing it to exert influence over legislation. This enables the company to maintain a monopoly on music rights and enjoy substantial revenues for an extended period, thanks to its significant market share. Bagdikian (2007, p. 49) argues that media power is political power. He reports that between 1994 and 2004, the recording industry donated approximately $13 billion to politicians in the United States, which influenced political processes to ensure the big corporations retained control over music production and distribution (Bishop, 2005, p. 457).

On the other hand, the acquisition of independent producers by major labels, highlighted by Hannaford (2007), is primarily aimed at entering new and often niche markets with significant potential that could not have been predicted beforehand. Furthermore, acquiring the most dynamic independent producers reduces the threat of strong distribution alternatives emerging from their combined forces, which is an important element of market advantage.

Both the merger of recording labels and the acquisition of independent labels give majors control over the release timing of albums. Since products in the recording industry can be considered imperfect substitutes and do not primarily compete on price, it is crucial for new projects launched in the market simultaneously to be distinct. This approach avoids direct competition and prevents album cannibalisation.

The strategy of acquiring independent labels specialising in different genres by a single larger entity was pioneered by Warner Bros., a film conglomerate, in the early 1960s. It established Warner Records, which pursued a diversification strategy by releasing music in various genres to secure market share in each segment. Such activities significantly increase costs, making it feasible only for companies with a sufficiently large structure to execute this strategy. The model created by Warner Records has been referred to as a *federation of labels* (Huygens et al., 2001, p. 26) and offers several advantages. Firstly, the labels can maintain their innovative approaches and continue their autonomous artists & repertoire search activities in the markets they specialise in and know well. With the support of the major label, they have a competitive advantage over potential new entrants in these markets. Secondly, the parent company can leverage economies of scale in production and distribution. For example, WEA[6] was established to distribute Warner Music recordings. Finally, organisational decisions are made at the head office, reducing the company's operating costs.

Warner's adoption of the multi-module company strategy allowed it to quickly gain market share (about 15%) and become the leader in the United States by 1969, just ten years after entering the recording industry (Huygens et al., 2001, p. 26). This success prompted other companies to follow suit, leading to the emergence of additional federations of labels and a decrease in the number of independent labels due to acquisitions (consolidation).

Catalogues held by labels are an important source of revenue due to copyright. When CDs were introduced in the early 1980s, consumers started replacing their LPs and cassettes, which significantly increased revenues for recording companies. The high prices of CDs, coupled with low production and marketing costs, proved beneficial for labels with a stock of old recordings. Revenues from catalogue use are estimated to account for a significant portion of a major label's total revenue and profits (Curien and Moreau, 2010, p. 28; Vogel, 2011, p. 253).

Controlling catalogues also provides an advantage in excluding rivals. Price competition is one aspect, with new releases generally sold at similar prices (Alexander, 1994, p. 3) due to the uncertainty of their success. However, already released products from catalogues can be sold at lower prices since their costs have already been recouped, thereby excluding some new releases from independent producers. Furthermore, the ownership of a broader catalogue facilitates the process of releasing compilations, as it requires consent from rights owners. Majors can also exchange catalogue credentials, further disadvantaging independent labels with limited stock.

Recording companies have expanded their use of catalogues in various ways. One of these is exporting catalogues to foreign markets, enabling the sale of local artists in different regions through international distribution networks. Additionally, licensing music to companies involved in producing entertainment products such as films, television programs, and videotapes has opened up new avenues for revenue generation in the music publishing sector (Huygens et al., 2001, p. 26).[7] The growth of this area has led to the acquisition of smaller publishing companies by major labels. This consolidation aims to reduce transaction costs associated with managing licences, and it often involves intra-group transactions within the larger music group, replacing external transactions.

Furthermore, recording companies themselves have become attractive targets for transnational entertainment and consumer electronics corporations.

The increasing revenue potential of recorded music, not just from phonogram sales but also through synergies with playback equipment sales and music promotion in films and other cultural products, has made them appealing partners. As a result, lateral mergers have occurred, with recording companies integrating into transnational corporations such as Time-Warner, Sony, Matsushita, and Bertelsmann.

2.2.5.2 *The importance of vertical integration*

The recording industry also evolves through vertical mergers, a process known as vertical integration. In this strategy, recording companies acquire control over different stages of production or the distribution of the product (Burnett, 2010, p. 16).[8] This includes acquiring recording studios, record pressing plants, and distribution companies. Vertical integration enables the rationalisation of the phonogram production process and facilitates synergy strategies (Gałuszka, 2009, p. 114). Control over promotion is also a crucial element, as recording companies aim to have control over the creation, performance, transmission, and purchase of music by all audiences at all times, following the principle of 'control as much as you can' (Bishop, 2005, p. 445).

Ownership of recording studios and pressing plants allows recording companies to have control over various phases of production, including the recording quality, production costs, and the efficiency of pressing. It also helps in managing the value creation chain of the company. Furthermore, such ownership helps reduce transaction costs. For example, Warner Music worked with Warner Music Manufacturing Europe, and BMG collaborated with Central Manufacturing Group. However, this does not mean that production was exclusively carried out within the group. The use of external companies allowed for greater flexibility in responding to market changes. For instance, in 1992, BMG produced 42% of its records with independent companies (MMC, 1994, p. 113). However, recording companies gradually shifted their focus from controlling production to controlling distribution and promotion. They significantly increased their investments in these activities, while studios and pressing plants were mostly sold to independent entities (Bernstein et al., 2007, p. 21).

While recording may require less investment compared to distribution and promotion, it is the effective distribution and promotion that can provide a competitive advantage in the market. This shift in strategy by recording companies is influenced by trends such as the increasing importance of distribution, rising costs of promotion, shorter availability of cultural products, and the concentration of demand on a smaller number of products, as observed in the cultural industries (Benghozi and Paris, 2008).

Distribution in the recording industry involves the transportation of records from pressing plants to retailers. It requires efficient order processing and a widespread network of retail locations, making the fixed costs associated with distribution, including logistics and organisational costs, significant. According to Alexander (1994, p. 8), establishing national-level distribution in a large market like the United States can cost around $100 million, creating high barriers to entry.

Due to the high costs involved and the potential for economies of scale in distribution, this aspect of the industry has become highly concentrated and controlled by major labels. In fact, at the turn of the 20th century, major labels were estimated to control up to 95% of global distribution (Alexander, 2002, p. 153). Control over distribution channels is considered a key element in gaining and maintaining a competitive advantage in the industry (Arditi, 2015, p. 105).

The integration of distribution stage in the recording industry began as early as the 1950s (Alexander, 1994, p. 7), although Vogel (2011, p. 230) places it more in the 1960s. Prior to this, major labels handled their own distribution within their networks, while independent distribution companies worked with independent labels. Changes in distribution occurred through two main processes. Firstly, major labels started acquiring independent distributors, reducing their number in the market. Secondly, by acquiring independent labels, major labels compelled them to shift from independent distributors to the major labels' distribution networks. With only a small number of distributors remaining in the market, independent labels had to rely on the networks owned by major companies, which could charge high prices for their services. This strategy increased the total costs for small rival firms. Additionally, major labels could secure the most promising artists from independent labels through the provisions of their distribution agreements.

The reduction in the number of independent producers in the recording industry had a significant consequence: independent distribution companies that solely relied on independent labels started to go bankrupt. This resulted in a concentration in distribution, with fewer distribution companies and reduced competition, while their power vis-à-vis their suppliers, the recording labels, increased. This situation further tempted major labels to acquire distribution networks.

Controlling distribution offers several advantages. Firstly, it enhances organisational efficiency and reduces transaction costs. Distributing music products involves inherent risks, as the success of a product is uncertain. It is challenging to capture all the transaction details in a contract between the producer and the distributor. Additionally, considering the significant promotional costs borne by record labels, ensuring optimal distribution arrangements becomes vital to maximise the promotional effect.

Secondly, international distribution control allows labels to develop a star system with economies of scale, ensuring that selected artists have presence in specific markets or even globally. With access to information on the various markets, major labels can plan their distribution and promotion strategies for specific artists in different markets.

Lastly, the possibility of control in distribution is linked to strategic objectives. Establishing a distribution network enables supplying wholesalers and large retailers, which allows for the application of economies of scale. Costs can be spread over a larger number of products. Furthermore, major distributors can offer wholesale prices and terms that are difficult for independent distributors working with independent labels to compete with. As a result, small companies aiming to reach geographically distant markets often have to rely on large distribution networks. By integrating distribution, major companies can exclude rivals, increase their costs, and potentially eliminate some productions from the market. This raises barriers to entry and increases the chances of success for products released by the owner of a particular distribution network.

The concentration of distribution networks and their control by major labels also have an impact on retailers. Distributors have the power to impose prices on shops and determine the level of discounts, often offering up to 15% of discs for free. This incentivises retailers to accept new releases into their stores. Furthermore, distributors have the ability to sell bundles of discs, which include both popular products and those that consumers are less likely to buy.

This highlights that distribution is one of the most significant elements of competition between companies in the recording industry. Alexander et al. (2015, p. 231) even argue that this type of control is a key factor enabling major labels to maintain their oligopolistic position in the market.

An example from the 1980s demonstrates the importance of control and smooth distribution, along with sales to end users, for recording companies. At that time, global distribution networks developed by major recording companies were already in place. However, in developing this system, the companies assumed all the risk of unsold records (Dannen, 2011, p. 181). Retailers could return excess inventory to the producers according to their contracts. While singles were typically destroyed, unsold LPs entered the secondary market. Many of these returns were purchased by intermediaries at significantly lower prices and distributed through their own channels. Since the recording companies did not specify the number of copies allowed to be returned in their contracts, they sometimes ended up receiving 100% reimbursement for unsold products. Additionally, the labels manufactured and distributed large volumes without properly analysing true market demand. This was done to appease their artists by promising them high sales figures, and since sales calculations were based on distributed albums rather than sold ones, returns were not accounted for. As a result, reported sales data were significantly inflated, leading to financial losses for the record labels. This was one of the reasons for the crisis that affected the industry in the late 1970s and early 1980s.

Before the digital breakthrough, and even today, physical sales to end consumers were primarily realised through specialised supermarkets, consumer electronics stores, or mass retail markets. Analyses show that the retail share of the latter has been consistently growing, with over 100,000 music titles offered to consumers. For instance, in the early 1990s, the UK's largest retailer had approximately 160,000 music products available (MMC, 1994). Retailers purchased music products from distributors at negotiated wholesale prices, which included discounts. To determine the retail price, retailers added around 30%–35% on top of the wholesale price, along with value-added tax (VAT). As retail prices for recordings were similar across price categories, retailers competed with each other to obtain the lowest wholesale prices and larger discounts.

Due to their market power, mass retail markets were able to exert pressure on both distributors and producers, requiring them to adapt their offerings to cater to mass consumer tastes (Boorstin, 2004, p. 36). As the offerings in these stores were homogeneous in nature, music by local artists produced by independent labels was often not available. Furthermore, music in these stores was used as a *loss leader*, sold below the purchase price. This strategy is employed to attract consumers and promote the sale of other products (Arditi, 2015, pp. 109–110). It is worth noting that this strategy has been utilised in the recording industry since its inception (McCarthy, 2011). This practice has become even more prevalent in the digital era, as will be discussed in the next chapter.

Record labels, through distributors, also compete for better exposure of their products in music stores. It is estimated that a product displayed in a prime location, such as near the entrance, on specially highlighted shelves, or in listening areas, sells three to four times better than if it were placed among other products without any particular distinction. In the case of albums by lesser-known artists, this could result in a sales improvement of up to 15 times. Stores charge fees to record labels or distributors for product placement, known as *price-and-positioning* fees, which typically amount to $1–1.5 per album in the United States (Power and Hallencreutz, 2007, p. 385). Additionally, stores impose other fees, such as fees for promotional posters in shop windows or participation in the store's advertisements, including television commercials or store circulars. These fees are in addition to customary discounts and can amount to several thousand dollars. Label representatives estimate that promotional fees in stores can even reach up to half of the budget allocated for marketing a product being introduced to the market (Power and Hallencreutz, 2007, p. 385). These practices stem from the fact that, due to limited display space and a wide array of offerings, retail entities are interested in accepting only those productions that can bring them the greatest profit, thereby limiting their selection to chart-topping releases. One of the consequences of the strong power of retailers is the ongoing reduction in the diversity of offerings.

Another consequence is the exclusion of indie productions from large-scale retail trade. Independent distributors and, consequently, independent producers face challenges in overcoming entry barriers established by the stores that dominate music sales and have a wide geographic reach due to their network structure. With a limited offering, they are unable to benefit from economies of scale and, therefore, struggle to compete on price with major distributors. As a result, indie offerings find their way into small, individual specialist shops and are primarily available at a local level.

In 1992, Nielsen introduced the SoundScan system, which revolutionised the recording of actual album sales in specific locations. This system, known as *just in time*, can be considered a pioneering application of sales data analysis not only for managing the supply chains of records to stores but also for record production (pressing). It is worth noting that this system played a significant role in the rise of hip-hop, as it unveiled the genre's substantial popularity among consumers. This inspired major companies to acquire small independent labels that were initially responsible for releasing this new genre (Arditi, 2015, p. 113).

2.2.5.3 The significance of promotion

In-store promotion is just one of the many forms of promoting music products. Both producers and consumers rely on media intermediaries to disseminate and receive information about new releases. The company that pioneered the effective evaluation of advertising and media promotion's impact on sales levels was Decca (Frith, 2017, p. 101). In the pre-digital era, it is estimated that less than 10% of music purchases were made by consumers who had never heard the music before (MMC, 1994, p. 120). The highest likelihood of purchasing an unheard album exists among fans of a particular artist. Therefore, selling records to consumers from different segments and promoting projects by emerging artists in the market heavily relies on their strong media presence. Since media buzz is as vital to the recording industry as the music itself (Frith, 1989, pp. 173–220), media outlets are utilised in several ways:

- they serve as traditional advertising channels for music projects;
- record labels feature artists' recordings in the media to introduce consumers to their music. This exposure reduces the risk of dissatisfaction with the purchase of an experience good (music) and minimises the cost of consumers searching for product information;
- artists make appearances on media broadcasts, often to promote their latest projects and build recognition among potential record buyers, gaining popularity and solidifying their status.

Promotional activities are managed by the marketing departments of major labels and their smaller-scale counterparts in independent labels. The costs of promotion are set at a level that ensures the highest possible sales, primarily achievable for large labels. Record companies estimate that the average investment in a new artist, including their compensation, master recording, pressing, distribution, and promotion costs, amounts to approximately $500,000.

Investments for established stars are significantly higher. For example, M. Jackson's contract with Sony was worth $65 million, and the Rolling Stones' deal with EMI-Virgin amounted to $44 million (Burnett, 2010, p. 23).

In terms of marketing costs, Vogel (2011, p. 244) estimates them to range from $100,000 to over $500,000. Benhamou (2008, p. 66) states that promoting an album to the top 20 best-selling records requires a budget ranging from €500,000 to as much as €800,000. These costs are both fixed and sunk, which causes only certain music projects to be promoted. This is not only due to the high expenses involved in activities such as producing music videos, releasing promotional materials, purchasing airtime, and securing space in the press and at retailers but also physical constraints. Radio and television stations have limited airtime to showcase new music releases, and there is a limit to the number of albums that can be featured as new releases in stores. As a result, record labels invest in artists who have the potential to generate the highest profits for the company, acting as gatekeepers in the realm of promotion.

Radio and television play a significant role in the distribution of music recordings and capturing consumer attention. There has been a symbiotic relationship between radio and the recording industry since the inception of this medium. The sheer fact that music occupies the most airtime on radio makes it the most popular and therefore the most effective channel for distributing recordings (Vogel, 2011, p. 9). For example, according to the results presented by Eurobarometer (Eurobarometer Survey, 2002), nearly 60% of Europeans (from the 15 member countries) listened to the radio daily, with 86.3% of them preferring to listen to music on the radio. A staggering 88.6% of respondents, when asked which medium they used to listen to music, answered that they listened to it on the radio and television, while only 62.3% used physical formats such as cassettes, CDs, and DVDs. The consequence of consumers' strong inclination towards listening to music on the radio is its impact on record sales. Research conducted by Warner Communications as early as 1977 revealed that 43% of the total population who was listening to music on the radio for at least ten hours per week were comprising 54% of all buyers and accounting for 62% of the total dollar market (Hull, 2004, p. 209). Some studies have indicated that television, particularly MTV and cable music channels, may have a greater influence on consumer purchasing behaviour than radio (Burnett, 2010; Caves, 2000, p. 149).

The main objective of recording labels is to maximise sales, which is heavily dependent on media exposure. However, securing airplay for new releases on radio stations is a difficult task, primarily due to the abundance of offerings and the limited broadcasting time in traditional media. As a result, only a select few artists and a small number of new projects can expect to find a place in aired programs. According to Burnett (2010, p. 81), approximately 7,000 singles and over 5,000 albums are released each year, with only around four new releases being featured on radio playlists weekly.[9] Nielsen SoundScan data suggests even higher figures, as the number of new releases in the

UK market ranged from 18,400 (1992) to almost 40,000 (1999) annually (Bourreau and Gensollen, 2006). In this case, gaining access to broadcast slots appears even more challenging.

In smaller markets, the situation is similar. In France, for instance, the number of new releases annually fluctuated between 3,314 (2003) and 1,231 (2007), while the number of singles ranged from 955 (2000) to 296 (2007) (Benhamou, 2008, p. 64). As for airplay, in France-Inter, a general French radio station where music represents only a fraction of the programming, approximately 400 different titles are broadcasted weekly (Les orpailleurs de la bande FM, 2002). Although young and promising artists are occasionally invited to these shows, like in most stations, the majority of airtime is dedicated to established and well-known figures. It can be expected that the tendency to include new releases in playlists is similar in other countries, so the chances of getting airplay and capturing consumer attention are at a comparable level.

With such a vast selection of music, programmers may struggle to make choices, and limited time prevents them from listening to all albums to determine the most interesting ones (ArtRock, 2004). Furthermore, despite the evident symbiosis between radio and the recording industry, their goals are not identical. Radio tends to target an older audience desired by advertisers, while record labels primarily cater to young people (Williamson and Cloonan, 2007). Therefore, record companies employ a strategy known as *payola* to influence programmers. Payola refers to the practice of offering financial, sexual, or other rewards in exchange for promotion (Shuker, 2017; Williamson and Cloonan, 2007, p. 188). The practice of paying radio DJs who also work as programmers (gatekeepers) and have the authority to decide which songs make it onto a radio stations playlist developed in the 1950s. However, its roots can be traced back to the 19th-century sheet music printing industry (Coase, 1979, pp. 270–286). This practice gained widespread attention in 1960 when one of the most prominent DJs at the time, A. Freed (credited with discovering rock and roll), was accused of accepting such bribes. It was argued that payola was immoral and deprived listeners of good music and should therefore be banned (Coase, 1979, p. 293).

Payola was particularly advantageous for small labels (Coase, 1979, p. 306) and was exploited by them, as illustrated in the story depicted in the TV series *Vinyl* (Janowska, 2016; Vinyl [TV series], 2023). The majors, as mentioned earlier, had (and still have) historical and financial ties to media conglomerates, which own radio stations and television networks. This allows them to influence the programming of these media outlets, including the selection of music to be featured. Although their inclination to resort to illegal methods may be lower, they also engage in payola practices, making it easier for them to limit the presence of small labels and potential newcomers on the airwaves. With greater resources to bribe playlist curators, they increased the costs of these activities, thereby raising entry barriers for indies. According to Coase (1979, p. 288), payola can be also seen as a form of advertising that promotes competition and increases musical diversity. It is likely that rock and roll flourished in the 1950s, thanks to this practice.

In the early 1980s, due to legal restrictions prohibiting record labels from engaging in the aforementioned practice, the institution of independent promoters (programmers) emerged as intermediaries between the labels and radio stations. It is estimated that by the mid-1980s, the entire industry was spending between $60 million and $80 million on what was called independent promotion (Knoedelseder, 1993, pp. 179–185).

Another way in which record companies leverage the media is through the exposure of artists themselves. Producers of primarily entertainment-based shows invite them as special guests. Such actions serve a dual purpose. Firstly, the labels solidify the status of the artists whose music they release, thereby increasing their popularity. This exposure not only helps sell the recently released album (new release) but also impacts the sales of other albums by the same artist, both previous and subsequent. As previously indicated, this is one of the significant factors influencing consumer decisions when it comes to purchasing recordings. Secondly, if the individuals invited to the show are popular and well-liked among consumers, the medium itself also benefits directly from such invitations. The program featuring a musical star gains higher viewership (listenership). The selection of guests for the show follows similar principles to the selection of tracks, taking into account the radio format, target audience to which the station directs its broadcasts, as well as the preferences of the audience, programmers, and pressures from the labels.

2.2.5.4 Overproduction and the star system as the main strategies of record companies

As previously mentioned, the goal of record labels is to maximise sales. Therefore, they employ the strategy of overproduction and concentrate the supply on a few products that are distributed and promoted. This results in pseudo-diversity, which Hannaford (2007) identifies as one of the main characteristics of an oligopoly. Garnham and Inglis (1994, p. 161) describe this phenomenon as artificial scarcity, which is maintained through actions such as vertical integration, allowing labels to control the release dates of individual products and ensuring their limited availability, as well as intensive advertising and copyright monopolies.

The strategy of overproduction entails producing far more than the market can absorb, in order to increase the chances of discovering a star (Alexander et al., 2015, p. 238). If successful, the star's success would be significant enough to compensate for the losses incurred in producing records by other artists whose works did not resonate with the audience. This is due to the economies of scale that can be achieved through the sale of the star's works in the market.

The star system is determined by two factors – the unpredictability of commercial success and mimetic behaviours of consumers (Curien and Moreau,

2010, p. 38) and involves producing a vast number of artists' works (hits), of which only a few with the greatest sales potential are promoted and distributed. It is worth further clarifying what or who a star is. Rosen (1981) defines stars as a small group of individuals earning large sums of money and dominating the fields in which they are employed. According to Benhamou's definition (2002), a star is a person, place, or company whose revenues depend entirely or partly on the economic exploitation of their popularity. In the star system, a small number of individuals (entities) capture a larger portion of the revenue in a given economic sector, which is also known as the *winner takes all* principle (Cook and Frank, 2010). However, Rosen's concept, suggesting that significant differences in earnings result from only minor differences in artists' talent, does not seem justified (Connolly and Krueger, 2006). Stars are created by consumers who desire to consume what others consume, so chance or a favourable set of circumstances plays a role, giving rise to the snowball effect (Adler, 2006). Undoubtedly, the *nobody knows* principle by Caves (2000) applies here. According to this principle, it is impossible to predict which artist will achieve success in the market.

The origins of the star system can be traced back to the 1930s when the popularity of radio posed a threat to the revenue of record labels. In order to regain their lost position, they had to create a new operating model. They focused on releasing a large number of records by a select group of performers and aggressively promoted them through radio. They enlisted the collaboration of renowned artists appreciated by the audience. The mass consumption of music was further strengthened with the introduction of jukeboxes, installed in bars (primarily in the United States). This equipment served as an effective channel not only for mass music promotion but also for its distribution, as the jukeboxes needed to be stocked with records (45 rpm discs).

Such a strategy allowed for the concentration of demand, resulting in increased sales of specific titles and performers. Moreover, the high fixed costs associated with recording, distribution, and intensive promotion were spread across a large number of units sold, which reduced the average cost per unit. Decca, which was the first to adopt the star system strategy, followed by other record companies, were able to increase in that way their revenue through economies of scale.

The flourishing of the recording industry and the dominant star system within it coincided with the birth of mass media – first radio, and later television. These mediums were the carriers of the emerging popular culture, which also included music. Through mass media connecting people living in different places and often in different times, a certain homogenisation was emerging in society: an increasing number of people had access to the same information, read the same newspapers, watched the same movies, and listened to the same music. Radio played a leading role in shaping stars, creating hits, and keeping songs, their authors, and performers at the peak of popularity. The most important function was performed by music charts, with the *Billboard*[10] chart being the most famous and respected measure of popularity. Recording companies built their financial success on hits and the stars who performed them, and radio and other mass media greatly assisted them in this endeavour. As Anderson (2006, p. 18) states, hits fill theatres, fly off shelves, and keep listeners and viewers from touching their dials and remotes. This system successfully persisted from its beginnings in the early 20th century until the digital revolution.

Increasing the chances of a product's success in the market is achieved through the aforementioned strategy of overproduction, which involves having a presence in all market segments and diversifying the offerings. However, adopting such a strategy increases fixed costs (production costs, with the initial and expensive element being the search for new talent), thus requiring a sufficiently large structure. This is ensured by label federations, as mentioned earlier. Producers are aware of the limitations associated with capturing consumers' attention, which is why they focus on intense promotion of only a few new releases. Furthermore, the highest promotion costs are incurred during the product's introduction to the market. As a result of these large-scale actions, a high volume of sales is achieved, but typically lasts for only two months before rapidly declining. Through this strategy, producers benefit from economies of scale, as they can significantly reduce the variable costs of promotion and the expenses incurred for each unit sold. Due to the uncertainty of success, the risk of failure for promoted novelties is reduced by promoting artists who have already achieved success or by promoting artists who fit into the created trend.

Notes

1 The authors invoke the term *hostile brothers*, proposed by K. Marx in *Theories of Surplus Value* (Marx, 2000). Hostile brothers join forces when it is in their interests to do so, the rest of the time they remain in conflict.
2 At the time, the same companies were producing playback equipment and phonograms.
3 This refers to the late 1980s and early 1990s. Later, the *big six* became the *big four* (after 2000) and eventually the *big three* (after 2012, when EMI was bought out by the other majors).
4 We do not discuss music in digital formats here; their characteristics will be presented in the next chapter.
5 There are typically two methods used to measure concentration within an industry. The first method is ownership concentration, which involves assessing factors such as profits, total turnover, and the number of employees within a company. However, since these specific figures are not provided, the second method of measuring concentration is often employed, which involves comparing the market shares of the major players in the industry (Burnett, 2010, p. 13).
6 WEA Corporation is indeed an abbreviation derived from the label names Warner Bros Records, Elektra Records, and Atlantic Records. It was created in 1970 by Warner to function as a distribution company (Bourreau and Labarthe-Piol, 2004; Passman, 2015).
7 Revenues from music publishing were growing at around 10% per year between 1982 and 1990.

8 The author distinguishes between two types of vertical integration – upstream and downstream, which means – on the one hand – the production phase and – on the other hand – the distribution phase of the finished product.

9 The US market.

10 Billboard is the first magazine about music, operating in the American market since 1894. Initially serving the advertising industry, it soon became the premier source of information on trends and innovations in music and related fields. It publishes charts of best-selling, most popular on-air, most frequently downloaded, and most profitable songs and albums (Billboard, n.d.).

Bibliography

Adler, M., 2006. Stardom and Talent, in: Ginsburgh, V.A., Throsby, D. (Eds.), *Handbook of the Economics of Art and Culture*. Elsevier, Amsterdam, pp. 895–906.

Alexander, A., Owers, J., Carveth, R., Hollifield, C.A., Greco, A.N., 2015. *Media Economics: Theory and Practice*. Routledge, Abingdon.

Alexander, P.J., 2002. Peer-to-Peer File Sharing: The Case of the Music Recording Industry. *Review of Industrial Organization* 20, 151–161.

Alexander, P.J., 1994. Entry Barriers, Release Behavior, and Multi-Product Firms in the Music Recording Industry. *Review of Industrial Organization* 9, 85–98.

Anderson, C., 2006. *The Long Tail: How Endless Choice Is Creating Unlimited Demand*. Business Books, London.

Arditi, D., 2015. *iTake-Over. The Recording Industry in the Digital Era*. Rowman&Littlefield, Lanham, MD, Boulder, CO, New York, London.

ArtRock, 2004. Wywiad z Piotrem Kaczkowskim [WWW Document]. ArtRock.pl. URL //artrock.pl//wywiady/123/wywiad_z_piotrem_kaczkowskim.html (accessed 4.27.21).

Bagdikian, B.H., 2007. *The New Media Monopoly*. Beacon Press, Boston, MA.

Benghozi, P.-J., Paris, T., 2008. Replacer la fonction distribution au cœur du management de la culture. Post-Print hal-00572826, HAL. URL https://hal.science/hal-00572826 (accessed 4.19.2021).

Benhamou, F., 2008. *L'économie de la culture*. La Découverte, Paris.

Benhamou, F., 2002. *L'Économie du star-system*. Odile Jacob, Paris.

Bernstein, A., Sekine, N., Weissman, D., 2007. *The Global Music Industry. Three Perspectives*. Routledge, New York, London.

Billboard, n.d. Billboard Charts [WWW Document]. Billboard. URL https://www.billboard.com/charts (accessed 10.12.20).

Bishop, J., 2005. Building International Empires of Sound: Concentrations of Power and Property in the "Global" Music Market. *Popular Music and Society* 28, 443–471.

Boorstin, E., 2004. *Music Sales in the Age of File Sharing. Department of Economics*. Princeton University, Princeton, NJ.

Bourreau, M., Gensollen, M., 2006. L'impact d'Internet et des Technologies de l'Information et de la Communication sur l'industrie de la musique enregistrée. *Revue d'économie industrielle* 31–70. https://doi.org/10.4000/rei.459

Bourreau, M., Labarthe-Piol, B., 2004. Le peer to peer et la crise de l'industrie du disque. Une perspective historique. *Réseaux* 125, 17.

Burnett, R., 2010. *The Global Jukebox: The International Music Industry*. Routledge, London.

Caves, R.E., 2000. *Creative Industries: Contracts between Art and Commerce*. Harvard University Press, Cambridge, MA, London.

Coase, R.H., 1979. Payola in Radio and Television Broadcasting. *The Journal of Law and Economics* 22, 269–328.

Connolly, M., Krueger, A.B., 2006. Rockonomics: The Economics of Popular Music, in: Ginsburgh, V.A., Throsby, C.D. (Eds.), *Handbook of the Economics of Art and Culture*. Elsevier, pp. 666–719.

Cook, P.J., Frank, R.H., 2010. *The Winner-Take-All Society: Why the Few at the Top Get So Much More than the Rest of Us*. Random House, London.

Coutinet, N., Moreau, F., Peltier, S., 2006. *Les grands groupes des industries culturelles*. Centre National de la Musique, CNM-IRMA.

Curien, N., Moreau, F., 2010. *L'industrie du disque*. La Découverte, Paris.

Czetwertyński, S., 2019. *Morfologia nieautoryzowanego kopiowania*. Wydawnictwo Uniwersytetu Ekonomicznego, Wroclaw.

Dannen, F., 2011. *Hit Men: Power Brokers and Fast Money Inside the Music Business*. Vintage, New York.

Dantec, A., Levy, F., 2005. *Stars et box office : un état des approches théoriques et empiriques*. Documents de Travail de l'OFCE.

Doyle, G., 2000. The Economics of Monomedia and Cross-Media Expansion: A Study of the Case Favouring Deregulation of TV and Newspaper Ownership in the U.K. *Journal of Cultural Economics* 24. https://doi.org/10.1023/A:1007599617438

Eurobarometer Survey, 2002. *Europeans' Participation in Cultural Activities (Eurobarometer Survey)*. Eurostat.

Ferstler, H., 2005. *Encyclopedia of Recorded Sound*. Routledge, New York.

Frith, S., 2017. *Taking Popular Music Seriously: Selected Essays*. Routledge, London, New York.

Frith, S. (Ed.), 1989. *Facing the Music: A Pantheon Guide to Popular Culture*. Pantheon Books, New York.

Frith, S., 1988. *Sound Effects: Youth, Leisure, and the Politics of Rock "n" Roll*. Pantheon Books, New York.

Gałuszka, P., 2009. *Biznes muzyczny : ekonomiczne i marketingowe aspekty fonografii*. Wydawnictwo Placet, Warszawa.

Garnham, N., Inglis, F., 1994. *Capitalism and Communication: Global Culture and the Economics of Information*. SAGE, Newbury Park, CA, London, New Delhi.

Gierszewska, G., Romanowska, M., 2017. *Analiza strategiczna przedsiebiorstwa*. Polskie Wydawnictwo Ekonomiczne, Warszawa.

Golat, R., 2008. *Prawo autorskie: komentarz dla praktyków*. Ośrodek Doradztwa i Doskonalenia Kadr, Gdańsk.

Hannaford, S., 2007. *Market Domination!: The Impact of Industry Consolidation on Competition, Innovation, and Consumer Choice*. Bloomsbury Publishing USA, New York.

Hendricks, K., Sorensen, A., 2009. Information and the Skewness of Music Sales. *Journal of Political Economy* 117, 324–369. https://doi.org/10.1086/599283

Hoffmann, F.W., Ferstler, H., 2005. *Pirated Recordings*, in: Ferstler, H. (Ed.), *Encyclopedia of Recorded Sound*. Routledge, New York.

Hull, G.P., 2004. *The Recording Industry*. Routledge, New York.

Hull, G.P., Hutchison, T.W., Strasser, R., 2011. *The Music Business and Recording Industry: Delivering Music in the 21st Century*. Taylor & Francis, New York, London.

Huygens, M., Van Den Bosch, F.A.J., Volberda, H.W., Baden-Fuller, C., 2001. Co-Evolution of Firm Capabilities and Industry Competition: Investigating the Music Industry, 1877–1997. *Organization Studies* 22, 971–1011.

IFPI, 2000. *Music Piracy Report 2000.* International Federation of the Phonographic Industry, London, URL https://www.irma.asso.fr/IMG/pdf/Piracy2000.pdf (accessed 4.19.21).

Janowska, A.A., 2016. *Show-biznes obnażony.* Recenzja serialu "Vinyl". URL https://kulturaliberalna.pl/2016/06/14/anetta-janowska-show-biznes-obnazony-vinyl-serial/ (accessed 4.18.21).

Knoedelseder, W., 1993. *Stiffed. Stiffed: A True Story of MCA, the Music Business, and the Mafia.* HarperCollins, New York.

Kominek, M., 1986. *Zaczęło się od fonografu.* Polskie Wydawnictwa Muczyzne, Kraków.

Laing, D., 2009. World Music and the Global Music Industry: Flows, Corporations and Networks, in: Tuulikki, P. (Ed.), *World Music: Roots and Routes. Studies across Disciplines in the Humanities and Social Sciences* 6. Collegium for Advanced Studies, Helsinki, pp. 14–33.

Les orpailleurs de la bande FM [WWW Document], 2002. l'Humanité. URL https://www.humanite.fr/les-orpailleurs-de-la-bande-fm-263515 (accessed 4.27.21).

Marx, K., 2000. *Theories of Surplus Value.* Prometeus Books, Amherst.

McCarthy, D., 2011. The Recording Industry as a Loss Leader: How Music Sales Are Used to Sell Other Goods. URL http://athingcalledmusic.com/wp-content/uploads/2013/10/DeanMcCarthy_MED7030_Assignment1-1.pdf (accessed 9.19.23).

MMC, 1994. *The Supply of Recorded Music.* Monopolies and Mergers Commission, London.

Noam, E., 2009. *Media Ownership and Concentration in America.* Oxford University Press, Oxford, New York.

Passman, D.S., 2015. *All You Need to Know about the Music Business.* Simon&Schoster, New York.

Porter, M.E., 2008. The Five Competitive Forces that Shape Strategy. *Harvard Business Review* 86, 78.

Power, D., Hallencreutz, D., 2007. Competitiveness, Local Production Systems and Global Commodity Chains in the Music Industry : Entering the US Market. *Regional Studies: Journal of the Regional Studies Association* 41, 377–390.

RIAA, 2022. U.S. Sales Database [WWW Document]. RIAA. URL https://www.riaa.com/u-s-sales-database/ (accessed 5.11.21).

Rosen, S., 1981. The Economics of Superstars. *The American Economic Review* 71 (5), 845–858.

Sánchez-Tabernero, A., Carvajal, M., 2002. Concentración de empresas de comunicación en Europa : nuevos datos contradicen los viejos mitos. *Communication & Society* 15, 129–162. https://doi.org/10.15581/003.15.1.129-162

Shemel, S., Krasilovsky, M.W., 2007. *This Business of Music: The Definitive Guide to the Music Industry.* Billboard Books/Watson-Guptill Publications, New York.

Shuker, R., 2017. *Popular Music: The Key Concepts.* Routledge, London, New York.

Strasser, R., 2010. *Music Business: The Key Concepts.* Routledge, London, New York.

Tschmuck, P., 2014. *Creativity and Innovation in the Music Industry.* Springer Berlin, Berlin.

Vinyl (TV series), 2023. Wikipedia.
Vogel, H.L., 2011. *Entertainment Industry Economics: A Guide for Financial Analysis*. Cambridge University Press, Cambridge, New York, Melbourne, Madrid, Cape Town, Singapore, Sao Paulo, Delhi, Dubai, Tokyo, Mexico City.
Wikström, P., 2020. *The Music Industry: Music in the Cloud*. Polity, Cambridge.
Williamson, J., Cloonan, M., 2007. Rethinking the Music Industry. *Popular Music* 26 (2), 305–322.

3 The impact of the digital revolution on the recording industry

3.1 Evolution of the recording industry product

In the recording industry's pursuit of cost reduction in music production and distribution through sound digitisation, as well as the introduction of digital sound recording methods and the compact disc (CD) as a digital medium, no one could anticipate that the consequences of these decisions would soon turn against the industry itself. Digitisation fundamentally changed the nature of its product.

3.1.1 Change in the character of music as a good

Through the process of dematerialisation (Bomsel et al., 2004), the product of the recording industry, namely the phonogram, underwent major changes. The previously inseparable attributes of the music product, namely the immateriality of its content and the materiality of its carrier, became separated. Dematerialisation involves minimising the use of scarce resources in the creation of new copies (Czetwertyński, 2015, p. 94), i.e., minimising the use of atoms to store information. Digitally recorded music can be also copied in any manner and any number of times without loss of sound quality. Therefore, the marginal cost (cost of producing an additional copy) has approached zero (Shy, 2004, p. 182).

Thanks to digitisation, music has become a digital information good. It can be transferred as a digital file between devices capable of playing it (computer, stationary player, portable digital player, smartphone). It can also be distributed in such a form over networks at costs close to zero. The only fixed cost here is the cost of internet connection. Music can be stored at much lower costs than physical storage media since compressed music files take up less space. Furthermore, it is sufficient to store one copy, the original, as buyers do not acquire the product in material form but merely make copies of the original file.

DOI: 10.4324/9781003414605-4

Information good

According to Varian (1999, p. 3), an information good is anything that can be digitised – a book, a movie, a recording, a phone call. This definition is similarly adopted by Curien and Moreau (2010, p. 25). In a broader sense, it can also be described as a good whose value lies in the information embedded in a medium (Wang and Zhang, 2009, p. 225) or as information that satisfies human needs through the use of carriers (media).

Based on Czetwertyński (2019, p. 113).

In the literature on the economics of intellectual property, which includes music, works of the mind are treated similarly to the production of information (Arrow, 1962). Information goods, in turn, possess two distinct characteristics: non-excludability and non-rivalry in consumption. These are also the characteristics of public goods. This means that using them does not prevent others from using them, and they are available to anyone who wants to access them.

Hesmondhalgh (2013, p. 17) argues that cultural commodities have always had the nature of public goods. For example, a live concert in a park exhibits non-excludability and non-rivalry characteristics, as listening to it does not prevent others from doing the same. Additionally, since such a concert takes place in a public space and is free, anyone can attend. However, it is difficult to agree with this classification when it comes to recorded music distributed on physical media. In this case, the product exhibits the typical characteristics of a private good, subject to the principles of rivalry and exclusion. If someone purchases a CD in a store, another person cannot buy the same copy. The availability of a specific product is also possible only upon payment of a specified fee.

In fact, the non-rivalry and non-excludability of cultural goods depend on the state of technology that enables their reproduction, transmission, and protection (Geffroy, 2007). Therefore, the digitisation of content, especially the dematerialisation of the carrier has made music acquire certain characteristics of a public good. In order to acquire a music file, all one needs to do is copy it, which allow other users to benefit from it. However, this characteristic only pertains to the technical possibilities of exclusion from consumption. Music, as a result of creative human work, is protected by copyright laws and therefore acquires the characteristics of a private good.

This change has significant consequences for the functioning of the recording industry, which has operated within the traditional economy and according to the principles of classical economics. This economics examines how the economy allocates scarce resources among unlimited competing needs (Hoskins et al., 2004, p. 3). However, widely accessible digital music, almost like water as predicted by David Bowie (Leonhard and Kusek, 2005, p. 3), has ceased to be a scarce resource and no longer fits within the boundaries of traditional market economics. This has led to the emergence of new business models in the industry and to the necessity of changes in intellectual property law, specifically copyright law, due to the incompatibility of existing legal regulations with the new digital reality.

Another significant aspect regarding the change of music characteristics is the conversion of recorded music into a service (Janowska, 2017). This has become possible through streaming technology. Today, consumers are increasingly foregoing ownership of music, whether in physical formats such as CDs or as digital files stored in computer or, more commonly, mobile phone (smartphone) memory. The increasing bandwidth and decreasing costs of mobile internet access enable users to access extensive music catalogues using permanent connection to the network. In that way, what is important is the access rather than the product itself (Rifkin, 2000).

3.1.2 Fragmentation of the traditional product of the recording industry

Since the introduction of analogue records, the fundamental product of the recording industry has been the album, a collection of an artist's tracks released on vinyl discs or cassettes. Singles, 45 rpm records, served as supplementary products to promote the main product. However according to Coleman (2005), the CD was never a suitable format for popular music; its capacity was better suited for recording symphonies rather than compiling a package of shorter songs. With digitisation, albums have been fragmented into individual songs, which have become the primary product of the recording industry. Currently, a significant portion of digital music revenue comes from the sale or usage (listening to) of individual tracks.

According to the International Federation of the Phonographic Industry (IFPI) report (2008, p. 7), in 2007, when the primary model for accessing digital music online was the sale of individual tracks, single sales accounted for a substantial 30% of digital revenue, compared to digital album sales, which only contributed 15% of revenue. The *Nielsen Music Mid-Year Report U.S. 2019* (Nielsen, 2019) reveals that digital album sales in 2019 accounted for a mere 6% of total sales, while physical album sales amounted to almost twice that figure (11%). The majority, over 80%, consisted of individual tracks, primarily in the form of streaming.

Meanwhile, the fragmentation of the industry's main product into individual tracks is not beneficial for producers. Bakos and Brynjolfsson (2000) have demonstrated that bundle sales, in the form of albums, actually yield greater benefits for the producer. Such a product is attractive to a larger audience than a single song. Different consumers will always find a track they like, even if the others do not pique their interest. As a result, albums are purchased more frequently, generating higher revenue for the producer.

Singles and albums are not the only digital products offered to consumers. In 2003, during the release of a new product (a new release from a known artist or a new artist), there were approximately ten different product formats available, with CDs and cassettes comprising the largest share of revenue. However, by 2007, there were over 100 formats, and CD sales accounted for only a few percent of revenue. For instance, during the release of J. Timberlake's album *Future Sex/Love Sounds*, there were 115 different product formats available, such as downloadable video files, phone ringtones, or full track downloads via phone, totalling 19 million units sold. CD sales constituted only 20% of the total revenue (IFPI, 2008, p. 6). Currently, streaming is the leading format, representing a significant 62.1% of the music industry's revenue in 2020. It proves a shift in consumer music habits reflecting a preference for accessing extensive online music catalogues rather than owning music (IFPI, 2020).

3.1.3 Evolution of formats available in mobile networks

Mobile telephony is an invention that has seen impressive development over the past few decades. According to the Universal McCann report (2007), at the beginning of the 21st century, the mobile phone became the most popular mobile device, surpassing portable music players, laptops, and game consoles. In 2022, the number of mobile subscriptions exceeded 8.5 billion (Statista, 2023b). As for smartphone penetration, the growth has been equally remarkable. Since the introduction of the first iPhone, a revolutionary product by Apple, in 2007, smartphone ownership has reached 68% of the population in 2022 (Statista, 2023a).

The beginnings of the mobile music market, accessible through mobile phones and mobile networks, date back to the late 1990s, when the market for personalising mobile phones emerged. The first interactive services were available in Scandinavia and Japan, offering monophonic ringtones and simple moving logos. Independent companies recognised the potential in the mobile market and provided these services (Strasser, 2010, p. 131). Subsequently, additional mobile formats were introduced, such as ringtunes, ring back tones, and full track downloads.

In the early 2000s, the first streaming services emerged, initially following an advertising model and later incorporating subscription models. French platform Deezer initially took the lead, followed by Spotify, which operated as both a computer and smartphone application. iTunes also joined the competition for music streaming consumers by acquiring Lala and integrating it into their music platform, now known as Apple Music. To this day, these three services remain the leading streaming platforms worldwide (Statista, 2021b).

3.2 Changes in music consumption

One of the effects of technological advancements is the evolution of music consumption, which aligns with broader trends in consumer behaviour. Scholars such as B. Barber, Z. Bauman, and J. Rifkin have written about these transformations. Barber (2008) discussed the infantilisation of consumers who, like children, prioritise the quick over the slow, the easy over the difficult, the immediate over the lasting, impulsivity over prudence, and individualism over community. Bauman (2008) interpreted new consumer habits in the context of postmodernity or liquid modernity. He argued that contemporary consumers are characterised by constant restlessness, a craving for change, movement, and a pursuit of diversity. They seek immediate access to products and derive instant satisfaction and benefit from their use. They desire novelty but are less concerned with ownership and primarily seek the experiences derived from consuming goods. Rifkin (2000) also discussed the shift from ownership to access, suggesting that sellers and buyers have disappeared from the market, replaced by providers and users, with products transforming into services of access to those products (Janowska, 2017).

Simultaneously, alongside these aforementioned changes, there is a tendency towards the deepening of time (Jung, 2009, p. 103), which is, in part, a consequence of the pursuit of change and the constant search for novelty, inevitably leading to a time deficit. This trend involves consumers multitasking to increase the number of activities they can perform within a day. Certain activities, such as listening to music, are now performed in situations that were previously unutilised for work or entertainment, such as commutes.

When discussing the growing consumer inclination towards constant novelty-seeking, it is important to introduce a distinction between different groups of music consumers and refer to Pierre Bourdieu's theory of cultural capital. According to Moreau (2008), consumer tastes are stable due to the costs associated with building cultural capital. An individual who has invested a significant amount of time in building cultural capital within a specific music genre is unlikely to invest it in new genres unless the expected utility outweighs the required investment. Therefore, younger individuals, whose cultural capital is usually minimal and thus does not require substantial investment, demonstrate a greater propensity for exploring new genres and artists. This is why new ways of accessing music that have emerged, thanks to the Internet, have predominantly been embraced by young people. This is supported by studies showing that millennials listen to up to 75% more music than the baby boomer generation (Resnikoff, 2016), facilitated by online music access.

3.2.1 Growing music consumption

One observed trend at the beginning of the 21st century was the increasing amount of time consumers dedicated to listening to music. Research conducted by IFPI (2004) in several global markets (United States, Canada, Australia,

UK, Germany) revealed that between 1997 and 2002, total music consumption (including physical and digital formats) increased by 30%. Millennials were the most significant music consumers, with the majority spending between three to over seven hours listening to music daily (Resnikoff, 2016). They can be aptly described as *musical omnivores* (Van Eijck and Majorana, 2013, p. 80). On average, in 2019, consumers spent approximately 18 hours per week listening to music, compared to 17.8 hours the previous year, as confirmed by the *IFPI Music Listening 2019 report* (IFPI, 2019). Streaming services also note that consumers are listening to music for longer periods (Krueger, 2019), often while engaging in other activities. A study cited in the aforementioned report reveals that 70% of respondents primarily listen to music in the car, as well as during cooking or cleaning (51%) (IFPI, 2019).

The intense growth in music consumption began with the emergence of Napster, the first file-sharing system for music between individual users, commonly referred to as piracy or extralegal sharing (Nordstrom, 2007). However, with the expansion of legal music access options, some consumers started using these methods. Music preferences from legal sources vary depending on consumer profiles and age. Trend followers are inclined towards streaming services, while those valuing quality prefer CDs and high-quality digital files (Im and Jung, 2016). On the other hand, older consumers lean towards premium ad-free models, while younger individuals prefer free ad-supported access (Weijters et al., 2014).

3.2.2 *Shift towards mobility*

The trend of listening to music on the move emerged in the 1980s with the introduction of the first portable music players, such as Walkmans, followed by Discmans, and later digital players, mobile phones, and smartphones. However, the roots of mobility can be traced back to the 1920s when radios were first installed in cars (Janowska, 2009).

The introduction of portable players for digital music, particularly Apple's iPod, which premiered in 2001, significantly intensified this trend, as evidenced by the rapidly growing sales of digital music (with an average annual growth rate of 85% until 2008) (Resnikoff, 2012a). The trend was further solidified with the integration of mobile players with mobile phones. Sony Ericsson was one of the first companies to adopt this approach, but Apple's iPhone became the clear leader in the market (Anderton et al., 2013). The advantage of mobile phones was the mobile internet connection, enabling direct access to digital music without the need for a computer or fixed internet connections. This became a key feature for consumers, as demonstrated by a survey conducted by the British mobile operator *3* among its subscribers in 2006 when mobile formats were just entering the market. The survey found that 76% of respondents aged 16–24 would immediately purchase a song they had just heard (IFPI, 2004).

Technological innovation and evolving consumer needs encouraged operators to collaborate with record labels and offer music packages to customers, often through subscription models (Wikström, 2020). Currently, there are numerous smartphone applications that enable music access, such as Spotify and YouTube, as well as music recognition apps like Shazam.

3.2.3 *Shift towards digital music consumption – ownership and access*

Listening to music on the go inevitably requires the use of digital formats. Research by Nielsen SoundScan (*The Nielsen Company & Billboard's 2011 Music Industry Report*, 2012) revealed that online sales revenue surpassed physical media sales for the first time in 2011. This applies to purchases made via computers as well as mobile phones and smartphones. Furthermore, IFPI data shows that in 2022, physical formats accounted for only 17.5% of revenue, while digital music accounted for a substantial 70.6% (IFPI, 2022). This trend can be explained by the hypothesis of the natural album replacement cycle (Arditi, 2015, p. ix), meaning that one form of the product replaces another, and by Coleman's suggestion (2005) that complex music products, such as albums, do not align well with popular music.

In the pre-digital world, consumers accessed music through radios or physical media, mostly full albums. With digital technology, they gained access first to the music libraries of other consumers through peer-to-peer networks (e.g., Napster) and later to individually sold tracks following the pay-per-download model. Streaming is an extension of this model.

The *IFPI Music Listening report* (IFPI, 2019) illustrates how consumer habits regarding music listening have changed significantly. A striking 89% of respondents stated that they listened to music through streaming platforms. The primary reasons for choosing them were immediate access to millions of songs, the ability to listen to chosen music at any time, and the convenience of using such platforms. In the United States alone, within a decade (2010–2020), streaming revenues grew from \$0.5 billion to \$10.1 billion (Statista, 2021c).

The rapidly increasing popularity of streaming services, particularly platforms like Spotify, confirms the suggestions of B. Barber and Z. Bauman that modern consumers constantly crave something new, seeking novel experiences, and the wide range of streaming platforms undoubtedly provides them. Furthermore, consumers no longer prioritise ownership of products; access, exposure to ever-changing music, and the experience of new emotions suffice (Rifkin, 2000).

3.3 The impact of digitalisation and ICT on the Porter's five forces in the music industry

Analysing the music industry using Porter's five forces model in the context of digitalisation and internet development raises several questions (Porter, 2001):

- What will be the influence of the Internet on the industry's structure?

- Will the Internet sustain or reduce firms' ability to gain a competitive advantage?
- Who will capture the economic benefits generated by the Internet?
- Will the entire profit shift towards consumers, or will firms be able to retain a portion of it?

This analysis attempts to provide answers to these questions.

3.3.1 Democratisation of music production, distribution, and promotion and the emergence of new producers

The phenomenon of democratisation in music production, distribution, and promotion entails several aspects. Firstly, it involves the reduction of equipment costs, enabling the recording of digitally formatted songs in acceptable quality under non-professional conditions, bypassing traditional recording studios. The cost of such production has significantly decreased (Waelbroeck, 2013, p. 396). Secondly, the Internet has nearly eliminated distribution costs through the availability of music on various platforms, including paid services like iTunes and Amazon Music, as well as free platforms such as artists' websites, social media, YouTube, and independent websites like Jamendo, SoundCloud, or Bandcamp. Peer-to-peer file-sharing platforms also facilitate direct music sharing between consumers. Thirdly, the development of Web 2.0 and social networking sites has reduced the costs of music promotion and dissemination of information. This applies to both fixed and marginal costs within the value chain (Curien and Moreau, 2010), with substantial reductions in marginal costs, nearing zero. These changes have influenced the circumstances of creation, production, distribution, promotion, and valuation of musical works (Andonova, 2015). The combination of these three elements has lowered the barriers to entry for new producers in the industry (Frost, 2007). Independent creators have become their own producers, distributors, and promoters.

In addition to individual creators, new independent record companies (indies) have emerged within the industry, joining the existing landscape of independent labels (Walzer, 2017). These are typically small-scale labels that operate within niche markets (Gałuszka, 2009, p. 54), releasing music genres outside the mainstream. They rely on independent distribution networks, often with a local reach.

The decline in music production costs has facilitated the emergence and growth of these independent entities in the industry. Pre-digital revolution, production costs amounted to around \$500,000 (Alexander, 1994), whereas today, the cost of producing a recording can be limited to computer hardware and software expenses (Strähle, 2018). Moreau (2013) states that digitalisation has reduced production and distribution costs by 35%. Further opportunities for funding new projects have also emerged, such as crowdfunding platforms, utilised by independent creators. They can be considered as new actors in the music production financing landscape alongside independent labels (Gałuszka and Bystrov, 2013).

Crowdfunding

It is a form of social financing that involves collecting monetary contributions from multiple individuals for a specific purpose indicated by the campaign initiator. Digital crowdfunding platforms serve as intermediaries for this process. They operate as online platforms hosting various projects, providing mechanisms for collecting funds and subsequently transferring them to the project initiators. These platforms also monitor the entire process and sometimes participate in the distribution of the funded product. Currently, the largest crowdfunding platform globally is Kickstarter, followed by Indiegogo.

Based on Gałuszka and Bystrov (2013), Godziszewski (2019), and Jain (2021).

Even before the digital revolution, independent record labels were known for their close relationships with artists on one hand, and their direct connection with audiences on the other. Some of these labels were founded by artists themselves to release, distribute, and promote their own works, as well as projects by other often affiliated artists. Indies typically represent creators who value artistic freedom and often specialise in niche genres with limited reach but dedicated fan bases. Similar to the pre-digital model, these labels serve as talent scouts and sources of innovation, diversifying the music offering and giving rise to new micro-markets (Sexton, 2009, p. 95; Waelbroeck, 2013, p. 396).

The shift in the balance of power in recorded music production is confirmed not only by industry practitioners but also by statistical data ('*Independent music is a growing force in the global market*,' 2015). While it is challenging to estimate the number of independent labels today, it is believed that there are several thousand worldwide, and in the early 21st century, they accounted for approximately 28% of the market share. Over the past few years, their market share has increased to nearly 32% (Curien and Moreau, 2010; Resnikoff, 2018; Statista, 2021a).

However, independent labels seeking to make the most of the opportunities offered by the digital and ICT breakthrough, such as global distribution and promotion, are compelled to rely on intermediaries that are entirely new entities in the music industry. These organisations, which represent independent labels, primarily focus on lobbying for their members and the artists they represent. Although they are not directly involved in recorded music production, they represent independent producers and thus constitute a new powerful force on the music market. One of the largest organisations of this kind is Merlin, based in London (*Merlin*, 2021), which primarily deals with digital music licensing for independent labels.

The activities of Impala, a European non-profit organisation representing independent labels, are much broader. Its mission is to strengthen the independent music sector, promote diversity and entrepreneurship, and facilitate access to financing (Impala, 2000).

In addition to independent labels (indies), new entities such as netlabels, also known as *virtual record labels*, have entered the industry. These initiatives, undertaken on the Internet by individuals or groups of varying degrees of formalisation, aim to promote and distribute music released under free licences in the form of digital files (Gałuszka, 2009, p. 241). They mainly focus on free distribution and promotion of music, without financial involvement in production or physical media releases, nor the acquisition of proprietary rights to recordings. Thus, they can be seen as new intermediaries in distribution and promotion rather than producers in the strict sense of the term.

An important aspect of democratisation, which involves lowering entry barriers at the production level, is the rapid growth of music available on the global network, resulting in an oversupply of music. On one hand, this positively contributes to the aforementioned diversity that consumers can enjoy. On the other hand, it leads to the disappearance of valuable projects among a mass of very low-quality products, as warned by Keen (2011). Prior (2012) also points out the influx of new amateurs, among whom only a few will become professionals. This further exacerbates the attention deficit among music consumers (Citton, 2014), increases the cost of seeking information for them, and creates conditions for the entry of new intermediaries, primarily at the level of digital music distribution.

Lowering entry barriers may also serve as an incentive for large companies operating in related industries, such as the concert industry, to engage in phonogram production. Established concert agencies, especially those organising tours for artists on the *A list*, the most popular ones, can take over their production from existing record labels, offering them services in both concert organisation and record production. They can leverage new promotion channels and concert tours, diversifying their operations and leveraging the synergy between different areas of the music industry to increase revenue. In this way, they can become new producers posing a threat to previously established companies. A prime example is the leading concert company Live Nation (*Live Nation*, 2021), which created a separate unit called Artist Nation to handle *360-degree deals* with performing artists. In 2007, they signed a comprehensive deal with Madonna covering her entire artistic activity, including recording (Waddell, 2007), and in 2008, they partnered with the renowned rapper Jay-Z (Song, n.d.).

It is worth noting that the recording industry is experiencing ongoing consolidation. Since 2012, only three majors have been operating in the market: Universal Music Group, Sony Music, and Warner Music, with their market share in recorded music amounting to approximately 70% (Eiriz and Leite, 2017; Statista, 2021a).

3.3.2 *Democratisation of music production and disintermediation in the supplier power*

Meisel and Sullivan (2002, p. 17) highlight in their analysis of the impact of the Internet on the legal and economic aspects of the music industry the elimination of retail sellers from the value chain. However, we are witnessing a broader process here, namely the elimination of various intermediaries, referred to as disintermediation (Malone et al., 1987).

Disintermediation

It refers to the gradual removal of various intermediaries from the value chain, made possible especially by the development of electronic connections between market participants, as described by Malone et al. (1987), although the term *disintermediation* itself was not used by these authors. According to this principle the distribution of a product or service occurs through a direct producer-to-consumer channel, eliminating an increasing number of intermediaries.

Jallat (2000) expands the original understanding of disintermediation, considering it as the elimination of intermediaries and the creation of a better trade environment, allowing consumers to engage in direct relationships with producers. According to Evans and Wurster (2000), disintermediation encompasses two phenomena. The first involves the direct sale of goods or services by the end producer to the end consumer, thereby reducing distribution channels (this definition aligns with the aforementioned ones). The second highlights the existence of new intermediaries who, using new distribution methods that involve lower costs, can compete with existing intermediaries in the market. This is referred to as reintermediation (Tuomola, 2004). In the case of creators, both aspects of this phenomenon are present, namely a clear shortening of the value chain in the phonographic industry (Wallis, 2001) and vertical production disintegration.

Production disintegration involves several stages. Firstly, recording studios can be eliminated. In the pre-digital era, studios were excluded from record label structures, indicating early vertical disintegration. Artists recorded in studios of their choosing or those recommended by record labels. An example is the independent label ECM, known for releasing jazz and classical music and prioritising the technical quality of recordings. They collaborate with selected music studios and trusted sound engineers (de Haro, 2021). The digital revolution has led to low costs of computer equipment and other recording-supporting tools, as well as sound editing software, eliminating the need for recording in professional studios, at least for mainstream music genres targeting a broad audience (Walzer, 2017, p. 28). This has lowered entry barriers for creators who often now record in *home conditions*. Sexton

(2009, p. 95) refers to them as *bedroom* producers. This shift has resulted in a crisis for traditional recording studios (Leyshon, 2009).

Furthermore, artists can take on the role of both the performer and the record label itself. Nordgård (2018) refers to discussions among industry professionals suggesting that record labels have become essentially unnecessary. In the traditional model, besides overseeing the recording process and providing artistic and organisational support, record labels financially supported various elements of the production process. However, with digitalisation, new intermediaries such as crowdfunding platforms assist artists in this area. Their activities strengthen the power of creators in the industry (Gałuszka and Brzozowska, 2017), as they lower the entry barrier for those artists who previously lacked sufficient funds to release their music, with their artistic activity mainly limited to live performances. An internationally known platform for funding music projects was Sellaband, which closed in 2010, but others like PledgeMusic, ArtisteConnect, Oocto, TuneFund, ArtistShare (Frej, 2014), and MegaTotal (Gałuszka and Brzozowska, 2017) continue to operate.

According to Gałuszka and Brzozowska (2017), researchers do not agree on the significance of crowdfunding platforms for the functioning of the phonographic industry. Some see them as a tool for the democratisation of production and an expression of artists' power over record labels in the market, while others argue that many crowdfunding music projects end in failure and that an artist must already have an established market position and audience to successfully carry out crowdfunding campaigns. A historical example is the campaign initiated in 1997 (before crowdfunding platforms existed) by fans rather than the music band itself. They decided to raise funds for Marillion's tour (Tuomola, 2004). Encouraged by the unexpected success, the band decided to finance their next album through crowdfunding, and the campaign was successful (Król, 2013). Therefore, crowdfunding appears as an alternative that allows bypassing gatekeepers in the traditional recording industry system and achieving success, thus shifting demand for music towards the *long tail*. However, it does not mean that every crowdfunding initiative is successful. Once again, the challenge lies in oversupply, limited time consumers can dedicate to finding information about music that interests them, and as a result, the dilution and fragmentation of demand, making it difficult to raise sufficient funds for specific projects.

Thirdly, creators can act as distributors of their music by placing it on social media platforms and streaming services. These platforms exemplify the aforementioned new intermediaries (Carrier, 2014), aggregators that can strengthen the power of independent artists relative to traditional record labels and build their own market power concerning both suppliers and music consumers (Pucheu, 2012, pp. 140–142). Among these new intermediaries, four platforms are worth mentioning as channels for artist promotion and distribution: CD Baby, established in 1998 in New York, Jamendo, founded in Luxembourg in 2005, SoundCloud, launched in Berlin in 2008, and Bandcamp, launched in California in the same year.

The distribution of paid recorded music in digital format is not obvious for lesser-known or emerging artists, as emphasised by Pucheu (2012, p. 138) and Haynes and Marshall (2018). This is due to the particular nature of music as an experience good and the social dimension of its consumption. It turns out that consumers rarely decide to purchase recordings from unknown artists, reducing the chances of success for these artists. Platforms that aggregate and utilise recommendation systems, including algorithms (Adiyansjah et al., 2019) and consumer opinions, play a significant role in this context. The situation is different for established artists who already have their audience (Nordgård, 2018, p. 74). Both psychological mechanisms, such as fan emotions, and economic mechanisms, such as a reduced risk of dissatisfaction with a purchased product created by well-known artists, come into play. Examples include actions by bands like Radiohead and Nine Inch Nails (Tschmuck, 2014, p. 193), which made their albums available digitally either completely free of charge or using a *pay what you want* model.

Fourthly, disintermediation also occurs at the promotion level, primarily within one of its functions – information dissemination. Frost (2007) refers to this understanding of disintermediation, stating that it offers benefits to consumers by lowering prices and providing better information. Moreover, it allows artists to inform audiences about their works and promote them directly using the tools offered by the Internet. Social media platforms, in particular, serve this purpose by enabling artists to build individual relationships with fans (Arditi, 2015). In turn, these fans, as members of the community gathered around their favourite artists, act as independent promoters and participate in promotion, supporting viral mechanisms of information dissemination online (Sexton, 2009, p. 98).

One of the first tools used for music project promotion was the social networking site MySpace, launched in 2003. The site not only facilitated direct music distribution from creators to consumers but also played a significant role as a promotional channel by showcasing artists and their image to fans. In 2007, at the height of its popularity, MySpace hosted approximately 3 million music bands on its platform (Tournès, 2012, p. 137). Currently, leading platforms for independent artists to present their projects include YouTube, as well as SoundCloud, Bandcamp, Jamendo, and social media platforms like Facebook or Tik-Tok.

It is worth noting that individual musicians, as authors and/or performers, often share their work online for free. They act as *loss leaders* (Moreau, 2013), offering a product below cost on the market to attract consumers and encourage them to purchase other products. Recorded music serves as a promotion for live concerts, which currently generate significantly higher earnings for artists than record sales, and as an opportunity for merchandising, the sale of artist-related merchandise (Magis, 2012, p. 74). Concerts are also a distribution channel for physical albums, which concertgoers enthusiastically embrace, driven by the emotions associated with experiencing live music. Thus, the effect of synergy and supporting one revenue source with another is utilised.

In summary, it can be concluded that, on one hand, the global network, personal computers, and content digitisation have gradually weakened the oligopsony that was prevalent in the phonographic industry. Artists can now build their careers not only through the demanding system of selection (gatekeeping) employed by major record labels. They are also not required to produce full albums, sell their works in traditional stores, and receive only a fraction of the amount for which they are sold. Artists have gained the power to make decisions about their own creativity – its production, protection, distribution, and promotion.

The diagram presented in Figure 3.1 illustrates the current forms of relationships between various participants in the phonographic market.

From the other perspective, it is clear that these new possibilities particularly benefit well-established artists in relation to record labels. Thanks to their popularity among consumers, these artists can operate in the market as independent entities, and their strong brand ensures sufficient buyer interest. Consequently, their bargaining power vis-à-vis record labels noticeably increases. However, the situation is different for lesser-known, niche, or emerging artists. Gaining recognition among consumers amidst the abundance of offerings

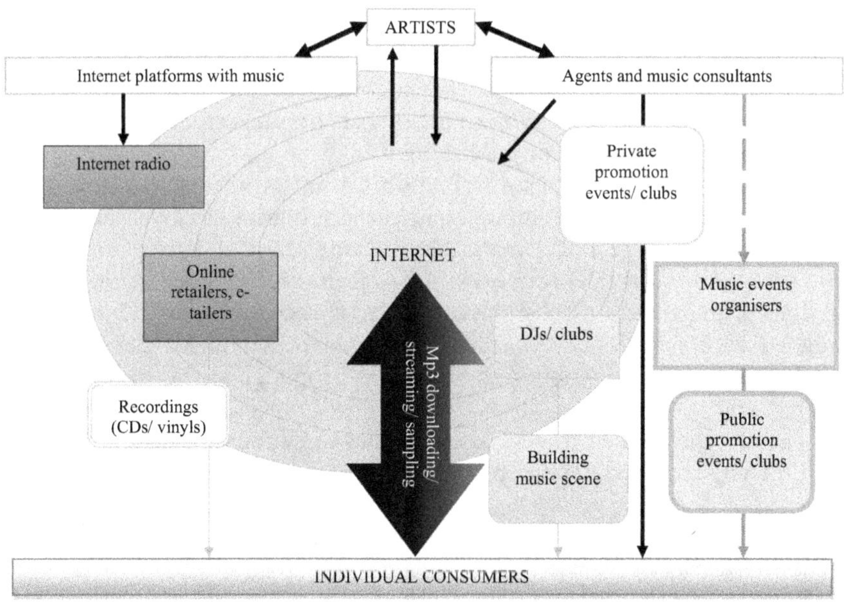

Figure 3.1 The relationships between individual participants in the phonographic market following the digital and ICT revolution. Based on Lewis et al. (2005, p. 354).

(Prior, 2012), which increases the cost of information search for consumers, and building their own audience are equally challenging, although these are different types of challenges compared to the pre-digital era. Despite the theoretically infinite possibilities provided by new technologies and the initiated process of disintermediation, it still requires time, resources, or the involvement of new intermediaries who, thanks to the same technologies, have significantly lowered the entry barriers into the industry.

3.3.3 The power of buyers in the digital world

Thanks to Web 2.0, the power of individual users and the networks they create has increased (Funk, 2008). This means that music consumers now have the opportunity to participate in activities related to music production, distribution, and promotion (Blank and Reisdorf, 2012), effectively intervening in the value chain at various stages. This has led to a certain weakening of the traditional oligopoly in the music industry, which primarily relied on controlling the distribution of products to consumers and the flow of information about them.

3.3.3.1 Music distribution

The area where the previous control of record labels, especially majors, has diminished in favour of consumers is distribution. In the late 1990s, with the emergence of Napster and other peer-to-peer (P2P) networks, distribution took place in an unauthorised and widespread manner (Arditi, 2015; Tschmuck, 2014). Consumers exchanged music among themselves without providing proper compensation to the owners of intellectual property rights, usually record companies or publishing firms.

The loss of control over distribution channels, which was held exclusively by major record companies in the pre-digital era, was an undeniable consequence of the dematerialisation of physical music carriers and the proliferation of P2P networks. As a result, record labels started taking actions primarily against P2P networks and music consumers. These actions aligned with the *piracy panic* narrative, which demonised the other side of the conflict and portrayed them as bad people engaging in bad actions (Patry, 2009).

The measures taken by record companies to eliminate illegal distribution and thereby reduce consumer power in this area were broader and included:

- filing lawsuits against internet users and companies facilitating piracy in the network;
- lobbying for the extension of copyright protection, thus strengthening the monopoly on works held by record companies, and limiting consumer rights regarding the use of purchased products by eliminating exceptions such as fair use in copyright law;

- lobbying for the creation of regulations that facilitate the easier prosecution and punishment of internet users for copyright infringement and the circumvention of technological protections of creative products;
- employing technological solutions such as Digital Rights Management (DRM) to secure files against illegal copying, as well as distributing fake or damaged files to discourage unauthorised music sharing;
- conducting information campaigns to highlight the harmful effects of unauthorised file sharing on the Internet.

Regarding lawsuits, the Recording Industry Association of America (RIAA) in the United States[1] was the most effective in this regard, having filed around 18,000 cases (Wikström, 2013, p. 153). For example, in 2009, an individual was fined $1.92 million for sharing 24 songs on the Internet (Interia, 2009). Approximately 5,500 cases took place across 18 European countries (Wikström, 2013, p. 153). A study conducted in 2003 revealed that higher penalties for piracy result in reduced demand for illegal goods (Hui and Png, 2003). The industry also fought against illegal internet services. In 2001, Napster was shut down based on a court decision following a lengthy legal process (Arditi, 2015, p. 63; Sinnreich, 2013). In 2009, The Pirate Bay, a website that provided links to illegally distributed materials on the Internet, garnered significant attention. Its creators were sentenced to one year in prison and ordered to pay a $3.6 million fine (Gontarek, 2009).

Due to their affiliation with large multinational corporations, record labels were able to leverage their market power and political influence to exert pressure on legislative bodies (DiCola, 2013). This occurred at both national and international levels. For example, in Poland, there has been a discussion for several years about expanding the private copying levy to smartphones, with the funds intended to support the Professional Artists Support Fund. Due to lobbying by organisations representing importers and electronic equipment manufacturers, the adoption of the levy and especially the determination of the list of devices subject to the fee proved problematic (Ziemska, 2021). In the United States, the Digital Millennium Copyright Act[2] was passed as a result of lobbying (Benkler, 2006, p. 413), and in the UK, the Digital Economy Act 2010[3] was enacted. In France, in 2008, a law was proposed to allow the cutting off of individuals from the Internet without prior court decision for copyright infringement. A special government agency called HADOPI was assigned to handle this. The law was approved by the French parliament in May 2009 and has been criticised by both the public and researchers (Bortzmeyer, 2016; Meyer, 2017).

Similar examples can be found at the international level. One of the first was the Trade-Related Aspects of Intellectual Property Rights (TRIPS) agreement developed within the framework of the World Trade Organization, heavily promoted by the United States (Janowska, 2012). In 1996, the WIPO Copyright Treaty was amended to adapt copyright law to technological changes (Wikström, 2013, p. 155). Furthermore, in Directive 2001/29/

EC of the European Parliament and of the Council of 22 May 2001 on the harmonisation of certain aspects of copyright and related rights in the information society, it is stated:

> Copyright and related rights play a crucial role in the Information Society as they are essential to the creation and marketing of new products and services, as well as to the creation and dissemination of creative works. An effective and balanced system for the protection of copyright and related rights is one of the main ways to ensure cultural creativity in Europe and the necessary conditions for its dissemination, and to guarantee the availability and independence of creators, artists, and performers.

However, in regulations, the economic interest represented by large companies is often prioritised over consumer rights (Lessig, 2004). An example of this is the Gallo Report adopted by the European Parliament in 2010, which was assessed as highly restrictive, equating file sharing on the Internet with the production of counterfeit drugs or car parts (Fundacja Panoptykon, 2010).

The Anti-Counterfeiting Trade Agreement (ACTA) was also intended to address issues related to intellectual property protection. Secret negotiations on this document involving representatives from the United States, the European Union, Switzerland, Australia, Japan, and other countries took place from 2008 and resulted in the first version of ACTA, which was officially made public in October 2010 (Cisek, 2009). According to critics, ACTA would have given the music and film industries a weapon that obliges internet service providers to carry out policing functions against network users, which contradicts the principles of democracy and freedom (La Quadrature du Net, 2010). Ultimately, ACTA was rejected by the European Parliament, but it is worth noting that this was the first instance where the European Parliament used its powers granted by the Lisbon Treaty to reject an international trade agreement (Parlament Europejski, 2012).

In 2019, the European Union adopted Directive 2019/790 of the European Parliament and of the Council on copyright and related rights in the Digital Single Market and amending Directives 96/9/EC and 2001/29/EC. It is commonly referred to as ACTA 2 (Cydzik, 2019). Internet rights organisations, such as Communia (International Communia Association, 2019), criticised the directive, particularly Article 13, which introduced the obligation to filter content for copyright compliance. Even though this directive has been compared to the ACTA agreement, it was adopted with controversial provisions (Dziennik Gazeta Prawna, 2019).

As the focus shifted from content ownership to content protection in the industry (Lewis et al., 2005, p. 354), music producers began investing significant resources in technological solutions that could allow them to maintain control over the market. In response to the growing popularity of the open mp3 format, they proposed the Secure Digital Music Initiative (SDMI), which, however, did not gain acceptance among consumers (Arditi, 2015, p. 7). Another solution was the implementation of digital rights management (DRM) technologies, aimed not at eliminating piracy entirely but rather making copying more difficult and costly. In other words, DRM aimed to create an artificial scarcity of digital goods (Hesmondhalgh, 2009).

DRM (digital rights management)

It is a system for managing digital rights (often referred to by opponents as digital restrictions management) based on cryptographic mechanisms or other content hiding methods designed to prevent unauthorised use of electronic data against the wishes of the content provider. While the intention behind such mechanisms was to protect the copyrights of creators, in practice, they could be used to limit the use of data in computer and multimedia systems.

Based on Dhingra (2017) and Finck and Moscon (2019).

DRM was applied to both CDs and digital files. Its main objective was to restore exclusivity (the ability to exclude unauthorised users from accessing a particular good) in relation to digital information by protecting against copying and restricting usage. This was intended to maintain the incentive for innovation (creation), which is lacking in the case of public goods, which music products have become in the digital world. DRM algorithms also allowed for offering different versions of the same product, such as varying quality (with a limited number of playbacks or legal copies). This enabled price discrimination among different consumer segments by the producer.

Unfortunately, such protections have two fundamental drawbacks. Firstly, they are often circumvented by users, which means that the original aim of making unauthorised copying more expensive is not achieved. Secondly, they restrict the use of products by their legitimate purchasers. Older CD players often couldn't play DRM-protected albums, rendering them unplayable. Additionally, music producers began to dictate on which devices recordings could be played, further limiting the rights and freedoms of consumers, facilitated by their strong market position. There was also a lack of general DRM standards, meaning that different manufacturers employed different protection algorithms (Gałuszka, 2009, p. 256), making it even more complicated for consumers to legally use these products.

In 2006, Sony BMG released CDs protected with an algorithm called a *rootkit*, which installed software on users' computers that facilitated hacking (a *backdoor*) (Buskirk, 2006). After consumers discovered this, the company was not only obligated to recall and replace the CDs with this protection but also faced legal action (Osorio, 2007). Another concerning issue was the collection of information about online music service customers using protective algorithms. Music platforms collected data about consumers, such as monitoring their behaviours, while also gathering necessary information about the number of downloads or plays to facilitate copyright settlements. Record labels often utilised such data for marketing purposes, usually after paying the platforms for access (Maasø and Hagen, 2020).

By adopting DRM, record companies incurred significant costs in developing the technology and became dependent on software providers. Additionally, DRM discouraged consumers from making legal music purchases due to the associated restrictions. Undoubtedly, this was one of the reasons why peer-to-peer file-sharing networks remained highly popular. From an economic welfare standpoint, these actions by the industry can be seen as an inefficient allocation of resources.

In the recording industry, recognising the problematic nature of DRM, a decision was made to provide music online without DRM. The eMusic platform was the first to do so (from its inception), followed by Amazon.com and later Napster (the legal service that replaced the original peer-to-peer Napster). In 2009, iTunes, the leader in digital music sales, also adopted this approach (Wikström, 2013, p. 102). These platforms (except for the first mentioned) primarily offer music from major labels. In the case of streaming services, the issue of protection resolved itself to some extent since the technology does not involve downloading the entire song to the device; instead, music playback occurs in a continuous system without storing the full track.

Consumers, whose freedom to access music online faced increasing control from record labels, began to retaliate against the music industry. They not only bypassed technical protections and continued to share music files on peer-to-peer networks but also engaged in hacking actions, organised demonstrations, and protested against imposed limitations. For instance, in late September 2010, the websites of the Motion Picture Association of America (MPAA) and RIAA were taken down. They were attacked by hackers as part of *Operation Payback*, which served as a form of punishment, retaliation, or protest against the aggressive actions of intellectual property protection organisations (Maj, 2010). The trial of The Pirate Bay website owners and negotiations surrounding the ACTA agreement sparked demonstrations in various countries against internet freedom restrictions (Bielenia, 2013; Piłat, 2012). In Poland, internet users decided to protest against the statement made by a popular artist named Kazik, who publicly expressed that he considered the unauthorised downloading of any album from the Internet by users as a personal loss. In response to these remarks, the *Strata Kazika* (Kazik's Loss) website was launched. Internet users who copied albums for personal use or downloaded music from the Internet would report it on the website, and the cumulative potential loss in Polish złotys suffered by Kazik would be calculated (Majdan, 2012).

The recording industry, apart from legal and technological defence against music and broader culture piracy by internet users, has also initiated a series of informational campaigns aimed at spreading awareness about copyright laws and the consequences of their violation. IFPI launched the *Pro Music* campaign, RIAA prepared the *Music United* project in the United States, and a similar initiative promoting legal music called *Respect the Value of Music* started in the UK (Wikström, 2013, p. 153). In Poland, the *Legal Culture* program was launched in 2010, aimed at educating consumers and promoting legal sources of culture (Fundacja Legalna Kultura, n.d.). At the same time, consumer rights organisations advocating for broad access to cultural goods, such as La Quadrature du Net in France or the Modern Poland Foundation in Poland, also carry out independent informational activities. In Poland, the *Prawo Kultury* (Culture Law) project is being implemented (PrawoKultury, n.d.). Its website provides information on copyright law, publications, legal positions, and a course on intellectual property law. In the EU, one such organisation is Communia, which works towards the public domain, increasing access to culture and knowledge, and limiting the expansion of restrictive copyright laws (International Communia Association, 2011).

It is worth noting the benefits that distribution occurring outside the official channels controlled by phonographic companies brought to them. Internet research companies such as Big Champagne or WebSpins, which collected data for RIAA and similar organisations to sue internet users sharing music, also gathered information about the specific content circulating in informal networks. This served as a basis for market observation of trends and musical preferences of internet users (Arditi, 2015, p. 13). It turns out that in an era where *knowledge is power*, consumer actions deemed illegal by the industry became a source of additional value and new revenue streams, especially for rich companies (often majors) that could afford to collect such data. This means that the initial increase in buyer power over businesses, manifested in the functioning of informal music circulation, ultimately contributed to creating market advantage for the largest phonographic companies as well as for new intermediaries.

3.3.3.2 Music promotion

With the development of the Internet, record companies, in addition to traditional promotion channels, started utilising digital channels as well. However, the principle remained similar: information was directed towards consumers in a top-down configuration. It was only with the tools that developed within the framework of Web 2.0 that the cost of information search, incurred in the pre-digital world, decreased and, consequently, the information asymmetry between leading industry entities and consumers diminished. The latter gained access, first of all, to official information from other markets, as well as information directly disseminated by artists. Secondly, they could create and spread such information themselves on a global scale. A characteristic feature of information transmitted on the Internet is its viral nature (Cruz and Fill, 2008).

Various intermediary platforms became tools for exchanging information about music products, which Meck (2001) refers to as *cybermediaries*. Among them, we can mention recommendation and ranking systems provided by online stores and streaming platforms such as Amazon and Spotify, social and music-social platforms, formerly MySpace and currently YouTube, Facebook, and SoundCloud. They allow consumers, on the one hand, to access information more easily, particularly opinions about the desired product, considered more credible than those disseminated by record labels. On the other hand, consumers can create such opinions, comments, and rankings using the offered tools. The consumer has become an opinion leader, tastemaker, innovator (McDonald and Alpert, 2007), and thus an initiator of word-of-mouth marketing, actively participating in product promotion. The flow of information about the product is presented in Figure 3.2.

As noted by Wikström (2013, p. 162), the rapid exchange of information that occurs on the Internet is difficult to control, partly due to its viral nature. Paradoxically, this has increased uncertainty regarding the success of music products created by record companies. While the risk of failure, known as the *nobody knows* principle, has always been present in the music industry, record labels could mitigate the risk by controlling promotional channels, such as developing star system. Currently, consumers have certain influence on the flow of information about products. They play a "key role in the success of a new product by conveying opinions to other consumers who may be interested in its benefits" (Arnould et al., 2007, p. 600).

In recent years, music recommendation on platforms has become largely automated. Based on users' listening history, built-in algorithms recommend music that they might like. One innovative recommendation mechanism is used by the service Pandora, which functions like an internet radio. It employs an algorithm called the Music Genome Project, which analyses songs based on 450 attributes and suggests new songs tailored to users' tastes. As a result, consumers receive personalised music content (Frej, 2014). Such easily accessible recommendations are enthusiastically utilised by consumers.

One might argue that this is an opportunity to confirm the long-tail hypothesis formulated by Anderson (2006). However, research on these systems reveals challenges related to consumer characteristics and the *cold-start* problem. Regarding the first issue, automated recommendation systems do not fully consider different consumer types when suggesting subsequent songs (Celma, 2010), leading to consumer dissatisfaction with such recommendations. The cold-start problem relates to the technical aspect and occurs

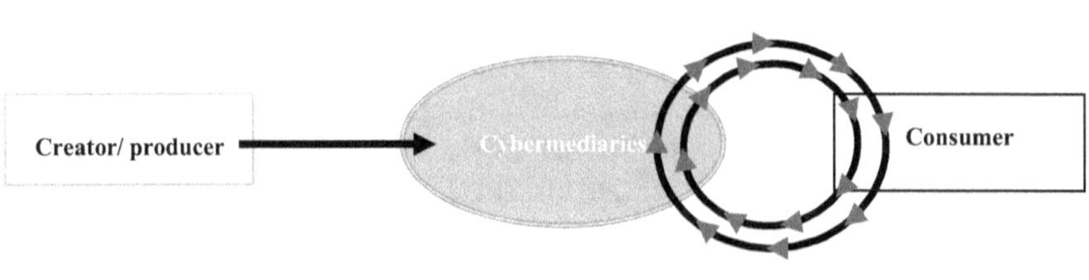

Figure 3.2 Flow of information about products in the digital world. Based on Meck (2001).

when songs that have not yet been listened to are not recommended to other consumers due to the lack of data about them. They cannot be properly profiled (Van Den Oord et al., 2013). Another difficulty lies in the specific nature of music products, which distinguishes them from other cultural products such as films or books, as well as from regular products (Schedl, 2019). This necessitates adapting recommendation algorithms to this particular type of product, which poses a challenge in terms of their effectiveness and introduces uncertainty regarding the success of specific songs (Lupker and Turkel, 2021). Research confirms that the long-tail theory does not hold true for automatic recommendations, as already popular songs are favoured among listeners (Kowald et al., 2020). Furthermore, platforms using automatic, as well as human-based recommendation systems, represent a new form of gatekeeping in the music industry known as *algo-torial power* (Bonini and Gandini, 2019). This places consumers in a situation of limited choice, and information overload increases the cost of searching for products and information about them.

Record companies seek to leverage the informational and networking activities of consumers to their advantage. One strategy is creating engaging content that includes commercial messages related to a music project. If such information resonates with consumers, a viral marketing campaign can lead to success. This was the case with the Nine Inch Nails album *Year Zero*, which was essentially part of an interactive multimedia project (Wikström, 2013, p. 163). In Poland, such an example can be seen in the promotion of D. Podsiadło's album Małomiasteczkowy (Kasprzyk, 2020).

Another way the industry harnesses the activities of internet users, who act as tastemakers, is by collecting information to profile consumers and study their preferences (Maasø and Hagen, 2020). This is facilitated by processing big data (Matz and Netzer, 2017). Today, it is easier for companies as consumers voluntarily provide such information through social platforms, including music platforms. Effective use of data allows for significant risk reduction and trend forecasting (Lyons et al., 2019).

3.3.3.3 Participation in production

Another area where entry barriers have significantly decreased is production. And it's not just about consumers transforming into creators, as mentioned earlier, but firstly, it involves participating in the production of works, creating derivative works, remixes, and creatively supporting favourite artists in their projects (Gamble, 2018). Jenkins (2006) referred to this phenomenon as *participatory culture*, Lessig (2008) as *remix culture*', and Tapscott and Williams (2008) as *wikinomics*. It can also be described as *prosumption*, a concept defined by Toffler in the 1970s (2006; Bruns, 2013). Secondly, participation in production also includes consumers contributing to the financing of cultural projects, including music (Marchegiani, 2018), as already discussed in this chapter. This means that consumers have a direct impact on the music offerings available online, eliminating the traditional intermediaries such as record companies.

Music fans actively engage as prosumers by creating videos for their favourite songs, making compilations of official music videos, or recording their own versions (cover songs) of popular tracks. They also participate in various contests related to their favourite artists. Wikström (2013, p. 158) provides examples of fan productions that used Japanese anime or Star Trek characters as a basis for creating their own music videos. Another interesting example is the use of a photo taken by a Polish fan, M. Kokowski, for the cover of Madonna's single *Sorry* (Frej, 2014).

However, such activities have become the essence of the conflict between cultural fair use and copyright fair use (Collins, 2010). On one hand, thanks to technology, consumers have engaged in amateur remixing of content for which the record companies and other creators held exclusive rights. Lessig (2004) advocated for the legalisation of these activities. On the other hand, the companies demanded respect for intellectual property rights and payment for the use of copyrighted content by prosumers.

However, copyright holders used this conflict to strengthen their position in the market. Firstly, by allowing such amateur activities and establishing frameworks for them, record and publishing companies could control and stimulate these fan activities (Rayna and Striukova, 2016, p. 17), thus providing a space for what is known as 'controlled creativity' (Tschmuck, 2014, p. 240). Secondly, these types of behaviours serve as a valuable source of data for the industry, allowing for the prediction of consumer taste evolution and reducing the risk of failure for new projects in the market (Lyons et al., 2019). Thus, the principle of *nobody knows* transforms into *somebody knows*. Thirdly, the creative actions of fans driven by passion and without expectations of compensation (Sandi and Triastuti, 2020) become unpaid labour essentially benefiting music producers (Gajjala et al., 2017; Sugihartati, 2020). Gamble and Gilmore (2013) refer to this phenomenon as *co-creative marketing*, which companies employ to increase the value of their products. Prosumer activities add additional value to the value chain, which is appropriated by record companies.

Another area in which the influence of consumers on music production has become apparent is through financing it via crowdfunding platforms. This has already been discussed in previous sections of this chapter. Wikström (2020, p. 176) refers to this type of support as patronage. He also states that music-related projects on the largest international crowdfunding platform, Kickstarter, account for approximately 20% of all projects. The fundraising model is based on product versioning, meaning that depending on the amount invested by a supporting individual, they receive a different product from the creator. In this way, consumer groups with varying willingness to pay for a product can become part of an artistic project as cultural patrons.

However, crowdfunding implemented within the model developed by Kickstarter and other similar platforms has one fundamental drawback. It does not provide a constant source of income for the creators, even if a large sum is raised for a specific artistic project. One platform that addresses this issue is Patreon (2013). Through Patreon, creators can manage groups of their fans, known as patrons, who provide regular support. Research shows that a large number of creators, including musicians, receive monthly support of over $2,500 through this platform (Regner, 2021). This type of financing is based on close relationships between fans and their favourite creators. These relationships are built on effective communication. Patrons directly influence the activities of the creators and the shaping of their image by either engaging in support or discontinuing it.

The conflict between music-producing institutions and consumers is undoubtedly evidence of a power shift in the music industry. At a certain point, record labels lost control over the most important elements of their operations, such as distribution, promotion, and production, which had previously ensured their efficient and highly profitable functioning as gatekeepers of the music market. Consumers have partially taken control over these aforementioned elements of the value chain, albeit through the utilisation of new business models (primarily streaming), big data, and Web 2.0 tools the power dynamics remain in a precarious balance. Benkler (2006, p. 441), analysing the concept of collaborative production, stated that the activities we currently witness online are part of a model referred to by E. Moglen as *anarchistic distribution*, and this form of activity may completely replace the recording industry. However, the Web 2.0 revolution has proven to be a double-edged sword – because at the same time, dominant entities in the industry, such as record companies, can utilise consumer activities performed for free to increase the value of their products and acquire valuable information about their tastes and behaviours to strengthen their oligopolistic position in the market.

3.3.4 Unauthorised copies of music files as substitutes?

In the pre-digital era, substitutes for music products offered by record companies could be divided into two categories, based on either the carrier or the content itself, i.e., the music. One may wonder how much digitisation has changed this matter.

Thanks to much easier access to both the product and information about it in the digital world, consumers can easily and inexpensively (in terms of search costs) discover works by creators or performers they were previously unfamiliar with. Firstly, this is enabled by an immense, unregulated offering, unlike the controlled model of the traditional model. Secondly, review and recommendation systems provided by digital intermediaries on platforms offering physical (e.g., Amazon) or digital (e.g., Spotify) products suggest alternative music to consumers. The selection is based on increasingly advanced algorithms that analyse consumer behaviour and build individual profiles, including musical preferences (Andjelkovic et al., 2019; Song et al., 2012). The suggested product can be considered an imperfect substitute, a song or artist similar to what the consumer is currently seeking. Therefore, the threat of substitutes in the new model is greater than in the traditional model. This tendency is favoured by changes in consumer behaviour, which are intensively evolving in contemporary economy.

Due to digitisation, the issue of substitutability of the medium has taken on a new dimension. It has enabled the creation of nearly perfect copies of songs at a cost close to zero. This, combined with other factors mentioned earlier, facilitated the creation and widespread distribution of unauthorised copies online. They could be considered substitutes for paid files, as they competed based on price. Moreover, since free is always better than paid, users downloaded many more songs than they would have been able to legally purchase. To limit the risk of such substitutes, record companies implemented digital file protection measures (Lewis et al., 2005). However, an illegal copy can be seen as an imperfect substitute due to its illegal nature, potentially reducing its usefulness for consumers who may fear the legal consequences of their actions (Belleflamme and Peitz, 2014).

The substitutability of physical music, such as CDs, by digital files remains a subject of debate. Firstly, the technical quality of recording is higher on a CD. Secondly, a CD contains additional materials, such as lyric booklets or photographs. Therefore, for some consumers, both of these products would be imperfect substitutes, as Moreau highlights (Moreau, 2013). The same applies to other digital formats. These products were introduced to the market to satisfy the demand of various consumer groups and allow the producer to capture a larger portion of consumer surplus through price discrimination. Additionally, when pirate copies compete with regular products, the producer feels compelled to offer lower-quality products to consumer segments less willing to pay for music (Belleflamme and Peitz, 2014, p. 7). This bears some analogy to the strategy employed in the traditional model, initiated by Warner Music, which involved acquiring different labels to establish a presence in various market segments, genres, and artists.

Arditi (2015, p. ix) approaches the issue of substitutability of mediums in a different way. He claims that replacing old mediums with new ones that emerged through technological advancements was a constant practice in the recording industry. He calls it the *album replacement cycle*, whose aim was to sell the same music, for which recording companies already held the rights, to the same consumers but in a different form. This was a significant source of revenue for the industry. The fundamental difference between the pre-digital and digital eras is that the labels used to introduce new carrier to the market while maintaining full control over distribution. Only with the introduction of the mp3 format and its independent proliferation did control over distribution drastically decline. Moreover, due to product fragmentation, the issue of substitutability does not seem as straightforward. While CDs have lost popularity to digital formats due to technological advancements, their utility remains higher for certain consumer groups.

Despite the aforementioned uncertainties, with the development of digital technologies, unauthorised copies of products, known as pirate copies, distributed by consumers using peer-to-peer networks, were recognised as substitutes for legal products that significantly threatened the recording industry. These copies were often initially sourced from legally purchased compact discs by some consumers.

Music piracy

This is an issue that has not yet been fully clarified, especially when it comes to terminology. The term is used in both academic literature and popular discourse (Czetwertyński, 2019, pp. 129–130; Kariithi, 2011, p. 133) with varying meanings, which requires clarification.

With the emergence of copying tools and blank media, consumers began copying content such as books, music, or movies for personal use or commercial purposes without the permission of the rights holders. These rights holders were either the authors themselves or, more often, publishers: publishing companies, record labels, or film studios. It was these entities that started using the term *piracy* and introduced emotional arguments into discussions about this phenomenon. In one of his essays, Stallman (2002, p. 195), the creator of free software and founder of the Free Software Foundation, criticised the use of the term *piracy* to describe unauthorised copying. He argued that comparing illegal copying to attacking ships at sea and murdering people was unjustifiable. He proposed using neutral terms such as *prohibited copying* or *unauthorised copying* or even *sharing information* instead.

Van Wijk (2002) defines piracy as 'the unauthorised reproduction of legally protected intellectual resources.' According to the simplest definition proposed by Johns (2009), piracy is the 'commercial violation of legally sanctioned intellectual property.' Karaganis (2011, p. 2) uses the term piracy to describe the 'ubiquitous and increasingly digital practice of copying that goes beyond the boundaries of copyright law.' The International Federation of the Phonographic Industry (IFPI) on its website refers to copyright infringement instead of piracy (although 'copyright' is often translated as 'author's right,' in the Anglo-Saxon legal system, it specifically refers to the right to copy). On the other hand, Arditi (2015) emphasises that copyright infringement means the unauthorised commercial reproduction of copyrighted content and is only informally referred to as piracy. He highlights that it was the industry that expanded this definition to include refusal to pay. He cites Litman's argumentation (2001), which notes that 'currently, piracy seems to describe every unlicensed activity.'

Czetwertyński (2019, pp. 133–143) draws attention to two important words found in the proposed definitions: *copying* and *unauthorised.*

In the case of copying, it refers to information (content) and its carrier, but in the context of goods like music, the content is the essence of the process. On the other hand, the term *unauthorised* relates to the permission granted by the author for copying their works. Therefore, he proposes the following definition: 'unauthorised copying is the exact reproduction of original works for which the author has not given permission.' It is important to distinguish between copyright infringement and fair use. In the case of fair use, the author does not grant permission for copying (lack of authorisation), but according to the law, permission is not required, and the person copying does not need to seek it. Other definitions also emphasise the term *commercial*. In the case of listening to music online from unauthorised sources, it is difficult to label users as pirates because the source owner has a commercial purpose, not the user, and different legal systems regulate these issues differently.

In literature and intellectual property documents, piracy is referred to as the illegal copying, distribution, and sale of recorded music and sheet music by individuals or organisations. In the Trade-Related Aspects of Intellectual Property Rights agreement, it is defined as the infringement of copyright and related rights. Traditionally, it is divided into three categories: (1) bootlegging – unauthorised recording of concerts for sale; (2) counterfeiting – unauthorised act of copying recordings, including duplicating packaging, for commercial purposes; (3) piracy in the strict sense – producing illegally recorded music for sale. This has been a problem in the music industry for over 100 years (Frost, 2007).

In the context described above, the understanding of piracy as downloading music files from illegal sources by consumers seems questionable.

Digital piracy can be divided into two main types: (1) commercial piracy, which involves making copies for subsequent sale; and (2) non-commercial piracy, which involves users sharing cultural goods, including music, for the purpose of discovering new works (sampling effect), as well as traditional social behaviours that involve both sharing cultural products and consuming them together. In this case, such actions become a subject of dispute regarding the boundaries of so-called fair use.

However, piracy depends on time and place, making it a relative phenomenon. Despite common international regulations developed by WIPO, such as the Berne Convention of 1886 (WIPO, 1928), copyright issues are regulated at the national level. The duration of copyright protection differs between EU countries (EP, 2006) and the United States (Hatch, 1998).

Moreover, in countries without legislation on copyright, one cannot speak of copyright infringement (Aigrain, 2012; Karaganis, 2011; Latrive, 2007; Strasser, 2010).

Music piracy is not a new phenomenon (Latrive, 2007), but its intensity has never been as pronounced as in the first decade of the 21st century. According to IFPI, the ratio of legal to illegal music, which was available on the Internet at the time, changed dramatically. While in 1999, only 36% of the circulating music came from unauthorised sources (IFPI, 2000), by 2009, it was as high as 95% (IFPI, 2009). Representatives of record companies, particularly organisations such as IFPI and RIAA, considered piracy, i.e., downloading music by consumers from unauthorised sources, as the main cause of the crisis that began in the industry in the early 21st century and as a threat to the interests of creators and the entire recording industry. According to them, piracy is a source of a drastic decline in revenues, erodes culture, destabilises legitimate economic activity, deprives countries of millions of dollars in taxes from the sale of legal music, and causes investment losses (IFPI, 2007). Marshall (2019, p. 148) questions this argumentation and suggests that even in pre-digital times, the economic value of recorded music was too high, which led to mass file sharing by internet users as a reaction to that situation. Additionally, the prices of music products had been declining since the 1990s, indicating a decrease in the value of the entire recording industry. Arditi (2015, p. xxii) refers to the statements made by representatives of the recording industry as a *piracy panic narrative*, arguing that such statements are biased and do not reflect the factual situation. This is also reflected in the conclusions formulated in the book *Music by Numbers* (Osborne and Laing, 2020), in which the authors state that the losses calculated by representatives of the recording industry do not align with reality.

With the development of streaming technology, internet users have started to engage in stream ripping, which involves saving music and music videos transmitted via streaming networks (originally not intended for saving, but only for online listening) on their devices, mainly on computers, using specific applications. IFPI (2019) still considers the creation of unauthorised copies of music to be a significant threat to the industry, although according to the organisation's estimates, only 28% of surveyed users employ illegal stream ripping tools. Interestingly, RIAA had been publishing regular reports on the impact of piracy on the recording industry for over a decade, but the last available report on the organisation's website dates back to 2012 (RIAA, 2020). This may suggest that the significance of informal music circulation in the network for the recording industry's condition has decreased in the past decade. However, a significant portion of consumers still prefer to use unauthorised sources for music (Jugović Spajić, 2021). The *2019 MusicWatch's Annual Music Study* revealed that stream ripping is becoming an increasingly common practice. In the United States, the number of stream rippers increased from 15 million in 2017 to 17 million in 2018 (Kelley, 2019).

Researchers studying the impact of piracy on the music industry do not agree on its actual dimension (Waldfogel, 2012). On one hand, Liebowitz (2004, 2005, 2013), in several publications, demonstrates the thesis that the sharing of digital music by internet users had a significant impact on the decline in CD sales. Waelbroeck and Peitz (2004) state that according to research conducted between 1998 and 2001, digital piracy could be responsible for a 20% decrease in CD sales. On the other hand, according to research by Oberholzer and Strumpf (2007), the impact of file sharing on music purchases is incalculable. Similar opinions are shared by Latrive (2007), Karaganis (2011), Murillo (2013) and Tschmuck (2014). Zentner (2006) estimated this impact at 7%. Waelbroeck (2013, p. 391) suggests that with the emergence of legal sources of digital music, this impact has significantly decreased. Huygen and a group of researchers (2009) stated that file sharing has a positive effect on social welfare. Filiciak et al. (2012) even argue that those who share the most music online also make the largest legal music purchases, while Moreau (2013) emphasises that the sale of CDs continued to grow and only collapsed in 2001, during the rise of peer-to-peer (P2P) services. Aguiar and Martens (2016) also found a positive correlation between consumer use of streaming services and digital music purchases on platforms. According to Arditi (2015, p. ix), the emergence of the first P2P services simply disrupted the cycle of replacing vinyl records with CDs, thus depriving record companies of control over distribution.

There are hypotheses suggesting that piracy may also have positive implications from the perspective of various market entities and even human civilisation as a whole. De Kosnik (2020) argues that in the event of the collapse of civilisation, digital copies, mainly private and likely obtained without authorisation, will become the cultural archive. Regarding the narrower perspective of the market itself, piracy may impact the profitability of music rights holders. This occurs for several reasons. Unauthorised copies can increase the value of original products by serving as samples, thereby reducing the risk associated with the nature of music as experience good. The sampling effect was discussed by Liebowitz as early as 1985. It consists of consumers listening to pirate copies to get acquainted with a song before deciding to purchase it (Waelbroeck, 2013), and thus, such copies serve strictly informational purposes. Duchêne and Waelbroeck (2006), as well as Peitz and Waelbroeck (2006), examined that such consumer behaviour particularly benefits lesser-known artists, while popular artists may suffer from this phenomenon.

Digital music files also generate network effects. A classic example of a digital product that exhibits this effect is computer software (Belleflamme and Peitz, 2012). In the case of cultural products, including music, utility is mainly manifested in the non-economic but social realm. Listening to certain genres of music can be associated with prestige and can influence the image-building of users within their social circles. It can also be a manifestation of a lifestyle or belonging to specific subcultures (Witt, 2016). Aigrain (2012) argues that file sharing without direct or indirect financial transactions, i.e., in a non-commercial mode, is justified. He highlights that file sharing has social and cultural value, thus creating positive external effects.

In light of the above conclusions, it seems reasonable to state that the hypothesis of substitution between physical and digital formats is true only under certain conditions and depends on various factors. It can even be argued that the phenomenon of much greater significance is the fragmentation of demand, which signifies the emergence of consumer segments with new needs and new music consumption habits.

3.3.5 Technology and competition in the recording industry

A series of technological innovations, such as compressed music formats, P2P networks, personal computers, tablets and smartphones, and fast internet connections (both fixed and mobile), have changed the landscape of competition among companies operating in the recording industry. In the traditional model, the advantage relied primarily on access to distribution and promotion channels, as well as a strategy that involved developing a star system to benefit from economies of scale in sales. The advantage was held by large recording companies, as these activities were costly.

The barriers to entry into the market, both in terms of distribution and promotion, have been significantly lowered, as their costs have almost reached zero. This has allowed not only independent artists and producers to enter the industry but also new entities that could directly reach consumers through new technology. The same technology has also enabled the entry of new players who have approached music distribution in completely new ways (Tschmuck, 2014, p. 190) through dedicated online platforms and mobile networks. Therefore, distribution channels have undergone significant fragmentation. The share of majors in global revenue, which reached 90% in the 1990s, declined to only 69% in 2018 (Mulligan, 2019). While they attempted to create their own online distribution platforms, they failed to gain a significant market share, in part because they hesitated to grant permission to competing label-owned platforms to distribute their recordings (Porter, 2008, p. 90).

Among the factors that contribute to the growth of online music sales, increased legal restrictions on illegal file sharing in P2P networks are mentioned. According to representatives of the recording industry, these restrictions lead to a growing number of internet users gravitating towards paid forms of music consumption instead of illegal and free downloads. However, there is a lack of empirical evidence that unequivocally confirms this claim (as discussed above). It appears that for many consumers, incentives to pay for music online may include a wide offer, user-friendly functionality of platforms, and additional innovative options such as playlist creation, recommendation systems, mobility, and metadata describing individual tracks or albums (Waelbroeck, 2013, p. 393).

3.3.5.1 Pioneering forms of online music distribution

A pioneering website in terms of online music distribution was IUMA (Internet Underground Music Archive) (Burnett, 2010, p. 147), founded in 1993 before the emergence of the standard World Wide Web. By the end of 1994, IUMA offered digital songs free of charge from over 500 mostly independent artists. Although it disappeared from the web in the early 21st century, it became a driving force behind the changes that began in digital music distribution.

In 1997, the platform mp3.com was created, enabling artists to distribute their work online. In 2000, an additional and innovative functionality called my.mp3.com was launched. It allowed users to access their personal music library from any computer connected to the network by uploading their favourite music to the platform. Today, this type of solution is referred to as cloud storage and serves users for online content storage. To facilitate the process of uploading music to the platform, the owner of mp3.com purchased a collection of CDs, loaded all the tracks onto their hard drives in mp3 format. Therefore, users who wanted to utilise the service no longer needed to compress the songs and upload them to the platform. They simply had to insert the original CD into their computer drive, and the program automatically recognised the tracks and associated the compressed files with the CD owner. However, representatives of the recording industry accused the website owner of unauthorised copying of copyright-protected works. The owner was charged with making mechanical copies for commercial purposes without permission from the rights holders, which resulted in a fine of $118 million. In 2001, the platform was acquired by the conglomerate Vivendi Universal (Lessig, 2004).

3.3.5.2 Distribution of music on physical media via the Internet

The first platform to utilise the Internet for the distribution of physical music products was CD Now (Burnett, 2010, p. 147). It offered over 140,000 CDs, cassettes, and mini-discs, accompanied by descriptions, artist biographies, and popularity rankings. This model was adopted and developed by the creators of the largest online store today, Amazon.com, which was founded in the United States in 1995. Initially, the store sold books, but soon expanded its range to include music in the form of CDs and cassettes. Amazon operates in various local markets, with the largest ones being the United States, Germany, the UK, and Japan. Its revenue reached $15.7 million just one year after its launch.

The distribution of CDs and cassettes via the Internet is an extension of traditional distribution, primarily controlled by major labels. The products available there are mostly from major corporations. Online stores like Amazon function as specialised supermarkets, fitting into the traditional distribution scheme in that regard. However, physical supermarkets, both general and specialised, have a strictly local reach. In the case of large online stores, their reach is inherently global, eliminating the need for producers to rely on their own extensive distribution networks since the store takes care of the distribution process. For this reason, the aforementioned model could be an opportunity for all those record labels for whom utilising the intermediation of major corporations proved to be too costly.

For independent producers, Amazon's marketplace system, developed by the company, can be beneficial. It acts as an intermediary for the sale of goods from small external entities. Transactions occur directly between the buyer and the small entity, with Amazon collecting a commission. One significant advantage of this approach is the ability to leverage the store's advanced customer information collection and product recommendation system (Smith and Linden, 2017). Additionally, the review system contributed by buyers encourages purchases and, in the case of experience goods such as cultural products (in this case, music), reduces the risk of buyer dissatisfaction. This system allows small publishers without promotional resources to sell niche products recommended by Amazon's customers (Passman, 2015, p. 80).

Numerous similar platforms operate in local markets, also offering music on physical media. Thanks to the Internet, they can overcome geographic limitations and operate on a national or even global scale. Unfortunately, although their catalogues of albums appear more extensive than those of physical stores, these products are often not available in practice. This is due to the necessity of utilising physical distribution centres in a particular country or region, which are burdened with the limitations of the physical world, such as storage and distribution costs. Therefore, the offerings of such stores must be limited and are constrained accordingly. They are therefore competitively inferior to other forms of online distribution on the market.

3.3.5.3 First regular platforms for digital music distribution

Due to the high number of early internet ventures that ended in failure, known as the dot-com crash (Atkinson et al., 2010, p. 7), which occurred in the mid-2000s, trust in the Internet and advertising revenues in this medium declined. This led to the withdrawal of many companies, including major players in the music industry, from investing in online activities. This created an opportunity for independent entities to enter the market.

One such initiative was the peer-to-peer (P2P) file-sharing network called Napster. It was the first network of its kind that allowed individual internet users to exchange music files. Napster was created in 1999 by S. Fanning and S. Parker (Bishop, 2005, p. 459), students at Northeastern University. Within nine months of its launch, the service gathered over 10 million users, and after 18 months, it was being used by approximately 80 million people (Lessig, 2004). Napster was shut down after a series of legal battles in 2001, but before its closure, other P2P systems started emerging on the Internet

(Wikström, 2013, p. 149), such as Audiogalaxy, eDonkey, Gnutella, Kazaa, eMule, LimeWire, BitTorrent, as well as Freenet and GNUnet. These P2P systems offered users new ways of accessing music, posing a threat to the interests of record labels. Previously, they had a monopoly on delivering music to consumers and reinforcing their hegemony by directing their customers through an intricately constructed labyrinth of their products. Competition was not welcome (Bishop, 2005, p. 459).

Simultaneously with the emergence of P2P systems, new entities focusing on legal digital music distribution entered the industry. From 1998, the eMusic service operated online in a subscription model. It offered over 150,000 mp3 tracks from approximately 600 independent labels, and after 13 years of negotiations, its catalogue expanded to include tracks from major labels. The service has always provided music without DRM protection. Starting in 2001, major labels also attempted to launch their own online music services, such as MusicNet, Connect, and Pressplay. With extensive music catalogues, control over global distribution, and significant financial resources, the then *big four* majors could have successfully become leaders in online music distribution following the *winner-takes-all* principle (Moreau, 2013). Unfortunately, the inertia of these massive organisations proved too significant, and the launched platforms failed to meet consumer expectations (Tschmuck, 2014, p. 190).

Majors had to surrender the field to new players, namely Apple and mobile network providers. In 2003, a new major player entered the market: Apple's iTunes, an online music distribution platform (Tschmuck, 2014, p. 191). Initially, it was only available to users of Apple computers and iPod owners. A single track initially cost \$0.99, while the price for a full album was \$9.99. By the end of 2008, the company made DRM-free music available while differentiating file prices at \$0.69, \$0.99, or \$1.29. These changes resulted from pressures exerted by record labels seeking influence over song prices and competition, for example, with Amazon, which had already offered DRM-free songs (Chudziński, 2009). For many years, iTunes has been the leader in the global digital music market, thanks in part to the integration of the platform with music and the iTunes application, as well as portable music players such as iPods (Tournès, 2012, p. 135), and later iPhones. Tschmuck (2014, p. 195) suggests that the digital music store was not a profitable venture but primarily served as an incentive for consumers to purchase complementary goods, such as portable music players and smartphones.

As stated by Gałuszka (2009, p. 220), the sale of music in digital format has always been on the verge of profitability. Part of the revenue, \$0.47 out of the \$0.99 file price, had to be given to the record label that owned the rights to the music. Therefore, companies engaged in the sale of digital music products had to either negotiate better terms with record labels and payment settlement institutions (e.g., PayPal or credit card payment service providers) or seek new business models. The first option is easier to implement for larger entities with greater market power, such as iTunes or Amazon, enabling them to operate more efficiently in the market and exclude smaller rivals.

Following the new trend in music consumption, characterised by access rather than ownership (Sanchez, 2016), which began to intensify with the growing popularity of the Spotify service, Apple decided to launch its streaming platform Apple Music. However, this only occurred in 2015. In 2019, it became evident that the business model relying on the sale of individual songs had reached its limits, as revenues not only from streaming but also from the sale of physical compact discs proved higher than those from online purchases of individual songs (Meisenzahl, 2019).

3.3.5.4 Leading models of online music distribution: pay-per-download, subscription, and freemium models

The pay-per-download (à la carte) model was the first online sales model adopted by major music stores like iTunes and Amazon. Purchases were made similarly to other online transactions. Consumers would find a desired track on the platform, pay for it online, and download it to their device. They became the owners and could listen to the music endlessly, transfer it to portable digital players, or burn it onto CDs. Initially, DRM restrictions limited the freedom of using these digital files, such as restrictions on the number of devices they could be copied to.

Currently, there are still numerous platforms operating under this model. However, the majority of them are local independent music platforms, often owned by mobile operators like Orange, Vodafone, or O2. This indicates that legal music availability online is not truly a global phenomenon. Copyright laws pose a fundamental limitation as they need to be negotiated individually in each market, as there is no international copyright law.

The subscription model was the second most popular model online, where consumers paid a monthly fee in exchange for unlimited access to a catalogue of songs (Waelbroeck, 2013). However, at that time they needed to download the tracks to their device before listening to them. Once the subscription expired, the downloaded files could no longer be played due to DRM restrictions aimed at preventing unauthorised copying.

Today, subscription-based streaming platforms like Spotify and Tidal also operate based on this model. This technology allows music to be listened to without the need to fully download the tracks, similar to radio broadcasting. The subscription model aligns with the previously described sampling effect. Consumers can familiarise themselves with the music and later purchase it on physical media or buy concert tickets and other additional products associated with the artist.

Paying a relatively low subscription fee for unlimited access to vast music libraries appears to be a favourable concept, especially for consumers who listen to a lot of music and seek interesting new releases. They can enjoy an unlimited number of tracks for a relatively small fee, comparable to the price of a single compact disc. The unit cost per track, especially when listening to a substantial amount of music within a month, is significantly lower compared to purchasing individual tracks. Consequently, this model has become dominant in the market. By the mid-point of 2022, approximately 616 million users subscribed to streaming services (Mulligan, 2022). A study conducted in the United States in the first half of 2021 revealed that as many as 47% of Americans above the age of 13 subscribed to some form of music service, including streaming platforms, internet radio, and audiobook services (Smith, 2021b). The market shares of individual platforms are depicted in Figure 3.3.

The leading platform operating within the subscription model is Spotify, which was established in Sweden at the end of 2008. However, it can be considered a mixed model of freemium vs. premium. Freemium users have access to the platform in exchange for listening to advertisements (tripartite transaction model). On the other hand, registered users who subscribe enjoy unlimited access to the catalogue of songs and can listen to them offline. The platform also allows users to create playlists, share them with friends, or see what celebrities are listening to. Based on listening history, the service also suggests new releases to users. Spotify can be accessed via computers by logging in through the website, but the most popular method of use is the smartphone application.

According to Tschmuck (2014), subscription-based services report constant losses, mainly due to high fees paid to music rights holders. Although the owners of these services complain about the need to allocate a significant

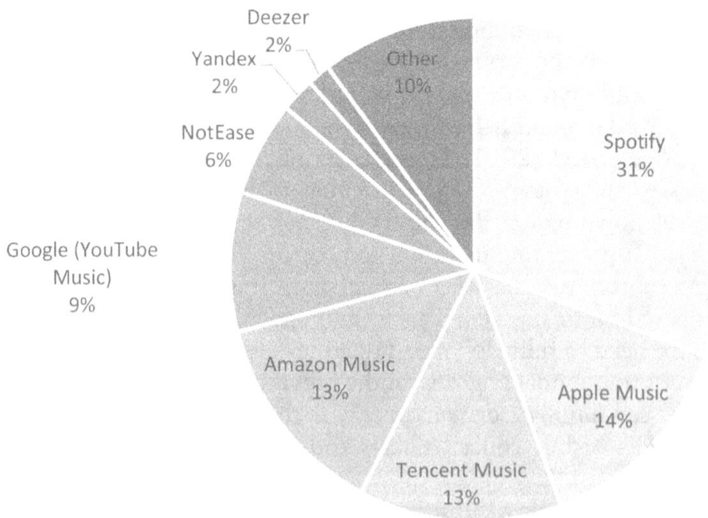

Figure 3.3 Global music streaming subscription market, Q2 2022.
Source: Mulligan (2022).

percentage of revenues to rights holders, they are criticised, especially Spotify, for their very low fees paid to artists. Industry reports indicate that eight out of ten music creators earn less than £200 per year from streaming services (The Ivors Academy, 2020). The payment for individual songs played in the streaming system is indeed very low, as shown in Figure 3.4. For comparison, the Bandcamp service (n.d.), which directly connects artists and consumers, on average, passes 82% of revenues from fans to the artists.

Streaming services have also faced criticism regarding the compensation system for rights holders and, consequently, creators, which is based on a pro-rata system. It has been problematic since the early development of streaming platforms (Resnikoff, 2012b). The fees collected from subscribers are pooled together and then distributed at the end of each accounting period based on the share of plays an individual rights holder or creator has received on the platform. This type of model favours certain music providers and can lead to abuses, such as the use of algorithms to artificially increase the number of streams for specific songs (Ingham, 2021), which has been alleged against platforms like Tidal (Sanchez, 2021).

At the beginning of the 21st century, during the peak popularity of the first P2P network, Napster, the prospects for success of paid music platforms seemed rather bleak. In 2001, they generated only $1 million in global revenue. Nevertheless, attempts were made to create online proposals for alternative business models for informal music circulation networks (Dubosson-Torbay et al., 2004). One of those models is the specific freemium vs. premium model employed by the independent music promotion and distribution platform, SoundCloud (Hesmondhalgh et al., 2019), where the revenue is generated not from listeners but from creators. The platform offers

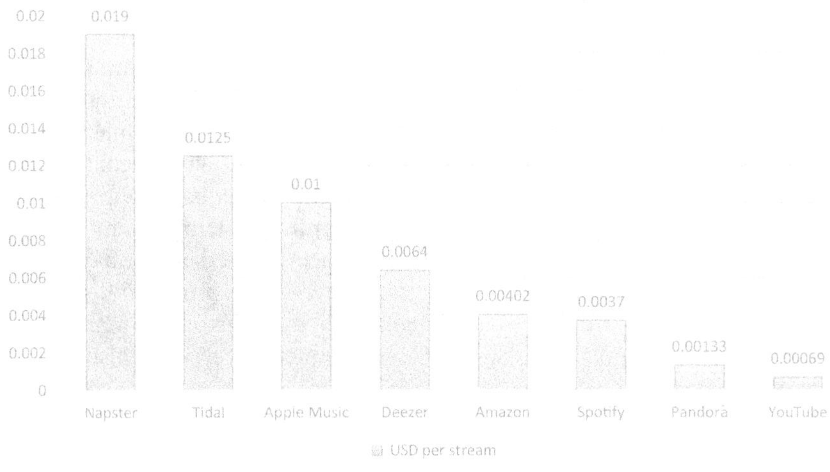

Figure 3.4 Music streaming – who pays best? (2021, USD).

Source: Sanchez (2021).

three types of memberships (SoundCloud, n.d.): Basic, which provides basic options such as a maximum of three hours of music that can be uploaded and basic statistics; Pro Unlimited, which includes an innovative method of compensating creators based on the plays of their songs and access to listening statistics; and Repost, primarily used to facilitate the distribution of independent music through major online music platforms. Unlike other streaming platforms, SoundCloud rewards artists based on individual consumer behaviours, meaning that creators receive a portion of the subscription fees from those consumers who actively listened to their music in a given month (Ingham, 2021; Smith, 2021).

3.3.5.5 Mobile music distribution

The beginnings of the mobile music market date back to the late 1990s, and one of the factors that accelerated its development was the exhaustion of the business model used by mobile network operators. As a result, they began to seek new sources of revenue (Vlachos et al., 2006). Previously, their model revolved around providing voice and text services, but with the advancement of mobile data transmission technologies, it became clear that operators possessed a digital channel (Peppard and Rylander, 2006) that could be used for the distribution of more advanced content, as well as a customer base potentially interested in new services.

Mobile phones quickly became fashionable gadgets, used not only for communication but also for work and entertainment, including music listening (IFPI, 2014). As their popularity grew, so did the demand for customisation. Thus, the shift towards mobile music was one of the effects of the interest in products allowing phone customisation, with ringtone service being one of the earliest examples.

The aforementioned trends coincided with the ongoing crisis in the music industry. Therefore, the opportunity to use mobile networks for music distribution was an appealing prospect for record labels that were losing control over global music distribution. Through collaboration with mobile network operators, they gained access to customer databases, allowing them to stimulate and control consumer behaviour. Thus, a kind of feedback loop emerged: on one hand, content providers needed a new music distribution model, and on the other hand, mobile technology providers needed new offerings for their consumers. Consequently, the latter entered the music industry as a new intermediary – a distributor of digital music. Smartphone manufacturers, starting with Apple and its innovative product, the iPhone, also became part of this system.

In November 2003, O2 network in the UK became the first mobile operator to offer a service for downloading songs to mobile phones. Sprint introduced a similar service in the United States, signing agreements with three major record labels at the time: Warner Music, Sony BMG, and Universal Music. Record labels became more involved in collaborations with mobile network operators, proposing joint music projects to networks such as British 3, T-Mobile, and O2 (IFPI, 2004, 2005).

In 2005, a business model called the *dual model* was introduced. It allowed mobile network users who purchased a song through the mobile channel to download it without additional costs via the stationary internet and transfer it to any mobile device. T-Mobile was the first to implement this model, followed by Sprint in the United States, Orange in Europe, three in the UK, and Muzodajnia Plus in Poland.

In 2005, music available through mobile networks accounted for nearly half of the revenue from digital music. It essentially became the driving force behind the development of 3G technology, attracting consumers, particularly those between the ages of 18 and 35, as the first entertainment product within mobile telephony (IFPI, 2006). Music consumed on the go quickly became a lifestyle trend (Arditi, 2015, p. 32).

During this period, master tones (ringtones) gained significant popularity. In Europe and Japan, they accounted for 50% of the ringtone market, while in the United States, their sales revenue reached 60% of the total ringtone sales revenue. The fastest-growing markets in this area were Japan and South Korea. In Japan, mobile music accounted for 96% of digital music sales, generating revenue of $211 million. In South Korea, out of the 40 million mobile network subscribers (out of a population of 48 million), 10 million were 3G subscribers. This high penetration of mobile network users, especially in terms of third-generation telephony, led to the flourishing of the mobile music market. The hit service that originated in the Korean market and subsequently spread to other markets was called ringback tone, and it significantly boosted the overall revenue from mobile music sales (IFPI, 2005, 2006).

In 2006, Asian markets still dominated the ranking of markets with the highest sales of music through mobile networks. In Japan, South Korea, India, and China, a total of 25% of global digital music was sold. Japan and Korea became countries with a mobile culture, where the penetration of technologically advanced devices, equipped with 3G at that time, as well as the development of 3G services, were significant. In Japan, out of 100 million mobile network subscribers, 70 million were 3G subscribers. Consequently, in 2007, 40% of the sold songs were master tones, downloaded through 3G services (IFPI, 2007). South Korea became the first market in mid-2006 where digital music sales surpassed physical sales, reaching a 57% market share.

In Europe, the development of mobile music, despite the high level of mobile phone market penetration, was much weaker compared to other markets. The rapid growth of broadband internet connections and the emergence of numerous online music platforms undoubtedly captured a significant portion of mobile channel customers. Italy unexpectedly became the leader in this region due to its relatively well-developed 3G technology, followed by France. In 2007, this market flourished noticeably in the UK, where 43% of subscribers owned music phones and used them for music listening

(IFPI, 2008). On the other hand, the largest music market in the world, the United States, did not succumb as quickly to the trend of accessing music through mobile networks, as fixed-line access dominated the market.

One of the reasons for the significant dynamics of the mobile music market's development was the rapid increase in sales of mobile phones with advanced music features. Initially, Nokia was the leader, followed closely by Samsung, which surpassed Nokia in terms of phone production only in 2011. Other major players included Motorola, Ericsson and Sony Ericsson, and finally Apple (Bouwman et al., 2014). In early 2009, Nokia launched the Nokia Music Store, a music file store for downloading music to mobile phones, available in 15 global markets (IFPI, 2010). Another concept introduced by Nokia was the Nokia Comes with Music model, which offered free access to the entire music library of 4.5 million tracks within a one-year subscription (Lindvall, 2008).

Sony Ericsson, continuing the tradition of the iconic portable Walkman, introduced a series of Walkman-branded phones to the market. Similar to Nokia, Sony Ericsson launched a music platform at the end of 2008, allowing owners of their phones to access music. Thus, Sony Ericsson's Play Now Plus began operating in the Swedish market.

In 2007, with the release of the first iPhone, Apple took steps to enter the mobile distribution market. In 2009, they acquired the streaming service Lala, which was intended to transform into a new streaming service (Buskirk, 2010) and become a competitor to the growing Spotify.

Notably, the Korean company Samsung played a role in the success of mobile music in Asian markets. In 2009, they started producing smartphones as competitors to the iPhones. In 2012, Samsung acquired the American streaming service mSpot (Kovach, 2012), which was transformed into MusicHub, a streaming service designed for Samsung smartphone users (Ulloa, 2014a). After launching the new Milk service in 2014, operating on a freemium model supported by ads, Samsung entered into an agreement with the French platform Deezer to provide music to Galaxy smartphone users.

An innovative strategy for the industry was Samsung's 2013 agreement with American rapper Jay-Z, through which users of the application available on Samsung Galaxy smartphones received a free digital version of Jay-Z's album *Magna Carta Holy Grail* five days before its official release. Samsung paid $5 each in advance for 1 million albums (Arditi, 2015, p. xi), which proved beneficial for both parties. Jay-Z's album achieved platinum status in just one day, while Samsung found a new way to market its smartphones.

Both device producers such as Apple, Nokia, Sony Ericsson, Samsung, and mobile network operators invested in the sale of digital music when it became clear that music on the Internet was in high demand. These companies, well-established in other areas of the market, entered the industry as new intermediaries in music distribution. It was intended to complement their core business, generate additional revenue, and stimulate sales of their primary products or services. Music and mobile devices, along with access to mobile networks, became complementary goods, with music serving as an add-on. Apple, for example, successfully launched the sale of portable music players, which became iconic devices for young people. Although the company initially earned little from music sales (Wingfield, 2008), their extensive catalogue attracted numerous buyers who also became interested in mobile music players and their successor, the iPhone. In this case as well, digital music played the role of a loss leader (Moreau, 2013). Similar mechanisms were at play for other companies offering mobile music devices: Nokia, Sony Ericsson, and Samsung. The opportunity to purchase access to music along with a phone aimed to increase customer loyalty to the brand, thereby reducing the risk of customers turning to competing brands (churn).

When it comes to mobile network operators, faster and easier access to music was one of the main motivations for customers to purchase 3G and higher services. Here too, music acted as a loss leader. Offering it for free allowed operators to increase revenue from mobile data sales. Music fans were willing to pay for higher limits to consume more. As this model became widespread to the point where individual networks could no longer leverage a competitive advantage in this area, they abolished limits on music, which became the norm for consumers (Ulloa, 2014b). Music services owned by mobile operators became less popular with the rise of independent streaming services such as Spotify, Tidal, Deezer, or Amazon Music, available on smartphones (Resnikoff, 2011a).

The weakening position of record companies in the industry is evidenced not only by the significant decline in the value of music, which became an add-on increasing the sales of complementary goods, such as mobile internet access. It is also indicated by the entry of new intermediaries, IT giants such as Google, offering the Android operating system and smartphones under their own brand; or Apple with its smartphone. These companies also launched cloud-based music storage services for consumers. It is worth noting that when the mp3.com platform was launched in 1997, operating under the same model, its owners were accused by the music industry of copyright infringement. However, several years later, record companies did accept such practices (Resnikoff, 2011a, 2011c), signifying an important shift in the balance of power in the industry.

3.3.5.6 Internet as a new channel for music promotion

In the traditional model, music promotion was conducted through media such as radio, television, print, and direct sales. Entry barriers were high due to time and space limitations for advertising, costs, difficulties in getting new songs on playlists, and the close relationships between major record labels and media outlets.

In the case of music, promotion on radio and television served not only as an incentive to purchase but primarily as metainformation, fulfilling three complementary functions. Firstly, it allowed consumers to assess whether a particular product suited their taste, thus creating a sampling effect. Secondly, metainformation was crucial for consumers to discover products and be aware of their existence. This saved consumers the cost of individually searching for information[4] about emerging music projects. And thirdly, if the use of a product was complex, metainformation facilitated its optimal utilisation (insufficient utilisation could occur due to misunderstanding or underestimation of a work due to inadequate cultural capital). As informational goods, including music, possess these characteristics, metainformation is considered one of the fundamental ways to create their value (Moreau, 2008, p. 2).

Media also served as opinion-forming institutions, creating trends and contributing to the building of cultural capital in an atmosphere of trust. Consumers did not have to make individual judgements about the quality of a work; it was enough for it to be popular, which, in the case of pop culture products, guaranteed its quality and trendiness.

The Internet, as a new promotional channel, fulfils all the aforementioned functions, allowing the experience, information, and optimal utilisation of goods. A revolutionary change in the case of the Internet is, firstly, the issue of access to this promotional channel. While access was highly limited in traditional media, in the case of the web 2.0 version of the Internet, entry barriers for independent entities have essentially been reduced to zero. Any creator can now utilise this promotional channel because the costs of such activities are significantly lower compared to accessing traditional media. Moreover, there are no limitations in terms of space and time for broadcasting.

Matching, the connection of supply with demand, is also much more efficient on the Internet.[5] Independent producers and even artists themselves have the opportunity to directly reach their audience through individual websites. They can also utilise newly emerged online platforms, which, despite acting as intermediaries in the exchange, eliminate the main disadvantage of traditional intermediation systems – information asymmetry. This means that consumers can actively search for information and access complete data about specific products.

It is worth mentioning one more element related to information, namely its reach and the relationship between reach and the value of information. It is generally accepted that the greater the reach of information dissemination about an informational good, the higher its value (Moreau, 2008, p. 4). In the traditional system, this property was used by majors to promote products on a global scale. As a global medium, the Internet allows for unlimited information dissemination. However, the drawback of this system is the excess of data within it, which is why the creation of value for a good in the Internet involves not only the reach of information about it but also its position in search engine systems, i.e., the chance of being found (as previously mentioned).

New intermediaries, platforms supporting independent music distribution and promotion, play a significant role in this context. In the 1990s, the

MIT-developed service called Ringo emerged, which functioned as a *personal music recommendation* service (Burnett, 2010, p. 146). Classification was based on the preferences of recipients. Consumers would send an email to the website and, in response, receive a list of artists to rate on a scale from 1 to 7. Based on this data, recommendation lists were created, suggesting artists worth attention or not.

Currently, various social or music-oriented platforms serve as tools that facilitate the dissemination of information about lesser-known artists. Thanks to these platforms, the cost of information dissemination has significantly decreased. Both independent creators and major producers make use of these platforms. In turn, consumers can discover new artists recommended by friends on the platform through the same mechanisms. For example, the first music-oriented social platform, MySpace, launched MySpace Music in 2008 in collaboration with major labels, offering users the ability to stream music, watch videos, and purchase mp3 files (Resnikoff, 2008). In addition to its role as an informational platform, the social service also began to function as a music distribution channel, capable of competing with the most efficient online sales platforms due to its popularity. However, MySpace has lost significance over time to platforms such as Facebook, Instagram, Twitter, Snapchat, as well as music-dedicated services like Soundcloud and Bandcamp. These platforms allow consumers to create their own playlists, share them with other users, recommend songs, and build rankings. They function as personalised radio stations that suggest new releases based on user preferences (Resnikoff, 2011b).

From the above considerations, it can be inferred that the competition among companies in the music industry has changed significantly compared to the traditional model. The Internet has enabled the emergence of new channels for music distribution and promotion, but majors no longer have control over them. Currently, new intermediaries dominate distribution and promotion, particularly those backed by IT giants that capture a significant portion of the recorded music value. It seems that these new, large entities will tend towards concentration and the formation of a new oligonomy. This is due to the lower search costs for consumers and the greater market power of these major platforms, both in relation to content providers (record labels) and consumers. Hannaford (2007) pointed out this trend, noting that the traditional oligopoly of record labels is effectively being replaced by an oligopoly of new intermediaries, including companies like Apple, Amazon, Google, and Spotify. Although these companies may appear to support small producers, their actions lead to the disappearance of traditional small music stores and smaller music services, thereby eliminating competition (Figure 3.5).

In the new oligonomy, the dominant entities that have gained significant market power are primarily the new intermediaries. They entered the industry and its value chain at the distribution and promotion stages. Their strength is mainly derived from technological innovations, which is why the largest and most influential music distributors, especially in the digital realm that currently dominates the market, belong to the realm of new technologies (ICT).

This is evident in the case of Apple's iTunes platform, which, as the first digital music distribution system, achieved near-global reach by scaling its operation model to local markets. The key factor here was the synergy effect that occurred between hardware, such as personal computers and music playback devices like iPod and iPhone, and software, such as the music player and library management program on user devices (iTunes), as well as the online music distribution service (iTunes Store).

Another important platform is the Amazon store, which, leveraging its leading position in the global market for goods distribution, also launched an online service for distributing digital cultural content, including music. Amazon initially distributed books but later expanded its operations to other cultural and creative goods such as CDs, DVDs, computer games, and other consumer goods. Thus, it not only possessed effective information systems that could be adapted to new needs but also had the appropriate negotiating position with major players in the music industry.

When Spotify entered the market, it revolutionised the way music is consumed, shifting from an owning model to an access model. The platform originated in Sweden as a startup in response to the growing piracy of

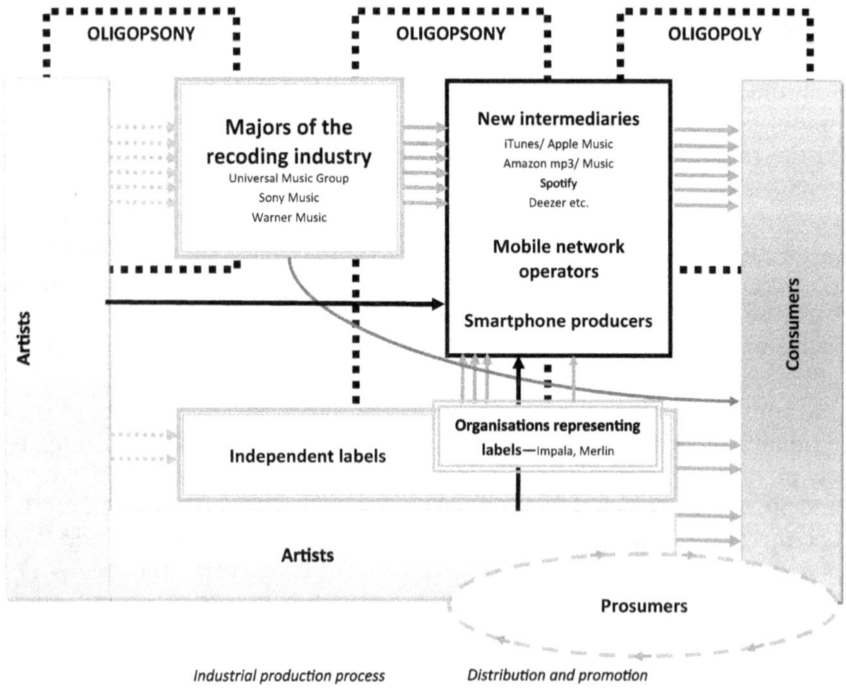

Figure 3.5 New oligonomy in the recording industry. Drawing by the author.

music and aimed to provide a better alternative to free file-sharing networks while properly compensating music rights owners (BBC, 2018). Currently, it is the leading streaming service in the world in terms of user numbers, although the same content delivery model has also been adopted by Apple and Amazon. Unfortunately, despite the significant global growth in streaming revenues over the past few years, accompanied by an increase in the number of users, the remuneration for rights owners, especially creators, remains very low. According to estimations, for a creator to earn the minimum wage in the highest-paying service, Napster, in the United States, their song would need to be streamed over 77,000 times. On YouTube, which pays the least, a song would require over 2 million views (Sanchez, 2021). Therefore, even though consumers have started to pay for music, the music industry, and particularly music creators, have not become the beneficiaries of this change.

Notes

1. Not all actions taken by the RIAA were successful, as seen in cases such as Capitol Records vs. Thomas-Rasset or Sony BMG vs. Tenenbaum.
2. The Digital Millennium Copyright Act (DMCA), introduced as a Green Paper in 1994, a White Paper in 1995 and enacted in 1998, regulates digital rights management in the United States (Arditi, 2015; WolnaKultura, 2009). Under this law, circumventing protective systems became illegal in the United States.
3. The UK Digital Economy Act regulates the operation of digital media.
4. The issue of search costs in economics was first addressed by Stigler (1961). These costs arise when a consumer seeks the lowest price for a particular product and increase with each subsequent search attempt.
5. This function of promotion is mentioned by Stigler (1961, p. 216).

Bibliography

Adiyansjah, Gunawan, A.A.S., Suhartono, D., 2019. Music Recommender System Based on Genre Using Convolutional Recurrent Neural Networks. *Procedia Computer Science*, The 4th International Conference on Computer Science and Computational Intelligence (ICCSCI 2019): Enabling Collaboration to Escalate Impact of Research Results for Society 157, 99–109. https://doi.org/10.1016/j.procs.2019.08.146

Aguiar, L., Martens, B., 2016. Digital Music Consumption on the Internet: Evidence from Clickstream Data. *Information Economics and Policy* 34, 27–43.

Aigrain, P., 2012. *Sharing: Culture and the Economy in the Internet Age*. Amsterdam University Press, Amsterdam.

Alexander, P.J., 1994. Entry Barriers, Release Behavior, and Multi-product Firms in the Music Recording Industry. *Review of Industrial Organization* 9, 85–98.

Anderson, C., 2006. *The Long Tail: How Endless Choice Is Creating Unlimited Demand*. Business Books, London.

Anderton, C., Dubber, A., James, M., 2013. Understanding the Music Industries. Sage, Los Angeles, CA, London.

Andjelkovic, I., Parra, D., O'Donovan, J., 2019. Moodplay: Interactive Music Recommendation Based on Artists' Mood Similarity. *International Journal of Human-Computer Studies* 121, 142–159.

Andonova, Y., 2015. Promesses et paradoxes de la référence créative. *Les Enjeux de l'Information et de la Communication* 16, 5–15.
Arditi, D., 2015. *iTake-Over. The Recording Industry in the Digital Era.* Rowman & Littlefield, Lanham, MD, Boulder, CO, New York, London.
Arnould, E., Price, L., Zinkhan, G., 2007. *Consumers.* Academic Internet Publishers, Southport.
Arrow, K.J., 1962. *Economic Welfare and the Allocation of Resources for Invention.* Princeton University Press, New York.
Atkinson, R.D., Ezell, S., Andes, S.M., Castro, D., Bennett, R., 2010. The Internet Economy 25 Years after.com. *Information Technology and Innovation Foundation* 35, 1–89.
Bakos, Y., Brynjolfsson, E., 2000. Bundling and Competition on the Internet. *Marketing Science* 19, 63–82.
Bandcamp, n.d. About Bandcamp [WWW Document]. URL https://bandcamp.com/about (accessed 6.8.21).
Barber, B.R., 2008. *Consumed: How Markets Corrupt Children, Infantilize Adults, and Swallow Citizens Whole.* W.W. Norton, New York.
Bauman, Z., 2008. *Płynna nowoczesność.* Wydawnictwo Literackie, Kraków.
BBC, 2018. How Spotify Came to Be Worth Billions. *BBC News.*
Belleflamme, P., Peitz, M., 2014. Digital Piracy: An Update. Available at SSRN: https://ssrn.com/abstract=2537269.
Belleflamme, P., Peitz, M., 2012. Digital Piracy: Theory, in: Peitz, M., Waldfogel, J. (Eds.), *The Oxford Handbook of the Digital Economy.* Oxford University Press, Oxford, pp.357–385.
Benkler, Y., 2006. *Wealth of Networks: How Social Production Transforms Markets and Freedom.* Yale University Press, New Haven.
Bielenia, H., 2013. Protesty przeciwko ACTA jako reakcja społeczeństw na niejawność dyplomacji. *Studia Podlaskie* 21, 279–299.
Bishop, J., 2005. Building International Empires of Sound: Concentrations of Power and Property in the "Global" Music Market. *Popular Music and Society* 28, 443–471.
Blank, G., Reisdorf, B.C., 2012. The Participatory Web: A User Perspective on Web 2.0. *Information, Communication & Society* 15, 537–554. https://doi.org/10.1080/1369118X.2012.665935
Bomsel, O., Charbonnel, J., Le Blanc, G., Zacaria, A., 2004. *Enjeux économiques de la distribution des contenus.* Cerna, Centre d'économie industrielle, Ecole Nationale Supérieure des Mines de Paris.
Bonini, T., Gandini, A., 2019. "First Week Is Editorial, Second Week Is Algorithmic": Platform Gatekeepers and the Platformization of Music Curation. *Social Media+ Society* 5, 2056305119880006.
Bortzmeyer, G., 2016. 14 septembre 2012 – Aurélie Filippetti critique la loi Hadopi, in: Le Livre Des Trahisons. Presses Universitaires de France, pp. 71–78. https://doi.org/10.3917/puf.sutte.2016.03.0071
Bouwman, H., Carlsson, C., Carlsson, J., Nikou, S., Sell, A., Walden, P., 2014. How Nokia Failed to Nail the Smartphone Market. Presented at the 25th European Regional Conference of the International Telecommunications Society, International Telecommunications Society, Brussels.
Bruns, A., 2013. From Prosumption to Produsage, in: Towse, R., Handke, C. (Eds.), *Handbook on the Digital Creative Economy.* Edward Elgar, Cheltenham, Northhampton, pp. 67–78.

Burnett, R., 2010. *The Global Jukebox: The International Music Industry*. Routledge, London.

Buskirk, E.V., 2010. Apple Kills Lala Music Service [WWW Document]. Wired. URL https://www.wired.com/2010/04/apple-kills-lala-music-service/ (accessed 6.5.21).

Buskirk, E.V., 2006. Sony BMG Settles Rootkit Scandal with Two States. Wired.

Carrier, M.A., 2014. No, RIAA, It's Not the End of the World for Musicians. Available at SSRN: https://ssrn.com/abstract=2602469.

Celma, Ò., 2010. Music Recommendation, in: Celma, Ò. (Ed.), *Music Recommendation and Discovery: The Long Tail, Long Fail, and Long Play in the Digital Music Space*. Springer, Berlin, Heidelberg, pp. 43–85. https://doi.org/10.1007/978-3-642-13287-2_3

Chalmers, D., Matthews, R., Hyslop, A., 2021. Blockchain as an External Enabler of New Venture Ideas: Digital Entrepreneurs and the Disintermediation of the Global Music Industry. *Journal of Business Research* 125, 577–591. https://doi.org/10.1016/j.jbusres.2019.09.002

Chantepie, P., Le Diberder, A., 2010. *Révolution numérique et industries culturelles*. La Découverte, Paris.

Chudziński, M., 2009. Apple: Muzyka bez DRM w iTunes [WWW Document]. Dziennik Internautów. URL http://di.com.pl/apple-muzyka-bez-drm-w-itunes-25314 (accessed 6.1.21).

Cisek, R., 2009. UE: Treść antypirackiego paktu wciąż tajna. Prawo Nowych Technologii. URL https://www.nowemedia.org.pl/ue-tresc-antypirackiego-paktu-wciaz-tajna/ (accessed 5.29.21).

Citton, Y., 2014. *Pour une écologie de l'attention*. Le Seuil, Paris.

Coleman, M., 2005. *Playback: From the Victrola to MP3, 100 Years of Music, Machines, and Money*. Da Capo Press, Cambridge, MA.

Collins, S., 2010. Digital Fair: Prosumption and the Fair Use Defence. *Journal of Consumer Culture* 10, 37–55.

Cruz, D., Fill, C., 2008. Evaluating Viral Marketing: Isolating the Key Criteria. *Marketing Intelligence & Planning* 26 (7), 743–758.

Curien, N., Moreau, F., 2010. *L'industrie du disque*. La Découverte, Paris.

Cydzik, S., 2019. Dyrektywa o prawach autorskich wpłynie na wszystkich [WYWIAD] [WWW Document]. Dziennik Gazeta Prawna. URL https://prawo.gazetaprawna.pl/artykuly/1411037,dyrektywa-o-prawach-autorskich-wplynie-na-wszystkich.html (accessed 5.28.21).

Czetwertyński, S., 2019. *Morfologia nieautoryzowanego kopiowania*. Wydawnictwo Uniwersytetu Ekonomicznego, Wrocław.

Czetwertyński, S., 2015. *Ekonomika kopiowania a korzyści społeczne*. Prace Naukowe Uniwersytetu Ekonomicznego we Wrocławiu 93–103.

de Haro, G., 2021. GPN in the Recording Industry. The Role of the Recording Studio. Interview.

De Kosnik, A., 2020. Piracy Is the Future of Culture: Speculating about Media Preservation after Collapse. *Third Text* 34, 62–70.

Dhingra, M., 2017. Digital Rights Management & Its Consumer Concerns. *International Journal of Engineering Research & Technology* 6, 438–441.

DiCola, P., 2013. Copyright Law, in: Towse, R., Handke, C. (Eds.), *Handbook on the Digital Creative Economy*. Edward Elgar, Cheltenham, Northhampton, pp. 187–196.

Dubosson-Torbay, M., Pigneur, Y., Usunier, J.-C., 2004. Business Models for Music Distribution after the P2P Revolution. Presented at the Proceedings of the Fourth

International Conference on Web Delivering of Music, 2004. EDELMUSIC 2004, IEEE, pp. 172–179.

Duchêne, A., Waelbroeck, P., 2006. The Legal and Technological Battle in the Music Industry: Information-Push versus Information-Pull Technologies. *IRL International Review of Law & Economics* 26, 565–580.

Dziennik Gazeta Prawna, 2019. Państwa UE przyjęły dyrektywę o prawach autorskich [WWW Document]. Dziennik Gazeta Prawna. URL https://serwisy.gazetaprawna.pl/prawo-autorskie/artykuly/1408202,panstwa-ue-przyjely-dyrektywe-o-prawach-autorskich.html (accessed 5.28.21).

Eiriz, V., Leite, F.P., 2017. The Digital Distribution of Music and its Impact on the Business Models of Independent Musicians. *The Service Industries Journal* 37, 875–895.

EP, 2006. Directive 2006/116/EC of the European Parliament and of the Council of 12 December 2006 on the Term of Protection of Copyright and Certain Related Rights (Codified Version), OJ L.

Evans, P., Wurster, T.S., 2000. *Net Stratégies*. Organisation, Paris.

Filiciak, M., Hofmokl, J., Tarkowski, A., 2012. *The Circulations of Culture-On Social Distribution of Content* [WWW Document]. URL https://ssrn.com/abstract=2246508, http://dx.doi.org/10.2139/ssrn.2246508 (accessed 3.04.21).

Finck, M., Moscon, V., 2019. Copyright Law on Blockchains: Between New Forms of Rights Administration and Digital Rights Management 2.0. *IIC* 50, 77–108. https://doi.org/10.1007/s40319-018-00776-8

Frej, J., 2014. Ewolucja konsumpcji muzyki w kontekście przełomu technologicznego. MA Thesis, SGH Warsaw School of Economics, Warszawa.

Frost, R.L., 2007. Rearchitecting the Music Business: Mitigating Music Piracy by Cutting out the Record Companies. *First Monday*. Fundacja Legalna Kultura, n.d. O fundacji – Fundacja Legalna Kultura [WWW Document]. URL http://fundacja.legalnakultura.pl/o-fundacji/13-ogolne/8-o-fundacji (accessed 5.29.21).

Fundacja Panoptykon, 2010. Parlament Europejski, głosami chadecji, otwiera drogę do zatwierdzenia ACTA [WWW Document]. Fundacja Panoptykon. URL https://panoptykon.org/wiadomosc/parlament-europejski-glosami-chadecji-otwiera-droge-do-zatwierdzenia-acta (accessed 5.29.21).

Funk, T., 2008. *Web 2.0 and Beyond: Understanding the New Online Business Models, Trends, and Technologies*. Praeger, Westport, London.

Gajjala, R., Dillon, J.M., Anarbaeva, S., 2017. Prosumption, in: Rössler, P., Hoffner, C.A., Zoonen, L. (Eds.), *The International Encyclopedia of Media Effects*. Wiley. https://doi.org/10.1002/9781118783764

Gałuszka, P., 2009. *Biznes muzyczny*. Placet, Warszawa.

Galuszka, P., Brzozowska, B., 2017. Crowdfunding: Towards a Redefinition of the Artist's Role–the Case of MegaTotal. *International Journal of Cultural Studies* 20, 83–99.

Gałuszka, P., Bystrov, V., 2013. Platforma finansowania społecznościowego jako nowy typ przedsiębiorstwa na rynku kultury. *Studia i Prace Kolegium Zarządzania i Finansów/Szkoła Główna Handlowa* 125, 145–162.

Gamble, J., Gilmore, A., 2013. A New Era of Consumer Marketing? An Application of Co-Creational Marketing in the Music Industry. *European Journal of Marketing* 47 (11/12), 1859–1888.

Gamble, J.R., 2018. With a Little Help from My Fans: The Transformative Role of the Consumer in Music Co-production. *Production Planning & Control* 29, 826–844. https://doi.org/10.1080/09537287.2018.1478148

Geffroy, A.-G., 2007. Analyse économique de l'évolution du droit d'auteur face aux nouvelles technologies. Presented at the Colloque les marchés de la musique et du cinéma, Institut National de l'Audiovisuel.

Godziszewski, B., 2019. Platformy crowdfundingowe w Polsce i na świecie - ile to kosztuje? Jakie prowizje? [WWW Document]. MamBiznes.pl. URL https://mambiznes.pl/finansowanie/platformy-crowdfundingowe-polsce-swiecie-76980 (accessed 5.19.21).

Gontarek, K., 2009. Apelacja The Pirate Bay odrzucona. Prawo Nowych Technologii. URL https://www.nowemedia.org.pl/apelacja-the-pirate-bay-odrzucona/ (accessed 5.28.21).

Hannaford, S., 2007. *Market Domination!: The Impact of Industry Consolidation on Competition, Innovation, and Consumer Choice*. Bloomsbury Publishing USA, New York.

Hatch, O.G. [R-U.], 1998. S.505 - 105th Congress (1997–1998): Sonny Bono Copyright Term Extension Act.

Haynes, J., Marshall, L., 2018. Beats and Tweets: Social Media in the Careers of Independent Musicians. *New Media & Society* 20, 1973–1993.

Hesmondhalgh, D., 2013. *The Cultural Industries*, 3rd ed. SAGE, Los Angeles, CA, London, New Delhi, Singapore, Washington, DC.

Hesmondhalgh, D., 2009. The Digitalisation of Music, in: Pratt, A.C., Jeffcutt, P. (Eds.), *Creativity, Innovation, and the Cultural Economy*. Routledge, London, New York, pp. 57–73.

Hesmondhalgh, D., Jones, E., Rauh, A., 2019. SoundCloud and Bandcamp as Alternative Music Platforms. *Social Media+ Society* 5, 2056305119883429.

Hoskins, C., McFadyen, S., Finn, A., 2004. *Media Economics: Applying Economics to New and Traditional Media*. Sage Publications, London, New Delhi.

Hui, K.-L., Png, I., 2003. Piracy and the Legitimate Demand for Recorded Music. *Contributions to Economic Analysis & Policy* 2 (1), 1–22.

Huygen, A., Helberger, N., Poort, J., Rutten, P., van Eijk, N., 2009. Ups and Downs; Economic and Cultural Effects of File Sharing on Music, Film and Games. TNO Information and Communication Technology Series.

IFPI, 2022. *Global Music Report 2023*. IFPI. URL https://ifpi-website-cms.s3.eu-west-2.amazonaws.com/GMR_2023_State_of_the_Industry_ee2ea600e2.pdf (accessed 6.30.23).

IFPI, 2020. *Global Music Report 2021*. IFPI. URL https://www.ifpi.org/wp-content/uploads/2020/03/GMR2021_STATE_OF_THE_INDUSTRY.pdf (accessed 4.27.21).

IFPI, 2019. *Music Listening*. IFPI. URL https://www.ifpi.org/wp-content/uploads/2020/07/Music-Listening-2019-1.pdf (accessed 4.29.21).

IFPI, 2014. *IFPI Digital Music Report 2014*. IFPI. URL https://www.scribd.com/document/25535464/Ifpi-2010-Report (accessed 6.5.21).

IFPI, 2010. *IFPI Digital Music Report 2010*. IFPI. URL https://www.scribd.com/document/25535464/Ifpi-2010-Report (accessed4.27.21).

IFPI, 2009. *IFPI Digital Music Report 2009*. IFPI. URL https://www.scribd.com/document/11289117/IFPI-DIGITAL-MUSIC-REPORT-2009-DMR2009 (accessed 4.28.21).

IFPI, 2008. *IFPI Digital Music Report 2008*. IFPI. URL https://www.scribd.com/document/431110111/ifpi-2008-pdf (accessed 4.27.21).

IFPI, 2007. *IFPI Digital Music Report 2007*. IFPI. URL https://www.musikindustrie.de/fileadmin/bvmi/upload/06_Publikationen/DMR/ifpi_digital-music-report-2007.pdf (accessed 5.11.21).

IFPI, 2006. *IFPI Digital Music Report 2006*. IFPI. URL https://www.musikindustrie.de/fileadmin/bvmi/upload/06_Publikationen/DMR/ifpi_digital-music-report-2006.pdf (accessed 5.26.21).

IFPI, 2005. *IFPI Digital Music Report 2005*. IFPI. URL https://www.musikindustrie.de/fileadmin/bvmi/upload/06_Publikationen/DMR/ifpi_digital-music-report-2005.pdf (accessed 6.4.21).

IFPI, 2004. *IFPI Digital Music Report 2004*. IFPI. URL https://www.scribd.com/document/456376078/IFPI-Digital-Music-Report-2004 (accessed 5.26.21).

IFPI, 2000. *Music Piracy Report 2000*. URL https://silo.tips/download/piracy-report-ifpi-music-june-2000 (accessed 9.20.21).

Im, H., Jung, J., 2016. Impacts of Personal Characteristics on the Choice of Music Consumption Mode: Purchasing CD, Downloading, Streaming, and Piracy. *Journal of Media Business Studies* 13, 222–240.

Impala, 2000. What We Do - IMPALA. URL https://impalamusic.org/what-we-do/ (accessed 6.4.21).

'Independent Music Is a Growing Force in the Global Market' [WWW Document], 2015. Music Business Worldwide. URL https://www.musicbusinessworldwide.com/independent-music-is-a-growing-force-in-the-global-market/ (accessed 5.18.21).

Ingham, T., 2021. SoundCloud Revolutionizes Streaming Music Payouts, Launching New Royalties System [WWW Document]. Music Business Worldwide. URL https://www.musicbusinessworldwide.com/soundcloud-is-about-to-revolutionize-streaming-payouts-launching-user-centric-royalties-for-100000-indie-artists/ (accessed 6.4.21).

Interia, 2009. Rząd USA popiera wysokie kary za dzielenie się plikami [WWW Document]. URL https://nt.interia.pl/internet/news-rzad-usa-popiera-wysokie-kary-za-dzielenie-sie-plikami,nId,686219 (accessed 5.28.21).

International Communia Association, 2019. Our Guidelines for the Implementation of the DSM Directive. International Communia Association. URL https://www.communia-association.org/2019/12/02/guidelines-implementation-dsm-directive/ (accessed 5.29.21).

International Communia Association, 2011. About. International Communia Association. URL https://www.communia-association.org/about/ (accessed 5.29.21).

Jain, A., 2021. These Are the Top 10 Crowdfunding Platforms [WWW Document]. Entrepreneur. URL https://www.entrepreneur.com/article/366972 (accessed 5.19.21).

Jallat, F., 2000. Désintermédiation et stratégie sur Internet: recomposition des filières, nouveaux acteurs et réintermédiation. *Revue Française du Marketing* 177/178, 69–82.

Janowska, A.A., 2017. Przemysły kultury w erze dostępu. *Studia i Prace Kolegium Zarządzania i Finansów* 158, 179-199.

Janowska, A.A., 2012. Problem globalnej ochrony własności intelektualnej, in: Molendowski, E. (Ed.), *Globalizacja i regionalizacja we współczesnym świecie*. Uniwersytet Ekonomiczny w Krakowie, Kraków, pp. 351–360.

Janowska, A.A., 2009. Muzyka w ruchu. W stronę konsumpcji mobilnej. *Studia i Prace. Zeszyty Naukowe KES, SGH* 17, 53–74.

Jenkins, H., 2006. *Convergence Culture: Where Old and New Media Collide*. NYU Press, New York.

Johns, Adrian., 2009. *Piracy: The Intellectual Property Wars from Gutenberg to Gates*. The University of Chicago Press, Chicago, IL, London.

Jugović Spajić, D., 2021. Piracy Is Back: Piracy Statistics for 2021 [WWW Document]. DataProt.net. URL https://dataprot.net/statistics/piracy-statistics/ (accessed 6.16.21).

Jung, B., 2009. Kryzys czasu, czas kreatywności i współpracy, in: Osiński, J., Sztaba, S. (Eds.), *Nauki Społeczne Wobec Kryzysu Na Rynkach Finansowych*. Oficyna Wydawnicza SGH, Warszawa, pp. 101–124.

Karaganis, J., 2011. *Media Piracy in Emerging Economies*. SSRC, New York.

Kariithi, N.K., 2011. Is the Devil in the Data? A Literature Review of Piracy around the World. *The Journal of World Intellectual Property* 14, 133–154.

Kasprzyk, I., 2020. *Marki osobiste artystów muzycznych jako element przewagi konkurencyjnej na rynku muzycznym*. MA thesis, SGH Warsaw School of Economics, Warszawa.

Keen, A., 2011. *The Cult of the Amateur. How Blogs, MySpace, YouTube, and the Rest of Today's User-generated Media are Destroying our Economy, our Culture, and our Values*. Nicholas Brealy Publishing, London.

Kelley, C., 2019. New Report Says Music Piracy On The Rise With 17 Million Stream-Rippers In 2018 [WWW Document]. Forbes. URL https://www.forbes.com/sites/caitlinkelley/2019/05/31/new-report-says-music-piracy-on-the-rise-with-17-million-stream-rippers-in-2018/ (accessed 5.1.21).

Kovach, S., 2012. In A Blow to Google Music, Samsung Buys Streaming Service mSpot [WWW Document]. Business Insider. URL https://www.businessinsider.com/samsung-buys-mspot-2012-5 (accessed 6.5.21).

Kowald, D., Schedl, M., Lex, E., 2020. The Unfairness of Popularity Bias in Music Recommendation: A Reproducibility Study. Presented at the European Conference on Information Retrieval, Springer, pp. 35–42.

Król, K., 2013. Crowdfunding – fani finansują muzykę [WWW Document]. crowdfunding.pl. URL http://crowdfunding.pl/2013/09/29/crowdfunding-fani-finansuja-muzyke/ (accessed 5.19.21).

Krueger, A.B., 2019. *Rockonomics: What the Music Industry Can Teach Us about Economics (and Our Future)*. John Murray, London.

La Quadrature du Net, 2010. La version « finale » de l'ACTA doit être rejetée [WWW Document]. La Quadrature du Net. URL https://www.laquadrature.net/2010/10/12/la-version-finale-de-lacta-doit-etre-rejetee/ (accessed 5.29.21).

Latrive, F., 2007. *Du bon usage de la piraterie*. La Découverte, Paris.

Leonhard, G., Kusek, D., 2005. *The Future of Music. Manifesto for the Digital Music Revolution*. Berklee Press, Boston, MA.

Lessig, L., 2008. *Remix: Making Art and Commerce Thrive in the Hybrid Economy*. Penguin Books, New York.

Lessig, L., 2004. Free Culture: How Big Media Uses Technology and the Law to Lock Down Culture and Control Creativity [WWW Document]. URL http://www.free-culture.cc/freeculture.pdf

Lewis, G.J., Graham, G., Hardaker, G., 2005. Evaluating the Impact of the Internet on Barriers to Entry in the Music Industry. *Supply Chain Management: An International Journal* 10, 349–356.

Leyshon, A., 2009. The Software Slump?: Digital Music, the Democratisation of Technology, and the Decline of the Recording Studio Sector within the Musical Economy. *Environment and Planning A* 41, 1309–1331.

Liebowitz, S., 2013. Internet Piracy: The Estimated Impact on Sales, in: Towse, R., Handke, C. (Eds.), *Handbook on the Digital Creative Economy*. Edward Elgar, Cheltenham, Northampton, pp. 262–273.

Liebowitz, S., 2005. Pitfalls in Measuring the Impact of Files sharing on the Sound Recording Market. *CESifo Economic Studies* 51, 439–477.

Liebowitz, S., 2004. Will MP3 downloads Annihilate the Record Industry? The Evidence so Far. *Intellectual Property and Entrepreneurship* 15, 229–260.

Lindvall, H., 2008. Why Nokia's Comes with Music comes with a Price [WWW Document]. The Guardian. URL http://www.theguardian.com/music/musicblog/2008/sep/25/nokia.comes.with.music (accessed 6.5.21).

Litman, J., 2001. *Digital Copyright*. Prometheus Books, Amherst NY.

Live Nation [WWW Document], 2021. Music Business Worldwide. URL https://www.musicbusinessworldwide.com/companies/live-nation/ (accessed 5.18.21).

Lupker, J.A., Turkel, W.J., 2021. Music Theory, the Missing Link Between Music-Related Big Data and Artificial Intelligence. *DHQ: Digital Humanities Quarterly* 15.

Lyons, F., Sun, H., Collopy, D., O'Hagan, P., 2019. Music 2025. *Music Data Dilemma: Issues Facing the Music Industry in Improving Data Management*. Intellectual Property Office, Ulster.

Maasø, A., Hagen, A.N., 2020. Metrics and Decision-Making in Music Streaming. *Popular Communication* 18, 18–31.

Magis, C., 2012. La musique comme valeur ajoutée: lorsque les éditeurs deviennent "marque de service". Une lecture critique des nouvelles stratégies d'éditeurs dans l'industrie culturelle, in: Matthews, J.T., Perticoz, L. (Eds.), *L'industrie Musicale à l'aube du XXIe siècle*. L'Harmattan, Paris, pp. 69–94.

Maj, M., 2010. Antypirackie strony wciąż celem ataków. Przesada? [WWW Document]. Dziennik Internautów. URL http://di.com.pl/antypirackie-strony-wciaz-celem-atakow-przesada-34207 (accessed 5.29.21).

Majdan, K., 2012. Twórca "Straty Kazika": Dość szantażu moralnego w przemyśle muzycznym, piractwo to zdrowa kultura [WWW Document]. naTemat.pl. URL http://natemat.pl/28953,tworca-straty-kazika-dosc-szantazu-moralnego-w-przemysle-muzycznym-piractwo-to-zdrowa-kultura (accessed 5.29.21).

Malone, T.W., Yates, J., Benjamin, R.I., 1987. Electronic Markets and Electronic Hierarchies. *Communications of the ACM* 30, 484–497.

Marchegiani, L., 2018. From Mecenatism to Crowdfunding: Engagement and Identification in Cultural-Creative Projects. *Journal of Heritage Tourism* 13, 143–151.

Marshall, L., 2019. Do People Value Recorded Music? *Cultural Sociology* 13, 141–158.

Matz, S.C., Netzer, O., 2017. Using Big Data as a Window into Consumers' Psychology. *Current Opinion in Behavioral Sciences* 18, 7–12.

McDonald, H., Alpert, F., 2007. Who Are "Innovators" and Do They Matter?: A Critical Review of the Evidence Supporting the Targeting of "Innovative" Consumers. *Marketing Intelligence and Planning* 25, 421–435.

Meck, A., 2001. *Shopbots, Powershopping, Powersales: New Forms of Intermediation in E-commerce – An Overview*. Universität Augsburg, Augsburg.

Meisel, J.B., Sullivan, T.S., 2002. The Impact of the Internet on the Law and Economics of the Music Industry. *INFO* 4, 16–22.

Meisenzahl, M., 2019. Apple is Killing its Most-hated App, iTunes. Here's How it Went from a Popular Music Player to an Outdated Relic [WWW Document]. Business Insider. URL https://www.businessinsider.com/apple-discontinues-itunes-after-18-years-history-rise-and-fall-2019-10 (accessed 6.1.21).

Merlin [WWW Document], 2021. Music Business Worldwide. URL https://www.musicbusinessworldwide.com/companies/merlin/ (accessed 5.18.21).

Meyer, T., 2017. HADOPI: 2009 Graduated Response in France, in: *The Politics of Online Copyright Enforcement in the EU*. Springer International Publishing, Cham, pp. 165–204. https://doi.org/10.1007/978-3-319-50974-7_4

Moreau, F., 2013. The Disruptive Nature of Digitization: The Case of the Recorded Music Industry. *International Journal of Arts Management* 15, 18–31.

Moreau, F., 2008. Méta-information et économie numérique, in: Métadonnées (Mutations et Perspectives). Presented at the Séminaire IST et informatique, ADBS, Paris, Dijon, pp. 223–240.

Mulligan, M., 2022. Music Subscriber Market Shares 2022 [WWW Document]. MIDiA Research. URL https://midiaresearch.com/blog/music-subscriber-market-shares-2022 (accessed 6.12.23).

Mulligan, M., 2019. 2018 Global Label Market Share: Stream Engine [WWW Document]. Media Research. URL https://www.midiaresearch.com/blog/2018-global-label-market-share-stream-engine (accessed 5.18.21).

Murillo, A.C., 2013. Music Piracy and Illegal Sharing: Are Artists Being Affected? *Criterio Libre* 11, 113–124.

Nielsen, 2019. Nielsen Music Mid-Year Report U.S. 2019. Nielsen, nielsen.com.

Nordgård, D., 2018. *The Music Business and Digital Impacts: Innovations and Disruptions in the Music Industries*. Springer, Cham, Switzerland.

Nordstrom, C., 2007. *Global Outlaws: Crime, Money, and Power in the Contemporary World*. University of California Press, Berkeley, CA.

Oberholzer, F., Strumpf, K., 2007. The Effect of File Sharing on Record Sales. An Empirical Analysis. *Journal of Political Economy*, 1–42.

Osborne, R., Laing, D. (Eds.), 2020. *Music by Numbers*. Intellect Books, Bristol.

Osorio, A., 2007. EMI Stays Cool on Copy-Protected Discs, Evaluates Alternatives. Digital Music News. URL https://www.digitalmusicnews.com/2007/01/10/emi/ (accessed 5.29.21).

Parlament Europejski, 2012. Parlament Europejski odrzuca porozumienie ACTA [WWW Document]. Aktualności. Parlament Europejski. URL https://www.europarl.europa.eu/news/pl/press-room/20120703IPR48247/parlament-europejski-odrzuca-porozumienie-acta (accessed 5.29.21).

Passman, D.S., 2015. *All You Need to Know about the Music Business*. Simon & Schoster, New York.

Patreon, 2013. The Story of Patreon [WWW Document]. URL https://www.patreon.com/about (accessed 6.16.21).

Patry, W., 2009. *Moral Panics and the Copyright Wars*. Oxford University Press, Oxford.

Peitz, M., Waelbroeck, P., 2006. Why the Music Industry May Gain from Free Downloading—The Role of Sampling. *International Journal of Industrial Organization* 24, 907–913.

Peppard, J., Rylander, A., 2006. From Value Chain to Value Network. Insights for Mobile Operators. *European Management Journal* 24, 128–141. https://doi.org/10.1016/j.emj.2006.03.003

Piłat, A., 2012. *Protesty przeciwko ACTA w Polsce*. Jagiellonian University, Kraków.

Porter, M.E., 2008. The Five Competitive Forces that Shape Strategy. *Harvard Business Review* 86, 78.

Porter, M.E., 2001. Strategy and the Internet. *Harvard Business Review* 2001, 62–78.

PrawoKultury, n.d. O nas [WWW Document]. Prawo kultury. URL http://prawokultury.pl/info/o-nas/ (accessed 5.29.21).

Prior, N., 2012. The Rise of the New Amateurs. Popular Music, Digital Technology, and the Fate of Cultural Production, in: Laura Grindstaff, J.R.H., Ming-cheng Lo (Ed.), *Handbook of Cultural Sociology*. Routledge, London, p. 720.

Pucheu, D., 2012. Les labels "indé" et les nouveaux chemins de l'intermédiation, in: Matthews, J.T., Perticoz, L. (Eds.), *L'Industrie Musicale à l'aube Du XXIe Siècle.* Approches Critiques. L'Harmattan, Paris, pp. 129–153.

Rayna, T., Striukova, L., 2016. Involving Consumers: The Role of Digital Technologies in Promoting 'Prosumption' and User Innovation. *Journal of the Knowledge Economy* 12, 218–237.

Regner, T., 2021. Crowdfunding a Monthly Income: An Analysis of the Membership Platform Patreon. *Journal of Cultural Economics* 45, 133–142.

Resnikoff, P., 2018. Collectively, Indie Labels are Now Bigger Than Any Major Label. Digital Music News. URL https://www.digitalmusicnews.com/2018/05/20/indie-labels-major-label/ (accessed 6.4.21).

Resnikoff, P., 2016. Millennials Listen to 75% More Music Than Baby Boomers, Study Finds. Digital Music News. URL https://www.digitalmusicnews.com/2016/06/02/millennials-listen-more-music-baby-boomers/ (accessed 5.27.21).

Resnikoff, P., 2012a. Analyst: Post-iPod, the Digital Music Market Is In Serious Trouble… Digital Music News. URL https://www.digitalmusicnews.com/2012/11/07/postipod/ (accessed 6.5.21).

Resnikoff, P., 2012b. What Else? Deezer Stalls, SoundExchange, MOG, Maestro, Tenenbaum, Triplay, Jivox, Lana Del Rey. Digital Music News. URL https://www.digitalmusicnews.com/2012/08/23/latest-40/ (accessed 6.5.21).

Resnikoff, P., 2011a. Breaking: Spotify Now Offering Direct iPod Management, iTunes-Style Downloads. Digital Music News. URL https://www.digitalmusicnews.com/2011/05/03/spotify-11/ (accessed 6.5.21).

Resnikoff, P., 2011b. The Majors Really Hate the Cloud. Just Ask mSpot. Digital Music News. URL https://www.digitalmusicnews.com/2011/04/05/mspot-2/ (accessed 6.5.21).

Resnikoff, P., 2011c. Study: 81% of iTunes Collections Never Get Played. Ever. Digital Music News. URL https://www.digitalmusicnews.com/2011/05/25/itunes-4/ (accessed 6.5.21).

Resnikoff, P., 2008. 2008: The Year in Review. Digital Music News. URL https://www.digitalmusicnews.com/2008/12/29/year/ (accessed 6.5.21).

RIAA, 2020. Reports Archive [WWW Document]. RIAA. URL https://www.riaa.com/reports/ (accessed 5.11.21).

Rifkin, J., 2000. *The Age of Access: The New Culture of Hypercapitalism, Where All of Life is a Paid-for Experience.* J.P. Tarcher/Putnam, New York.

Sanchez, D., 2021. What Streaming Music Services Pay (Updated for 2021). Digital Music News. URL https://www.digitalmusicnews.com/2018/12/25/streaming-music-services-pay-2019/ (accessed 6.8.21).

Sanchez, D., 2016. iTunes Music Downloads Imploding: Down 22.1% In 2016… Digital Music News. URL https://www.digitalmusicnews.com/2016/09/20/streaming-revenue-overtakes-digital-downloads/ (accessed 6.1.21).

Sandi, Z.A., Triastuti, E., 2020. Fandom as a Reward Industry in Indonesia: Pleasures in Pop Music Fan Engagement and Participation within Online Social Networking. *SEARCH (Malaysia)* 12, 73–89.

Schedl, M., 2019. Deep Learning in Music Recommendation Systems. *Frontiers in Applied Mathematics and Statistics* 5, 44. https://doi.org/10.3389/fams.2019.00044

Sexton, J., 2009. Digital Music: Production, Distribution and Consumption, in: Creeber, G., Royston, M. (Eds.), *Digital Cultures: Understanding New Media.* McGraw Hill, Open University Press, Maidenhead, pp. 92–106.

Shy, O., 2004. *The Economics of Network Industries*. Cambridge University Press, Cambridge.

Sinnreich, A., 2013. *The Piracy Crusade: How the Music Industry's War on Sharing Destroys Markets and Erodes Civil Liberties*. University of Massachusetts Press, Amherst.

Smith, B., Linden, G., 2017. Two Decades of Recommender Systems at Amazon.com. *IEEE Internet Computing* 21, 12–18.

Smith, D., 2021a. SoundCloud Introduces "Fan-Powered Royalties" for Independent Creators. Digital Music News. URL https://www.digitalmusicnews.com/2021/03/02/soundcloud-fan-powered-royalties/ (accessed 6.23.21).

Smith, D., 2021b. Nearly Half of Americans Pay for Audio Entertainment, Study Finds. Digital Music News. URL https://www.digitalmusicnews.com/2021/06/17/audio-entertainment-subscription-study/ (accessed 6.21.21).

Song, Y., Dixon, S., Pearce, M., 2012. A Survey of Music Recommendation Systems and Future Perspectives. Presented at the 9th International Symposium on Computer Music Modeling and Retrieval, Citeseer, pp. 395–410.

Song, Z., n.d. 360 Deals and What Can Musicians Do to Protect Individual Income.

SoundCloud, n.d. Stand out with Pro Unlimited [WWW Document]. SoundCloud. URL https://checkout.soundcloud.com/pro?ref=t132 (accessed 6.4.21).

Stallman, R., 2002. *Free Software, Free Society: Selected Essays of Richard M. Stallman*. GNU Press, Boston, MA.

Statista, 2023a. Mobile Phone Subscriptions Worldwide 2022 [WWW Document]. Statista. URL https://www.statista.com/statistics/262950/global-mobile-subscriptions-since-1993/ (accessed 6.6.23).

Statista, 2023b. Global Smartphone Penetration 2016-2022 [WWW Document]. Statista. URL https://www.statista.com/statistics/203734/global-smartphone-penetration-per-capita-since-2005/ (accessed 6.6.23).

Statista, 2021a. Music streaming market share [WWW Document]. Statista. URL https://www.statista.com/statistics/653926/music-streaming-service-subscriber-share/ (accessed 4.28.21).

Statista, 2021b. U.S. Music Streaming Revenue 2020 [WWW Document]. URL https://www.statista.com/statistics/437717/music-streaming-revenue-usa/ (accessed 5.26.21).

Statista, 2021c. Global Recorded Music Market Worldwide by Label 2019 [WWW Document]. Statista. URL https://www.statista.com/statistics/947107/recorded-music-market-worldwide-label/ (accessed 6.4.21).

Stigler, G.J., 1961. The Economics of Information. *Journal of Political Economy* 69, 213–225.

Strähle, J., 2018. *Fashion & Music*. Springer, Singapore.

Strasser, R., 2010. *Music Business: The Key Concepts*. Routledge, London, New York.

Sugihartati, R., 2020. Youth Fans of Global Popular Culture: Between Prosumer and Free Digital Labourer. *Journal of Consumer Culture* 20, 305–323.

Tapscott, D., Williams, A.D., 2008. *Wikinomics: How Mass Collaboration Changes Everything*. Penguin, New York.

The Ivors Academy, 2020. 8 Out of 10 Music Creators Earn Less Than £200 a Year from Streaming [WWW Document]. The Ivors Academy. URL https://ivorsacademy.com/news/8-out-of-10-music-creators-earn-less-than-200-a-year-from-streaming-finds-survey-ahead-of-songwriters-and-artists-giving-evidence-to-a-select-committee-of-mps/ (accessed 4.15.21).

The Nielsen Company & Billboard's 2011 Music Industry Report [WWW Document], 2012. URL https://www.businesswire.com/news/home/20120105005547/en/The-Nielsen-Company-Billboard%E2%80%99s-2011-Music-Industry-Report (accessed 5.26.21).

Toffler, A., 2006. *Revolutionary Wealth*, 1st ed. Knopf, New York.

Tournès, L., 2012. *Du phonographe au MP3: une histoire de la musique enregistrée: XIXe-XXIe siècle*. Éditions Autrement, Paris.

Tschmuck, P., 2014. *Creativity and Innovation in the Music Industry*. Springer Berlin, Berlin.

Tuomola, A., 2004. Disintermediation and Reintermediation of the Sound Recording Value Chain: Two Case Studies. *Journal of Media Business Studies* 1, 27–46.

Ulloa, N., 2014a. Samsung Music Hub is Shutting Down in Almost Every Country... Digital Music News. URL https://www.digitalmusicnews.com/2014/05/23/musichub/ (accessed 6.5.21).

Ulloa, N., 2014b. T-Mobile Excludes Pandora, Spotify, iTunes Radio, and More from Monthly Data Limits... Digital Music News. URL https://www.digitalmusicnews.com/2014/06/19/streamingdata/ (accessed 6.5.21).

Universal McCann, 2007. Anytime Anyplace. Understanding the Connected Generation. Universal McCann, www.slideshare.net.

Van Den Oord A., Dieleman S., Schrauwen B., 27th Annual Conference on Neural Information Processing Systems, N. 2013, 2013. Deep Content-Based Music Recommendation. *Advances in Neural Information Processing Systems* 2643–2651.

Van Eijck, K., Majorana, M., 2013. Consumption Patterns, in: Towse, R., Handke, C. (Eds.), *Handbook on the Digital Creative Economy*. Edward Elgar Publishing, pp. 79–89.

van Wijk, J., 2002. Dealing with Piracy: Intellectual Asset Management in Music and Software. *European Management Journal* 20, 689–698.

Varian, H.R., 1999. *Markets for Information Goods*. Institute for Monetary and Economic Studies, Bank of Japan, Tokyo.

Vlachos, P., Vrechopoulos, A., Pateli, A., 2006. Drawing Emerging Business Models for the Mobile Music Industry. *Electronic Markets* 16, 154–168.

Waddell, R., 2007. Update: Madonna Confirms Deal with Live Nation [WWW Document]. Billboard. URL https://www.billboard.com/articles/news/1048045/update-madonna-confirms-deal-with-live-nation (accessed 5.18.21).

Waelbroeck, P., 2013. Digital Music, in: Towse, R., Handke, C. (Eds.), *Handbook on the Digital Creative Economy*. Edward Elgar, Cheltenham, Northhampton, pp. 389–398.

Waelbroeck, P., Peitz, M., 2004. The Effect of Internet Piracy on CD Sales: Cross-Section Evidence. *Review of Economic Research on Copyright Issues* 1, 71–79.

Waldfogel, J., 2012. Digital Piracy: Empirics, in: *The Oxford Handbook of the Digital Economy*. Oxford University Press, Oxford, pp. 1–12.

Wallis, R., 2001. Business as Usual or a Real Paradigm Shift in the Value Chain? The Example of the Music Industry's Response to E-commerce Technology and Ideology. Presented at the E-Work 2001 Conference, Venice, October.

Walzer, D.A., 2017. Independent Music Production: How Individuality, Technology and Creative Entrepreneurship Influence Contemporary Music Industry Practices. *Creative Industries Journal* 10, 21–39.

Wang, C.A., Zhang, X.M., 2009. Sampling of Information Goods. *Decision Support Systems* 48, 14–22.

Weijters, B., Goedertier, F., Verstreken, S., 2014. Online Music Consumption in Today's Technological Context: Putting the Influence of Ethics in Perspective. *Journal of Business Ethics* 124, 537–550.

Wikström, P., 2020. *The Music Industry: Music in the Cloud*. John Wiley & Sons, New York, NY.

Wikström, P., 2013. *The Music Industry: Music in the Cloud*. Polity, Cambridge, MA.

Wingfield, E.S.N., 2008. More Artists Steer Clear of iTunes. *Wall Street Journal*. URL https://www.wsj.com/articles/SB121987440206377643 (accessed 6.5.21).

WIPO, 1928. *Berne Convention for the Protection of Literary and Artistic Works*, WIPO.

Witt, S., 2016. *How Music Got Free*. Penguin, New York.

WolnaKultura, 2009. Problem DMCA czyli gdy wielkie korporacje tworzą prawo [WWW Document]. Wolna Kultura Wiki. URL http://wolnakultura.wikidot.com/problem-dmca-czyli-gdy-wielkie-korporacje-tworza-prawo (accessed 5.28.21).

Zentner, A., 2006. Measuring the Effect of File Sharing on Music Purchases. *The Journal of Law and Economics* 49, 63–90.

Ziemska, A., 2021. Opłata reprograficzna nie od smartfonów [WWW Document]. URL https://ksiegowosc.infor.pl/wiadomosci/5247915,Oplata-reprograficzna-nie-od-smartfonow.html (accessed 5.29.21).

4 In search of solutions

4.1 Copyright in the digital era

4.1.1 The role of copyright

The origins of copyright can be traced back to 1469 when the Republic of Venice granted publisher Johann von Speyer a privilege to publish works in exchange for introducing printing to the city. It was only 20 years later that the first protection for authors was granted. The *Statute of Anne*, also known as the *Act for the Encouragement of Learning, by Vesting the Copies of Printed Books in the Authors or Purchasers of such Copies, during the Times therein mentioned,* established by the British Parliament in 1709, was the first legal text referring to copyright. This document recognised authors' rights, marking a significant change as, previously in Great Britain, publishers held exclusive and perpetual rights to works. Although censorship was the primary concern, the economic aspect, specifically the ability to derive financial benefits from printing and selling works, was crucial (Benhamou and Farchy, 2014, p. 19).

The purpose of copyright was to strike a balance between the costs of restricting access to works and the benefits of incentivising further creation (Landes and Posner, 1989). In other words, it aimed to address market failure in the realm of cultural goods. This failure arises from the difficulties associated with protecting intellectual property rights and, consequently, financing creativity. Consumers who can freely access a work, especially if it is widely available or considered a public good, are reluctant to pay the author for it. On the other hand, authors who do not receive compensation lack sufficient incentive to create. Therefore, copyright was established to provide authors with protection and remuneration for the use of their works. These elements were intended to motivate continued creation (Demsetz, 1967, p. 356; Towse, 2001).

At the same time, copyright aimed to ensure broad access to cultural goods by incorporating temporal limitations on copyright monopolies. These limitations dictate that after a specified period, a work enters the public domain, allowing unrestricted use without the need for permission from creators or

DOI: 10.4324/9781003414605-5

rights holders and without the obligation to pay any fees. According to the provisions of the *Statute of Anne*, the protection granted to authors lasted for 14 years from the date of publication, with the possibility of a 14-year extension if the author was still alive. The 14-year term of protection also applied in the United States under the provisions of the country's first copyright legislation, the *Copyright Act* (US Copyright Office, 1790). Currently, in the European Union, copyright protection extends for 70 years after the author's death (EEC, 1993), while in the United States, the author's rights are protected for 70 years after their death or, in the case of corporate ownership, 95 years from publication or 120 years from creation, whichever period expires earlier (Hatch, 1998).

The possibility of particular use of works during the protection period was ensured by exceptions in copyright law. The first one is known as *fair use*. Benhamou and Farchy (2014, p. 36) list three objectives of its establishment. Firstly, in the physical world, controlling every use of a work was both unnecessary and impossible to maintain. This means that the losses caused by certain uses of works, such as playing music at private parties or making a few copies for friends, were too small and insignificant in terms of the overall revenues of the rights holders, so from an economic point of view, it was not worth taking action to collect fees. Moreover, controlling all such instances of use was impractical due to the high transaction costs. Secondly, the purpose of fair use was to provide the opportunity to use works in circumstances considered essential, such as by journalists or people with disabilities (fulfilling a special social interest). And thirdly, its existence aimed to serve the general public interest, specifically ensuring freedom of speech and access to works for educational or scientific purposes.

Another exception was the *first-sale doctrine*, also referred to *exhaution rule*, which meant that certain author rights were exhausted after the first sale of a product. This means that a purchaser of a compact disc (CD) with music has the right to resell it to another buyer without the permission of the rights holder and without the obligation to pay any additional remuneration. The legal basis for this rule in the European Union is Directive 2001/29/EC of the European Parliament and of the Council of 22 May 2001 on the harmonisation of certain aspects of copyright and related rights in the information society, which was further amended in 2019. In the United States, this is regulated by 17 U.S. Code §109 – Limitations on Exclusive Rights: Effect of Transfer of Particular Copy or Phonorecord.

Copyright law, in principle, assumes a balance between protecting the interests of the author or rights holder and the interests of society in terms of the right to access culture. As J. Stiglitz emphasises, intellectual property is not a natural right, it is a right created by people for the benefit of society (Latrive, 2007, p. 20). The interests of artists and creators should be protected not only because they are entitled to compensation for their work but also because artistic and cultural activities are a source of positive externalities and one of the pillars of sustainable development (Sabatini, 2019). However, in practice, corporations such as music publishing companies and record labels are the owners of the economic rights (the distinction between moral rights and economic rights is clearly marked in the case of *droit d'auteur*). Therefore, the law primarily protects the economic interests of these companies rather than the interests of creators (Latrive, 2007; Lessig, 2004a).

According to Lessig (2008), there are important flaws of copyright. He argues that copyright laws have become outdated and ineffective in the digital age, hindering rather than promoting creativity. The current copyright system serves as a means for corporations to safeguard their financial interests rather than fostering innovation and artistic expression.

4.1.2 *Balancing the interests of creators, rights holders, and consumers*

As long as music had a physical dimension, meaning it was tied to a carrier, the protection of intellectual property and transactions respecting it were in accordance with the applicable copyright law on the one hand, and market rules on the other. Rights management was relatively straightforward because all activities took place in the physical world. Collective management organisations collected appropriate fees from entities that used music in various ways, and then distributed the collected funds to rights owners. The sale of both music in the form of phonograms and the rights to use musical works, such as broadcasting and copying, were the basis for financing the activities of record companies and served as the primary incentive for innovation.

At that time, the fair use clause and the first sale doctrine provided consumers with a certain level of autonomy over their purchased music products, such as CDs and their accompanying content. The inseparable nature of the work and its physical carrier created the illusion that the buyer of a phonogram had the right to dispose of both its tangible and intangible parts. Due to the relatively time- and cost-consuming process of copying, as well as the lower quality of copies compared to the original, the act of dubbing CDs or cassettes occurred on a small scale and did not pose a threat to the well-being of record companies. This also held true for the resale of music products, which maintained a manageable level in terms of both magnitude and scope.

The dematerialisation of the carrier caused confusion among music enthusiasts regarding the concept of phonogram ownership. Only a few of them realised that a musical work is a separate entity, existing independently of the medium. This means that a consumer who purchases a tangible form of such a work, such as a compact disc, has the right to freely dispose of the carrier alone, while the content recorded on it is protected and subject to separate regulations. Research conducted in 2008 by the Recording Industry Association of Japan (RIAJ) revealed that as many as 80% of individuals using peer-to-peer (P2P) file-sharing systems were unaware that such actions were illegal (IFPI, 2008).

The Internet has transformed the scale of activities that were previously considered common social practices, such as sharing (Janowska, 2009). The online environment not only provided consumers with the technical capabilities to exchange music files at near-zero cost but also the ease of accessing and obtaining them for free created the illusion that such actions were morally acceptable. This perception stemmed from the unique characteristic of the internet as a free medium, providing access to costless resources. The inclination towards unrestricted use of resources published on the Internet, referred to by Lessig (2004a) as free culture, is a legacy of the Internet's early conditions, when it emerged. The development of the network was made possible by free communication protocols (TCP/IP) developed as part of a scientific project at Stanford University, operating outside the market system. Furthermore, the first programs enabling information exchange between computers, created in the late 1970s, functioned under public domain licences (not subject to copyright) (Castells, 2002).

As a result, the previous status quo, which represented a relative balance between protecting the interests of creators and music producers on the one hand and the public's right to access culture on the other, has been disrupted. The scales initially tipped in favour of consumers, granting them unrestricted access to an abundance of musical works. Additional factors, such as changes in consumer lifestyles and music consumption patterns, further reinforced this trend.

Record companies and affiliated music publishing firms, in order to maintain control over their works, took actions that ultimately limited consumers' rights. This was already discussed in Chapter 3 (in the context of music distribution), but it is worth revisiting two specific issues here: limitations on fair use and the first sale doctrine. Limitations on fair use were addressed through the implementation of digital rights management (DRM) measures in distribution systems. These measures allowed consumers to listen to files on specific devices or a limited number of times. However, these systems proved to be insufficiently effective and were eventually abandoned. As for the first sale doctrine, it sparked controversy concerning the resale of legally purchased digital works. Advocates for its abolishment argued that, firstly, digital works do not degrade with use, and secondly, the transaction costs associated with such resale, such as time and delivery expenses, are very low due to online sales. Consequently, there is no distinction between an original work purchased from a legal online service and a secondhand product, which led to the removal of entry barriers in sales to end users and the emergence of unfair competition. The streaming model partially addressed this issue, as the resale of music in digital file form is no longer a common practice.

In the search for solutions, the proposed alternative to stricter copyright law, sanctions, and technical protections was the liberalisation of copyright law, which was expected to bring numerous benefits to entities operating in the music industry. The idea was to embrace the concept of free economy (Baumann, 2013), where recorded music would be offered to ordinary users free of charge, while record companies would operate based on various business models that allow them to generate revenue from sources other than phonogram sales. Such a future for music was predicted by Attali (2015) as well as Leonhard and Kusek (2005). Given the declining value of recorded music and the development of new music distribution models like streaming, which do not provide satisfactory income for creators, this solution could seem attractive to both creators and consumers.

An extreme and completely utopian approach is the proposal to abandon copyright protection. Barrow (1996) refers to copyright as a relic of the pre-digital era. Meanwhile, Kinsella (2008), an American lawyer and theorist of libertarianism, believes that the existence of intellectual property rights is not necessary to encourage the production of creative works and innovation. He even argues that in the digital world, music is no longer a scarce good, and as long as goods are in abundance (free goods), there can be no conflict over them. Fogel (2006) also argues that copyright law does not actually protect creators because they are not the primary owners of their works. It mainly protects major record labels and the enormous profits they derive from the rights acquired from creators. An example is the 1997 Sonny Bono Copyright Term Extension Act (Hatch, 1998), also known as The Mickey Mouse Protection Act, enacted in the United States under the influence of lobbying by The Walt Disney Company to extend the protection of the character Mickey Mouse. The author suggests that music should be made available without charges, and as a result,

> we would see a return to an older and richer cosmology of creativity, one in which copying and borrowing openly from others' works is simply a normal part of the creative process, a way of acknowledging one's sources and of improving on what has come before. And the old canard that artists need copyright to earn a living would be revealed as the pretense it has always been.
>
> (Fogel, 2006)

Defenders of copyright, when presenting arguments for its preservation, often invoke the *natural right* of the creator to protect the fruits of their labour, placing it among fundamental human rights. However, Latrive (2007, p. 29) reminds us that the consumer's right to access and share creative works is equally natural. He cites the stance of I. Le Chapelier, an 18th-century French lawyer and politician who participated in the creation of the legal system in France, including droit d'auteur – copyright, from which its continental concept derives. Le Chapelier recognised that one cannot draw analogies between intellectual property and physical property, as he believed that they are two different forms of ownership. According to him, when an author publishes their work, they thereby hand it over to the audience, which – if the work is good – engages with it, reads it, listens to it, learns from it, repeats it, and makes it their own. The published work thus becomes public property.

In this case, the work belongs to both the author and the audience. It is in this approach that perfect balance manifests (Latrive, 2007, p. 30), where both sides of the market exchange system have their respective rights guaranteed: the author – the right to protect their property, and the audience – the right to access and share it. It should been noted that excessive restrictions in copyright law that overly protect author's rights can impede innovation and hinder the flow of ideas. Additionally, it may result in market monopolies. Conversely, if there are no intellectual property (IP) protections in place and everyone freely uses others' ideas, it can lead to a dilution of the benefits derived from investments and creative endeavours. Striking a balance between protecting rights and fostering innovation is crucial to avoid both stifling creativity and undervaluing intellectual property (Thetsidaeng, 2019).

4.1.3 *Creative Commons as the 'third way?'*

Lessig (2004a, b), an American constitutional lawyer, attempted to create a unique compromise, a kind of *third way* (Krzysztofek, 2006, p. 7), between the liberalisation of copyright law and its intense tightening. He emphasises the role of creators in his proposal, stating that they should have the right to their own creations and the ability to control them when they do not wish to relinquish control to traditional intermediaries. His concept, which complements the existing copyright law, is commonly known as Creative Commons (CC) and has a universal character.

For Lessig, the most important resources of today's society are symbols and creativity, as well as specific commons – the cultural common goods. They are threatened by what he terms *enclosure*, understood here as the increasing enclosure and restrictive application of intellectual property law. In an era of free and global information flow, it is increasingly difficult to enforce this law, giving rights holders a false sense of certainty that further restrictions and legal sanctions are the best solution. However, formal legal conditions, instead of stimulating creativity, increasingly hinder it and constitute one of the barriers to participating in online cultural sphere (Wilson, 2006).

In his book *Free Culture,* Lessig (2004a) presented the history of barriers in sharing culture and building new works based on the accomplishments of previous creators. That is why he developed the concept of CC licences, in which the traditional phrase *all rights reserved* was replaced with *some rights reserved*. The intention was to protect creators and their works while maintaining incentives for innovation, creativity, and inventiveness. According to Lessig (2004b), *remixing culture* can simultaneously serve as a means of learning and creation.

CC licences expand the application of traditional copyright law and work in favour of real creators, rather than corporations. It is up to the author to decide who can use their creations and in what way. This would allow new creators, just as it was practiced in the past, to draw from the achievements of previous generations without needing to seek permission or pay exorbitant sums to producers and publishers. Lessig, while criticising current trends in intellectual property law, also promotes the protection of creativity, freedom of expression and cultural autonomy. In doing so, he also works for the benefit of consumers, who, according to CC, have greater freedom to use the works they acquire.

There are six CC licences ("About CC Licenses," n.d.), each with different conditions under which the work protected by that licence is made available. Each licence includes a condition regarding attribution (referring to the author's moral rights) and additional terms. Additionally, there is the CC Public Domain licence, indicating the absence of copyright restrictions on the marked work (Figure 4.1).

These licences have been widely used by creators who share their works online, particularly those who do not have contracts with major corporations. Google and YouTube offer the possibility to search for works on the web based on the licence under which they are released. There is also a dedicated CC search engine for finding images and graphics – https://search.creativecommons.org, including those in the Europeana resources. Independent music distribution platforms such as Magnatune and Jamendo also offer music marked with CC licences. The founder of the latter, S. Zimmer, highlights that Jamendo wants to show that there are many talented artists who know how to take advantage of the opportunities offered by the Internet and can embrace innovative monetisation models. Their fans should be rewarded, not punished (Maj, 2009) for using free music.

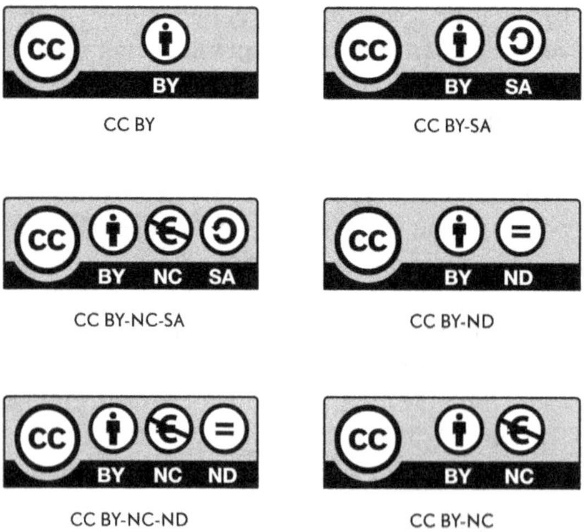

Figure 4.1 The six variations of the CC licences.

Source: Büsges and Designbüro (2014), https://commons.wikimedia.org/wiki/File:Open_Content_A_Practical_Guide_to_Using_Creative_Commons_Licences_web-29.png.

Some creators were initially concerned about sharing music online in this manner, fearing a loss of control. However, Lessig (2004a) argued that if traditional intellectual property laws cannot effectively protect creative works that are widely disseminated through digital technologies, then it might be worth considering abandoning their application. Instead of fighting against fans, artists should allow them to freely listen to and download recordings, thereby encouraging a deeper appreciation of their work. Such an approach could lead to a more supportive audience and enable artists to generate greater income from artistic activities in other areas such as concerts, merchandising, or music publishing.

Wikström (2020, p. 164) characterises CC licences as a utopian solution, acknowledging that they don't completely resolve the challenges of unauthorised copying and distribution of works online. However, CC licences can still be viewed as a significant recognition on the part of creators towards consumers. These licences serve an important informational function by providing clarity on the permissions granted for using works, which is particularly valuable for amateur creators involved in user-generated content (UGC) activities, including remixing or incorporating elements of others' works into their own.

One of the key advantages of CC licences is the reduction in transaction costs associated with seeking information about licensing rights. By clearly indicating the permissions and restrictions attached to a work, CC licences simplify the process of understanding how a work can be used. This accessibility lowers barriers for creators and encourages greater collaboration and creativity. It also empowers individuals to reuse and build upon existing works, fostering innovation and the creation of new artistic expressions.

Moreover, the use of CC licences can contribute to a more efficient and cost-effective approach to reusing works. The ability to easily identify the permissions granted by a CC licence streamlines the process of obtaining necessary permissions, saving time and resources. This facilitates the development of derivative works, encourages cultural exchange, and promotes a more open and participatory creative environment.

Looking ahead, CC licensing solutions have the potential to synergise with emerging technologies such as blockchain. Smart contracts, built on blockchain networks, could provide a secure and automated framework for managing intellectual property rights (Finck and Moscon, 2019). By leveraging CC licences as the foundation for these smart contracts, creators and users could benefit from transparent and efficient management of intellectual property in the digital realm. This could further enhance the accessibility, traceability, and enforceability of licensing agreements, ensuring that creators are appropriately recognised and rewarded for their work while enabling wider access and collaboration.

However, despite the widespread adoption of CC licences by creators, the issue of value capture within the production chain and the resulting challenges faced by artists in today's music market remain unresolved. However, it is important to recognise that this situation is not solely attributable to the actions of consumers who, taking advantage of the digital world's phenomenon of market failure, behave as free-riders by consuming cultural goods without adequately compensating the artists. The underlying factors lie in the evolving power dynamics of the recording industry.

Firstly, traditional recording companies continue to maintain a dominant position, exerting significant control over the distribution and promotion of music. Their established structures and practices still prioritise profit maximisation, leading to a concentration of power and limited opportunities for artists to fair compensation for their work. This concentration of power within a few major players has hindered the equitable sharing of value along the music value chain.

Secondly, the rise of new entities, particularly global music distribution platforms, has further shaped the industry landscape. Leveraging technological innovations, these platforms have revolutionised music consumption by offering consumers access to vast catalogues of music at low subscription fees or even for free, as well as relatively low information searching costs. Their ability to deliver immense value to consumers, such as unlimited music streaming and personalised recommendations, has established them as key players in the music ecosystem. However, this has also given them considerable bargaining power and the ability to dictate terms to other industry stakeholders, including artists. As intermediaries, these platforms have the potential to control the visibility and reach of artists' work, often determining the financial returns they receive.

While the use of CC licences represents a step towards greater openness and flexibility in sharing creative works, it alone cannot address the complex issues of value distribution and artist compensation. Therefore other cultural policy tools at both national and supranational levels started to be developed in the hope that they would solve the problem of fair remuneration for creators and broad access to cultural goods.

4.2 Other cultural policy solutions

4.2.1 Private copying levy

The private copying levy, also known as the blank media tax, which is fiscal cultural policy instrument (Throsby, 2010), is a specific fee imposed on importers or manufacturers of devices used for copying and of blank media. This category includes smartphones, computers, tablets, photocopiers, as well as CDs, hard drives, USB drives, and memory cards. The primary rationale for introducing this type of levy was the need to compensate creators and rights owners for the losses resulting from the fact that the mentioned devices and media were often used for making private copies of works, which in different legal systems is referred to as an exception or a limitation to the exclusive right of authors, permitted use, limitation to economic rights, restriction to copyright, fair use, fair dealing, act which does not constitute an infringement to copyright, or act not controlled by copyright (CISAC et al., 2020).

The private copying levy was first introduced in Germany in 1965 (Nikoltchev, 2011) as a response to the emergence of copying devices on the market, such as blank audio cassettes, VHS tapes, and later blank CDs and DVDs, which allowed for copying music and films for personal use. With the development of the Internet, including mobile internet, and devices for listening to music, such as digital music players, laptops, and smartphones, such copying has taken on a significantly larger scale than before. This required a revision of the approach to the private copying levy, particularly regarding the list of devices and media that the levy should cover.

The European Commission had intended to harmonise the provisions regarding this levy in the 1990s, but no action was taken at that time (Boyer, 2017). Some regulations were introduced by Directive 2001/29/EC of the European Parliament and of the Council of 22 May 2001 on the harmonisation of certain aspects of copyright and related rights in the information society, known as the InfoSoc Directive (Nikoltchev, 2011). Regulations at the national level were implemented in 22 out of 27 EU member states, excluding the UK, Ireland, Malta, Cyprus, and Luxembourg, although the adopted solutions varied in different systems. The private copying levy is collected from manufacturers, importers, or distributors, and the lists of devices and media it applies to, as well as the calculation methods, recipient groups, and the structure regulating the management of these levies, are different in respective countries (Marinescu, 2018).

Increased complexity of intra-EU trade was one of the main consequences of introducing this regulation. Moreover, the acceptance of the levy itself remains highly controversial. On 27 February 2014, the European Parliament adopted a resolution on the private copying levy, suggesting the need for a revision of Directive 2001/29/EC. The aim of these changes was to enable European citizens to create private copies of legally acquired content while compensating authors and rights owners for the losses incurred by such copying (Pereira, 2017). Article 60 of Directive (EU) 2019/790 of the European Parliament and of the Council of 17 April 2019 on copyright and related rights in the Digital Single Market and amending Directives 96/9/EC and 2001/29/EC addresses the issue of the private copying levy, but the regulations are rather suggestive, leaving member states with significant discretion in this regard.

In 2020, three organisations – the International Confederation of Societies of Authors and Composers (CISAC), the Bureau International de l'Edition Méchanique (BIEM), and Thuiskopie (a collecting society in the Netherlands) published a joint report summarising how the issue of private copying levies is regulated in different countries around the world. The report contains data for 2018 from national collective management organisations. It turns out that many countries do not have systems for compensating for private copying or collecting levies. Details are presented in Table 4.1.

Table 4.1 Number of countries with different private copying remuneration systems – breakdown by continents (2020)

Continent	*Countries with no private copying exception*	*Countries with private copying exception but no remuneration system*	*Countries with private copying exception but no collection and distribution system*	*Countries with both private copying remuneration and distribution system*
Africa	6	22	17	9
North and South America	12	18	1	4
Asia	14	24	6	2
Europe	2	3	11	29
Oceania	6	8	0	0

Own compilation based on CISAC et al. (2020).

According to the report, solutions regarding the regulation of copying works for private purposes and remuneration for creators and rights holders are primarily found in developed capitalist economies. These include European countries, the United States, Canada, Japan, and Israel. Interestingly, the exception for private copying does not exist in the UK, while Australia and New Zealand have such exceptions in their legal systems, but they have not implemented a remuneration system for creators and rights holders. A similar situation can be observed in South Korea, which is one of the leading markets for digital music sales (CISAC et al., 2020). This proves that the private copying levy is not widely regarded as a suitable solution that could help adequately compensate artists.

In literature, several contentious issues related to the private copying levy are emphasised (Poort, 2013). One of these issues is the difficulty in accurately estimating the actual harm suffered by creators and rights holders due to the application of copyright exceptions and unauthorised copying. Another concern is that individuals who do not engage extensively in copying activities end up financially supporting heavy users, as the levy paid by importers and distributors is incorporated into the prices of devices and media. Additionally, the system of redistributing collected fees to creators and rights holders relies on rough calculations, meaning that compensation remains disconnected from the actual use of works and provides a misleading market signal regarding their market value (Towse, 2008).

Furthermore, as emphasised by Lessig, we are currently experiencing a remix culture (Lessig, 2008), where UGC is being commonly produced. This means that cultural consumers are simultaneously becoming creators of new content by borrowing fragments from existing works, combining them, changing them, and providing them with a new artistic expression. However, such activities are often considered unauthorised usage, also referred to as piracy by rights holders, particularly by companies producing cultural content. Therefore, the private copying levy, in its current form, cannot apply to this type of activity, as it focuses on private copying complying with current legislation.

Moreover, private copying has become less common in the era of rapid development of streaming platforms, which provide consumers with access to unlimited resources of cultural works. It is true that streaming technology requires storing a copy of the work in the device's cache, but it is merely a technical copy and has nothing to do with private copying.

Lessig highlights the need for reform, advocating for a more balanced approach that empowers individual creators and encourages the sharing and remixing of creative works. He suggests that the focus should shift from strict control and restrictions to a system that embraces the potential of digital technologies and allows for greater collaboration and cultural exchange. The private copying levy could fill the gap in the proposed system and serve as actual compensation for creators for the use of their original works. However, a mandatory condition would be the recognition of UGC/remix as a legal activity.

The Polish case

In Poland, the private copying levy has been in place for over 20 years and is regulated in Article 20 of the Copyright Act ("Opłata reprograficzna – fakty i mity," 2021; Journal of Laws 1994 No. 24 item 83, 1994), although the list of devices and media was established only in 2003 (Ciechoński, 2021). In 2020 and 2021, this levy, particularly the list of devices and blank media to be included in the levy, became a subject of heated discussions (Orlikowski, 2021; Ziemska, 2021). The reason behind this was a draft act on the rights of a professional artist, in which the revenue from the private copying levy was intended to serve as the basis for creating a financial support system for professional artists. The draft was prepared with the involvement of artists and submitted for public consultations. Over a hundred organisations representing both cultural and creative sectors, consumer associations, IT-related organisations, as well as individuals, submitted numerous comments on this draft. The majority of these comments, mainly by organisations outside the artists' community were negative, criticising the private copying levy. On the Ministry of Culture and National Heritage's website, this levy was referred to as *compensation for fair culture* (MKiDN, n.d.). Opponents of the levy pointed out that currently, private copying occurs to a very limited extent due to changes in the way culture is consumed. Consumers now primarily rely on streaming platforms, where content is technically copied automatically in the memory of devices (such as computers or smartphones). Streaming services already charge fees, so there is no copying within the scope of permitted use. According to the draft act on the rights of a professional artist, which was revised following public consultations, the private copying levy will cover, among others, laptops, computers, tablets, and televisions but will not include smartphones. This decision highlights that the private copying levy is a political construct, a solution adopted because there are no alternative ideas concerning private copying and, importantly, which is not addressed in proposed legal changes, the utilisation of works within the so-called UGC.

4.2.2 Culture flat-rate: A flat fee for access to culture

At the turn of the 20th and 21st centuries, before the emergence of new content delivery platforms (particularly for music) that comply with existing copyright laws, there were discussions about the legalisation of peer-to-peer (P2P) services, where internet users shared content. The idea of introducing a system to compensate creators for lost revenues from informal circulation of culture began to surface (Fisher, 2007; Ku, 2002; Lunney Jr, 2001; Netanel, 2003). This system was called *culture flat-rate*, *global license*, *blanket licensing*, *creative contribution* (Aigrain and Aigrain, 2012), or *alternative compensation scheme* (Poort, 2013, p. 244). Advocates of this concept argued that a significant portion of the value in the cultural and creative industries' value chain was being captured by IT companies. It is through cultural and creative content, such as music, films, and video games, including those shared in unauthorised way by internet users, that increasingly advanced devices for consuming such content are being developed. Internet service providers, both fixed and mobile, as well as new online intermediaries distributing the mentioned content, also capture a substantial portion of the value.

In France, in 2001, two organisations representing musicians and managing neighbouring rights, ADAMI (Administration des Droits des Artistes et Musiciens Interprètes; Collective Management Organisation for the Rights of Performers) and SPEDIDAM (Société de Perception et de Distribution des Droits des Artistes-Interprètes; Society for the Collection and Distribution of Performers' Rights), proposed the concept of a global licence, which would allow internet users to freely exchange cultural goods online. In return, they would optionally pay an additional fee to internet service providers, which would later be distributed to creators and rights owners through collective management organisations. However, this solution was not implemented in France (Nikoltchev, 2011, p. 17).

In 2009, the Green Party proposed a similar system in Germany (Aigrain and Aigrain, 2012, p. 173) called *Kulturflatrate* (flat-rate for access to culture). Similar proposals were also considered in other European countries, such as the Netherlands, Belgium, Italy (Nikoltchev, 2011), and the United States. Non-governmental organisations representing artists and advocating for free culture were involved in lobbying for the adoption of such solutions and worked on proposing appropriate measures, including within the framework of Foro Internacional para la Cultura Libre (the International Forum for Free Culture [FCForum], 2015). This solution faced widespread criticism not only from internet service providers but also from governments (Aigrain and Aigrain, 2012, p. 138).

Nevertheless, new ideas continue to emerge regarding the issue of proper compensation for creators of content as well as performers. In the United States, discussions about implementing *blanket licensing* for small organisations involved in online music distribution were initiated by C. Doctorow, a prominent activist for internet freedom. He presented his proposal in an article (Doctorow, 2020) published on the website of an American non-profit organisation: Electronic Frontier Foundation. In the article, he argued that this solution could compete with the existing oligopsony in the music industry and would improve the situation for artists who are currently the most disadvantaged when it comes to revenue from the use of their music.

The concept of a culture flat-rate is based on similar assumptions to those behind the private copying levy. In exchange for an additional fee of 2%–5% for internet access paid by private users to internet service providers, the unauthorised use of cultural content, including music, would be legal. It would also allow for the reuse of disseminated content. Individual users would be able to exchange music in accordance with the common pre-digital practice of sharing cultural goods. They would also have the freedom to act as creators-participants in remix culture. Internet service providers would transfer the collected fees, for example, to collective rights management organisations, which would later redistribute the funds to creators and rights holders. This would provide them with compensation for potential damages resulting from the informal circulation of culture.

However, this seemingly logical solution has sparked many controversies similar to those that arose in relation to the private copying levy. Firstly, they revolve around how to determine the amount of such a fee in order for the sums transferred to creators and rights holders to adequately compensate them for potential harm. The challenge lies in finding a balance that reflects the value of the shared cultural content without burdening users excessively.

Secondly, if the fee were made mandatory, users who do not actively participate in free culture or engage in sharing may feel unjustly burdened by financing those who frequently access and share cultural works. This raises concerns about fairness and the potential for inequitable distribution of financial contributions. On the other hand, if payment were dependent on the user's decision, there could be a free-rider effect, where individuals choose not to pay but still benefit from the shared cultural content. This could undermine the sustainability of the system and create challenges in ensuring adequate compensation for creators and rights holders.

Thirdly, the global nature of the Internet poses challenges in terms of using and enforcing such a fee system. Content made available in countries where the flat-rate fee is not collected could create inconsistencies and difficulties in managing the cross-border flow of cultural works.

Fourthly, defining what constitutes non-commercial sharing, which would be permitted under such a system, presents a significant challenge. Drawing the line between personal use and commercial exploitation of shared content can be subjective and open to interpretation, making it difficult to enforce and ensure compliance with the intended regulations.

Lastly, the method of redistributing funds to creators and rights holders raises practical and logistical challenges. Determining fair and transparent distribution mechanisms that accurately reflect the contribution and value of each work in the shared cultural ecosystem is complex. Researchers in this field have put forward various proposals to address the issue of appropriate compensation for creators, but none of them offer a comprehensive solution. One proposed approach involved sampling user consumption of content (Fisher, 2007) or calculating the number of users sharing online content (Gratz, 2004). These methods aimed to gather data on user behaviour and engagement with cultural works to inform compensation schemes. However, these approaches may face challenges in accurately capturing the full spectrum of user activities and may not provide a precise measure of the value derived from individual works.

Fisher (2007, p. 3) also proposed using technology to track files on the network. In this approach, creators and rights holders who wish to receive compensation from informal circulation of cultural goods would need to register with a dedicated copyright office. Upon registration, each file would be assigned a digital identifier for tracking its transmission and utilisation across the network. Collecting societies would collect fees to remunerate creators and rights holders, and the redistribution would occur proportionally based on the popularity of works, similar to the payment system used by radio and television broadcasters. However, it is worth noting that this type of fund redistribution is currently employed by streaming services and has also faced criticism.

Alternatively, involving consumers in the decision-making process by allowing them to vote on which content should be remunerated has been suggested (Oksanen and Valimaki, 2005). This participatory approach seeks to incorporate user preferences and opinions in determining the distribution of funds. However, implementing such a system would require extensive infrastructure and mechanisms to ensure transparency, fairness, and broad participation.

Another proposal suggested monitoring peer-to-peer networks to control the specific content being downloaded (Netanel, 2003). However, this raised concerns about privacy infringement, as network monitoring could potentially encompass a wide range of content beyond copyrighted works. As a consequence, the law transforms copyright into a censorship (Senftleben, 2020). Additionally, focusing solely on content downloading fails to capture the actual utilisation or consumption of shared cultural works, e.g., the UGC.

The above idea, namely the obligation to verify content shared by users online, was imposed on internet service providers in accordance with Article 17 of the EU Directive 2019/790 dated 17 April 2019. The foundation of this solution lies in the argument named the *value gap*. It raises concerns about the excessive revenues earned by platforms that base their business models on UGC (such as YouTube or Instagram) and that are not obliged to provide appropriate compensation to the creators of the original content used in UGC (Senftleben, 2020). Article 17 has sparked numerous controversies, and Poland even filed a complaint against it with the Court of Justice of the European Union (MKiDN, 2022). The court dismissed the complaint, stating that in recent years, the online content market has become more complex, and therefore, it is necessary to provide greater protection to entities entitled to copyright protection, even if it may affect freedom of expression (DigWatch, 2021). However, although the provisions of the directive are controversial, they can be seen as an attempt to restore a certain kind of balance, in this case, between the creators of value, i.e., artists, and the entities, i.e., platforms, that capture a significant portion of that value.

While the proposals presented above offer potential avenues for exploring appropriate compensation models, they each come with their own limitations and complexities. Quoting Lessig: "legal culture, and hence, political culture, suffers a failure of imagination" (Lessig, 2004b). The challenge lies in finding a solution that strikes a balance between providing fair remuneration for creators and accommodating the diverse nature of cultural consumption in the digital age. Moreover, one significant obstacle to implementing the above solutions to access culture online is the legal status of file-sharing systems used by internet users for music sharing (peer-to-peer networks) as well as that of the UGC. In many countries' legal systems, including the EU (Nikoltchev, 2011), these systems are considered illegal. Therefore, before introducing any compensation system for creators and rights holders through user-led activities, it would be necessary to establish that file-sharing among users of copyrighted works as well as UGC are legally permissible and fall within the scope of fair use. Such a decision would be revolutionary in the history of copyright law and would require not only legal system restructuring but also a rethinking of business models in the cultural and creative sectors, including the music industry.

4.3 Utilising blockchain in the music industry

In 2015, the World Economic Forum recognised blockchain as one of the most promising and groundbreaking technologies ever invented by mankind.

According to forecasts, by 2027, as much as 10% of the global GDP could be stored in this system (WEF, 2015). M. Cuban, an American billionaire, refers to blockchain as the new Internet (101Blockchains, 2021), while O'Dair (2018, p. 17) calls it the Internet of value. Although it is commonly associated with cryptocurrencies, specifically Bitcoin, its applications extend far beyond the realm of finance. Advocates of this technology go as far as stating that it could serve as a solution for the administration of intellectual property rights, potentially displacing existing paradigms (Finck and Moscon, 2019).

4.3.1 Blockchain – a brief overview of the technology

Blockchain technology, specifically Blockchain 1.0, was initially widely applied in the financial sector when Nakamoto (2008) created Bitcoin – the first cryptocurrency based on this technology. Bitcoin served as a prime example of disintermediation, as it eliminated intermediaries from financial transactions. In the traditional system, banks acted as intermediaries, and transactions were conducted using currencies issued and controlled by governments. In the Bitcoin system, the credibility of transactions is not based on trust in intermediary institutions but is confirmed by a peer-to-peer network of distributed users known as *miners*. Additionally, transactions are secured through cryptography using public and private keys (Casey and Vigna, 2019, pp. 64–65).

In the extensive literature on blockchain (Gorkhali et al., 2020), it is commonly defined as a decentralised, distributed ledger of data grouped into interconnected blocks, with transactions being simultaneously transmitted to all participants in the system (Ciupa, 2019). According to Nakamoto's (2008) vision, the entire system is built upon three pillars: (1) a decentralised infrastructure necessary for circulation, issuance, and reporting of the so-called (2) representative of value and (3) a centralised set of rules that determine the process flow within the system (Ciupa, 2019). In other words, this technology lacks a central entity responsible for recording, supervising, and confirming transactions (Tasca et al., 2017). Everything occurs within a distributed network that stores identical versions of a database containing the complete history of all transactions conducted within that network (Arcos, 2018). The representative of value is the digital counterpart of a certain (physical) external object involved in a transaction. The representative of value is also referred to as a token or crypto asset (Böhme et al., 2015). Thanks to the centralised set of rules, there is no need to rely on a single entity to confirm transactions. Trust is instead based on the transparency of all activities, the immutability of records, the inability to make changes, the built-in consensus mechanism for determining correctness and continuity of records, and the built-in system for verifying actions (Chalmers et al., 2021). The technology itself is based on open-source principles, making its structure transparent, and due to its design and governing rules, there is no central failure point (O'Dair et al., 2016), which makes the entire system secure and resistant to hacking attacks (Schwab, 2016).

There is another important characteristic of blockchain, namely the classification of networks based on access rights to the database and the ability to create records. In practice, there are commonly public and permissionless networks, which are accessible to everyone, as well as private and permissioned networks, where selected entities can make changes (Mulligan et al., 2018). For example, the Bitcoin network is public and permissionless, meaning that any internet user equipped with appropriate computer hardware and software can become an active participant in the network, known as a node.

In 2013, a new concept emerged – Blockchain 2.0, known as Ethereum. It enables the application of this technology in non-financial areas (Beck, 2018), such as registering transactions using tokens, e.g., domain names, personal data records, property deeds, social welfare payments, bank account registrations, or transactions conducted using traditional currencies (Tapscott and Tapscott, 2018). What is innovative compared to first-generation blockchain is the ability to create smart contracts, which are sets of rules encoded as code or algorithms that self-execute under programmed circumstances and take actions according to those rules (Ciupa, 2019). These rules are directly attached to the blockchain, although, as pointed out by O'Dair (2018, p. 20), they are only as intelligent as the program they contain allows them to be, and they do not properly qualify as contracts in the legal sense of the word.

4.3.2 Can blockchain save the recording industry?

The launch of music platforms, especially streaming technology, has led to a significant number of consumers heavily relying on them, which resulted in increased revenues for the digital music sector. However, this system also has its drawbacks. Firstly, streaming platforms, such as the market-leading Spotify, are not profitable ventures. Secondly, the fees paid to rights owners remain at a very low level, significantly lower than in the pioneering pay-per-download model. This means that for individual creators, especially niche or less popular ones, the profit from digital recordings is small or nonexistent. Moreover, in the contracts of some artists, there is a lack of provisions regarding compensation from online sources, mainly streaming (Cooke, 2015). Thirdly, streaming platforms redistribute fees from consumers and advertising revenue proportionally based on the total number of plays for specific tracks on the platform. Consequently, the consumer does not directly pay the artist whose music they listen to but indirectly funds other artists. This kind of redistribution, instead of promoting musical diversity and the development of the long tail of consumption, favours hits and stars. This brings us back to the pre-digital model and the gatekeeping system employed by record labels. In the case of streaming services, the gatekeeper is the system itself. Additionally, the music content that users share on the internet or reuse it as UGC is not a source of income for rights owners, creating a *value gap* in the system (IFPI, 2018).

Blockchain, recognised as the most significant foundational technology since the Internet, generate high expectations for its applications across various industries. Artists, including musicians, have also seen it as a beacon of hope in addressing two key issues. Firstly, blockchain could provide them with access to both information about how their music is actually being utilised and reused in the online world, such as in UGC, as well as information about transactions involving their works. Secondly, blockchain technology could ensure that they are properly rewarded for their efforts and creative contributions (Verma, 2022). An additional expectation is that music artists releasing their songs directly on blockchain networks would eliminate the need for middlemen. Platforms operated by these networks would directly engage with consumers, thereby diminishing transactional expenses. Meanwhile, recording companies would primarily assume the responsibility of offering technical, production, and promotional support based on the specific terms of each agreement. In this way, this technology could empower musicians and increase the value captured by artists (Sitonio and Nucciarelli, 2018).

Blockchain technology is characterised by three features that facilitate its application in the context of music circulation in the digital environment. The first feature is decentralisation and dispersion, which means there is no central database that could be a weak point in the entire structure. The second feature is synchronisation, whereby identical copies of specific information are synchronised in different locations across the network, following the same rules. The third feature is transparency, particularly evident in public and permissionless networks, where all actions are visible to all users and can be monitored by them. By employing blockchain, any digital object with a defined value, including recorded music, can be created, registered, and exchanged in transactions that are decentralised, distributed, and transparent. Moreover, such exchanges are cost-effective and fast, which contributes to better music management, especially in terms of usage fees (Xu et al., 2019). Furthermore, it appears that the characteristics of this technology, such as creating scarcity and trust, along with the aforementioned features, align with the fundamentals of copyright law (Bodó et al., 2018). Generally speaking, blockchains and blockchain-based smart contracts are often depicted as the saviours that can utilise technology to enforce copyright law in a more effective and equitable way.

In recent years, several initiatives related to the utilisation of blockchain technology in the recording industry have emerged (Chalmers et al., 2021). Their objectives usually involve gathering data and metadata about music to create payment models for its usage in various exploitation fields. Initiatives aimed at funding music creation are also evolving. Analysis of such activities has already found its place in the literature, pointing to several areas where blockchain could positively impact the functioning of the recording industry. These areas include: (1) networked databases with information on copyright and related rights; (2) direct and simplified royalty payments;

(3) transparency in the value chain; and (4) access to alternative sources of funding (O'Dair et al., 2016).

4.3.2.1 Networked database on copyright and related rights

Every musical work, as mentioned in Chapter 1, is subject to both copyright (protecting the creator of the work, such as the composer and lyricist) and related rights (referring to performers' rights, as well as producers' and broadcasters' rights). The use of existing music such as placing it on streaming platforms, using it in advertising or video games, requires permission of the rights holder and often involves payment. Due to the abundance of available resources and the lack of territorial barriers to the circulation of digital music products, effective rights management is currently a significant challenge. There is a lack of a global database that would contain comprehensive information about all existing music (Torbensen and Ciriello, 2019). In 2003, the Recording Industry Association of America (RIAA) and the International Federation of the Phonographic Industry (IFPI) initiated the GRid project, which aimed to create a digital identifier for recognising digital music products in the network, such as individual tracks, albums, or bundles of tracks (IFPI, 2007). It is supposed to facilitate the remuneration of artists for the use of their works, but its use is not mandatory. As a result, many works exist on the network without such identification.

In 2008, an attempt to create the Global Repertoire Database, a unified, extensive, and authoritative repository that encompasses the worldwide ownership and management of musical works was made at the request of the European Commission (Isherwood, 2011). Unfortunately, due to the withdrawal of cooperation from collecting societies, the project failed in 2014. Since then, several similar initiatives have emerged, such as the Music Joint Venture and the International Music Registry (MusicAlly, 2016), as well as ICE, MusicBrainz, Gracenote or Discogs (Torbensen and Ciriello, 2019). Some of them have failed, and those that have survived have a siloed nature. None of them cover the global repertoire, and they sometimes provide contradictory information. Moreover, maintaining them in various separate, centralised archives makes them vulnerable to hacking. As a result, transaction costs have increased, transparency has decreased, and the time taken to complete a transaction, including payment for the use of a work, has prolonged.

Advocates of blockchain solutions have recognised that it could potentially resolve the issue of maintaining databases with music-related information, as well as ensuring the updating and reliability of such information, thereby facilitating the management of rights to works and eliminating unnecessary intermediaries (Tapscott and Tapscott, 2018). Each work uploaded to the network by its creator or other rights holders could include a hash, which is a unique fingerprint of copyrighted material, containing information about the rights along with a licence for its use, as well as contact details of the rights owner for permission and fee arrangements (metadata). The information stored in a distributed manner on the blockchain network would be timestamped and recorded for every change, with the identical copies ensuring its credibility. This would enable precise tracking of files that could serve as evidence of authorship and provenance. However, the prerequisite for this would be the establishment of a global registry enabling the transformation of potential benefits of blockchain and smart contracts into tangible advantages (Finck and Moscon, 2019).

Platforms distributing UGC would also benefit from this type of solution. According to the Directive (EU) 2019/790, these platforms are obliged to monitor the content shared by users, and with the use of smart contracts containing licensing information, the implementation of such control could be more efficient and cost-effective.

An attempt to create a blockchain-based initiative for musicians, Dot Blockchain Music (n.d.), was made by B. Rogers, a British musician and entrepreneur. However, the project's website hasn't been updated since 2017, which suggests that the project may no longer be active. Its aim however was to establish a database to streamline music licensing. The database would contain information about songs, including copyright details, performance dates, licensing and usage rules, payment information, contact details, as well as song lyrics and pictures.

I. Heap, a British musician and businesswoman, created the Mycelia for Music project (n.d.), which aimed to be a database of songs containing not only basic metadata such as authorship and licensing rules but also information about instruments, tempo, key, and even the circumstances of the song's creation or the artist's favourite coffee. This would provide significant facilitation for both the use of the songs and the utilisation of the artist's image. The platform was established in response to an ongoing issue faced by artists in the music industry, where they often do the most work but are the last to be compensated (Arcos, 2018). According to the artist, blockchain could help address this problem (Heap, 2017). However, the implementation of this idea seems to be more complicated, as the latest information on the website dates back to 2018.

The above examples demonstrate that although the idea appears to be valid, especially for music creators and copyright holders, its implementation is challenging. However, there are a number of independent platforms offering services to artists based on blockchain technology. These include Musicoin ("Musicoin Project," n.d.), a platform where users can listen to independent music for free, and artists receive immediate compensation. Another example is Revelator, a platform for managing digital products, song rights, and proposing redistribution of royalties owed to artists ("Revelator Pro Platform," n.d.). Another use of blockchain technology is Resonate, the first community-owned music streaming service managed collectively by artists, listeners, and service staff. It primarily offers a model where consumers only pay for the music they actually listen to ("Play Fair," 2015).

Nonetheless these solutions raise several concerns. The primary revolves around the substantial amount of information that needs to be gathered and processed. Another refers to an important concern about who would be responsible for managing such an activity and bear the undoubtedly significant costs. Artists themselves could possibly perform this work by uploading appropriately marked content to the network, but such a system would not only require appropriate competence from them but also leave room for errors and abuse. Validating the initial credibility of such data would be difficult, which is referred to as *garbage-in garbage-out* problem (Ito and O'Dair, 2019) unless penalties were imposed for introducing false or illegal music files into the network (Halgamuge and Guruge, 2022).

In addition, numerous blockchain-based initiatives exhibit a siloed nature. Due to the lack of metadata standards and classification, conflicts and interoperability issues may thus arise in data management. Solutions such as machine learning and AI could undoubtedly aid in organising data. However, research indicates that these technologies are still in the early stages of development and their effectiveness as support mechanisms remains uncertain (Ghildiyal and Sharma, 2021).

The Berklee Institute for Creative Entrepreneurship is actively working on blockchain solutions in the music sector. In partnership with MIT Media Lab, they have established the Open Music Initiative (n.d.). Its objective is to create an open-source protocol for the unambiguous identification of music rights holders and creators to compensate them for the use of their musical works (Panay, 2016). Representatives of the Open Music Initiative presented their idea at the World Economic Forum in 2020, which evokes the history of groundbreaking technologies such as the Internet and mp3. The academic community has played a significant role in the development of both inventions, not only due to the reputation of the involved institutions but also thanks to the talented individuals working on innovative projects and the financial and organisational support they received. However, it is undeniable that the success of such projects requires collaboration among various stakeholders representing artists, music recording and publishing companies, collective management organisations, as well as public institutions responsible for cultural policy implementation. The establishment of common metadata standards and verification systems would be essential as well.

4.3.2.2 *Direct and straightforward royalty payments through the use of smart contracts*

The aforementioned databases containing metadata about musical works, including licences and usage fees, could be the first step towards improving the functioning of sound recordings on the Internet, particularly when it comes to their identification and authenticity confirmation. The next step would be enabling direct payment of royalties to artists through the use of smart contracts. This could allow for the elimination of traditional intermediaries, such as music publishers, music labels, collective management organizations (CMOs), and online platforms.

From a technical perspective, this would involve creating (crypto) tokens as representatives of value for elements such as the musical work itself and metadata related to ownership, licensing terms, and remuneration. These elements would later be attached to the digital sound recording in a similar manner to how DRM systems functioned. Some initial models of this kind have already been developed, such as *trusted DRM* (Zhaofeng et al., 2018). As a result, when a consumer downloads, streams, or uses music available on blockchain networks, an algorithm – a smart contract – would automatically trigger the execution of the relevant licensing agreement and the transfer of royalties to the entitled entities (Finck and Moscon, 2019; Pons, 2017).

Appropriate licensing provisions would also allow for consumer segmentation (McConaghy et al., 2017) and, consequently, the application of different business strategies for each segment. In this case, CC licences could serve as a legal framework, clearly indicating who and how can one use a particular work. For example, regular users could freely use works for personal purposes. On the other hand, reusers, who use music marked with a smart contract, would be required to pay a fee either when incorporating the work into a new production or when their own work starts to generate revenue.

In this way, creative activity would not be hindered, as Lessig pointed out when discussing remix culture (2008). This is particularly significant for emerging artists or small independent companies operating in creative sectors. Arditi also mentions this (2015, p. xxvi), emphasising that independent artists have never been able to compete with artists promoted by large record companies, partly due to limited access to music licences needed for their own projects. In the traditional system, both reuse fees for works and transaction costs associated with intermediaries significantly increase expenses, which ultimately only larger players, such as established video game creators or film studios, can afford. Handke (2013) refers to a study conducted in 2012 by KEA European Affairs, which found that transaction costs related to intellectual property rights borne by online music sellers in Europe can reach up to €260,000, excluding the licence itself (Ranaivoson, 2012). The possibility of eliminating intermediaries in the value chain, such as collective management organisations or music publishing companies, would reduce transaction costs for entities utilising existing music, and as a result, a larger portion of the fee would go directly to the creators (Hirsch and Gruber, 2015).

Transaction costs also apply to the distribution of remuneration to entitled entities. For niche artists whose works are used to a limited extent, distributing remuneration is not cost-effective. The use of blockchain and smart contracts could help reduce or even eliminate these costs, as the fees for commercial use defined in the smart contract would be automatically transferred to the creators or rights holders in the form of micro-payments. By bypassing intermediaries, transaction costs would be reduced. Furthermore, fees would be distributed among creators based on actual usage, rather than, as is the case in the system employed by collective management organisations and streaming platforms, through a percentage-based division of fees collected from users. Moreover, the transaction would be executed immediately after the commercial use of the sound recording. Additionally, remuneration principles could be established in a way that each participant in the creative process, such as the lyricist, band members, or producer, receives a portion of the remuneration predetermined by an algorithm. Furthermore, if fees for usage were paid using tokens or cryptocurrencies, the entire process would take place outside the traditional financial system. As emphasised by Panay (2016), smart contracts would primarily be based on attribution, recognising authorship, and the fee would be a consequence of it. The first song in history for which remuneration was automatically transferred to the creators involved in the creation and recording process through a smart contract was "Tiny Human" by Heap (2017).

In addition to independent initiatives utilising blockchain in the music industry, established entities that have already achieved success in the market have also shown interest in the possibilities offered by this technology. In 2017, Spotify acquired the small company Mediachain Labs, which developed a system for image recognition on the web and assigning them attribution (in other words, identifying the creator) (Sanchez, 2017a). Spotify intended to utilise this technology to change the system of redistributing compensation to artists, whereby listeners would pay for the songs they actually listened to and to the artists themselves (Arcos, 2018, p. 443). Similarly, Sony started to develop a rights management system for digital content utilising blockchain (Sony, 2018), aimed to create a more efficient way of managing and demonstrating ownership of copyright-related information.

eMusic (2019a), a music service existing since 1998 that primarily features independent artists, has launched a blockchain-based system for redistributing compensation to creators and rights holders, operating on a similar logic as the aforementioned Spotify concept. The platform aims to address the criticism directed towards the compensation systems used by streaming platforms thus far. Its mission is to create a music distribution platform that maintains a balance between the offering and the compensation flowing among fans, artists, and music content providers (eMusic, 2019b).

4.3.2.3 Value chain transparency

The digital landscape has brought about significant changes in the value chain of the recording industry. With the emergence of digital music distribution platforms, new intermediaries have entered the scene, capturing a considerable portion of the value generated. However, the situation for creators has seen only marginal improvements. This shift has further exacerbated the existing information asymmetry within the industry (De León and Gupta, 2017). Despite the overall growth in global revenues from digital music distribution, primarily driven by streaming, the current model for redistributing compensation to creators for the use of their works remains flawed. As pointed out by Heap (2017), creators lack access to vital information regarding the accounting of their royalty payments and have limited insight into by whom, where, and how their music is being consumed or utilised (Tapscott and Tapscott, 2018, p. 243). Furthermore, the absence of standardised protocols and a unified data storage system, as previously discussed, gives rise to errors in the redistribution of royalties to artists (Torbensen and Ciriello, 2019).

The advent of blockchain technology has paved the way for enhanced transparency in transactional processes. By leveraging blockchain's inherent properties, such as immutability and decentralisation, it becomes possible to track and trace all digital cultural assets existing within the online realm (Stankovic, 2020). Leveraging data mining techniques, valuable insights can be extracted pertaining to the utilisation of music by diverse consumer segments. This includes geographic, demographic, and consumer behaviour data, which can contribute to a deeper understanding of consumers. Armed with this knowledge, industry stakeholders can engage in more effective planning of future music projects to attract larger audiences. Additionally, this data-driven approach can serve as the foundation for the development of new business models that revolve around recorded music, including the implementation of dynamic pricing strategies. For instance, music consumed during specific time periods could be offered at discounted rates, while during peak hours, prices may be adjusted accordingly. As an added incentive, loyal fans could be rewarded by artists with exclusive discounts on subsequent tracks (Sitonio and Nucciarelli, 2018).

The transparency provided by blockchain technology extends beyond consumer insights and enables more efficient management of derivative works. By gaining visibility into the entire value chain, including the role of intermediaries, it would become possible to optimise processes, reduce transactional costs, and, critically, eliminate unnecessary intermediaries. This streamlined approach ensures that a larger proportion of the generated value is directed towards the rightful creators, empowering them with increased revenues and a fairer distribution of compensation.

4.3.2.4 Access to alternative sources of funding

One of the consequences of the digital as well as information and communication technology revolutions is a shift in the financing system for music production. The abundance of unauthorised music consumption on the Internet has led to market failure, which traditionally was prevented by copyright law in the cultural sectors, including the recording industry. Unfortunately, new models, particularly streaming, have not solved the problem of insufficient compensation for rights owners, especially the creators, for the use of their music. Although the number of subscribers to streaming platforms has been growing, along with revenues from digital music, this does not translate into adequate earnings for musicians.

One solution that has emerged is crowdfunding for music projects, allowing niche, less popular, or even debut artists to pursue their musical endeavours. However, the possibilities of supporting artists through crowdfunding are limited and one-sided due to the structure of crowdfunding platforms, where creators raise funds by offering merchandise products or limited editions (special releases of albums or tickets to concerts with additional fan experiences). Additionally, crowdfunding platforms face challenges related to security, abuse, and illegal transactions (Zhao and Coffie, 2020).

Blockchain expands the possibilities of such music financing while securing transactions (Tapscott and Tapscott, 2018, p. 125), operating as blockchain crowdfunding (Dziuba, 2018). Artists could use such solution to raise funds by issuing tokens (NFTs – non-fungible tokens) and reward their fans with these tokens for listening to their music, recommending it, giving endorsements, or engaging in other actions that generate value for the musicians (De Filippi, 2015; Sitonio and Nucciarelli, 2018). In return for the received tokens, fans could later acquire special goods offered by the respective artist. Moreover, this could be done without the intermediation of crowdfunding platforms, solely by utilising the blockchain network, facilitating direct connections between individuals.

Tokens that users of blockchain-based streaming platforms could receive for listening to music could also contribute to the development of the long tail of music consumption. For example, tokens with higher value could be offered to listeners of less popular music. This way, artists could gain increased exposure, attract more followers, and generate greater income from their work (Behal, 2022). Such an idea could also help solve the problem of the so-called cold start faced by niche artists on traditional streaming platforms.

One example of using blockchain for music financing is the project of dance music artist Gramatik, who created his own cryptocurrency token to fund his artistic endeavours. Fans, as owners of these tokens, gained a share in the artist's royalties ("Etherscan. Token Gramatik," n.d.). Björk also utilised a virtual currency system called AudioCoins when releasing her album Utopia. The idea was that individuals who purchased the album would receive 100 AudioCoins worth around 25 cents as a gift. Those who promoted or shared the album with others would receive additional cryptocurrency coins (Sanchez, 2017b).

eMusic has also introduced an NFT service for consumers. Fans can purchase tokens of their favourite artists through the platform, along with additional features such as exclusive collectible images and music connected to the token. Interestingly, eMusic NFT operates on the Ethereum sidechain Polygon, which requires minimal energy consumption and has a low environmental impact (eMusic, n.d.).

Such concept however raises the question of whether artists could start earning from music adopting such an approach, as in this system, consumers are rewarded for purchasing legally distributed products and engaging in actions that support the artist. However, the challenge lies in a different aspect. Previously, consumers just had to pay for music be it a CD or access to a streaming service. Here, by paying, they receive additional benefits, such as exclusive content as well as better relationships with their idols. In that way, by building engagement with fans, particularly dedicated aficionado fans, artists augment revenue from other sources, not necessarily from recorded music.

The owners of the start-up PurpleThrone also have had the ambition to address the issue of inadequate compensation for creators who distribute their music on streaming services (Resnikoff, 2021). Their project involves a platform that utilises cryptocurrency and offers artists opportunities to earn income through various music-related services such as streaming, video productions, concert tickets and other events. The platform also enables the exchange of this cryptocurrency into traditional fiat currencies. Artists are associated with the platform similar to a music label, which allows them to earn revenue through diverse means from their creative work.

In 2019, Warner Music also showed interest in blockchain technology by acquiring a start-up that developed and popularised a crypto game based on Ethereum (King, 2019). The aim of this acquisition was to explore new digital products that could be sold using the new Flow blockchain network.

Despite the promising potential of the solutions mentioned earlier, there are still significant concerns surrounding certain aspects, such as the storage of metadata-enriched music and the implementation of micropayment methods. Addressing these issues would inevitably require the involvement of either existing or new intermediaries (Finck and Moscon, 2019), as achieving complete disintermediation does not seem feasible (Bodó et al., 2018) due to the vastness of the Internet, the abundance of music content, and the fragmented attention of users.

While smart contracts could contribute to standardising licensing terms and conditions for copyrighted works across different uses and jurisdictions (Finck and Moscon, 2019), the divergent legal systems in various countries present a challenging obstacle to overcome. Furthermore, blockchain-based solutions encounter additional difficulties related to interoperability between older and newer systems, potential errors in smart contracts with their implications for transactions, and establishing trust in private blockchain networks (Stankovic, 2020).

Resolving these challenges may take considerable time since achieving the overall effectiveness of the entire system requires reaching critical mass (Savelyev, 2018). Only then can the network effect truly manifest itself. Moreover, existing industry players, particularly those that capture significant value within the music supply chain, may resist transparency in their operations. These entities include record labels, music publishers and online music distribution/streaming platforms. They may even form consortia to consolidate power and strengthen oligonomy within the music industry, relying on strong, private blockchain networks. It is crucial for any blockchain-based music platform to offer an integrated solution that effectively addresses the business challenges faced by the music industry and incentivises all relevant stakeholders according to their diverse interests; otherwise, it is likely to face failure (Ciriello et al., 2023). As a consequence, the hope of a complete transformation into a musician-centred ecosystem with minimal intermediaries within the music industry may remain unfulfilled (Cooperative, 2018).

Bibliography

101Blockchains, 2021. Mark Cuban Predicts Blockchain Is the New Internet. 101 Blockchains. URL https://101blockchains.com/mark-cuban-predicts-blockchain-is-the-new-internet/ (accessed 6.8.21).

Aigrain, P., 2012. *Sharing: Culture and the Economy in the Internet Age*. Amsterdam University Press, Amsterdam.

Aigrain, P., Aigrain, S., 2012. *Dzielenie się. Kultura i gospodarka epoki internetu*. Fundacja Nowoczesna Polska, Warszawa.

Arcos, L.C., 2018. The Blockchain Technology on the Music Industry. *Brazilian Journal of Operations & Production Management* 15, 439–443.

Arditi, D., 2015. *iTake-Over. The Recording Industry in the Digital Era*. Rowman & Littlefield, Lanham, MD, Boulder, CO, New York, London.

Attali, J., 2015. *Une brève histoire de l'avenir*. Fayard, Paris.

Barrow, E., 1996. Rights Clearance and Technical Protection in an Electronic Environment. Presented at the Electronic Publishing in Science ([Paris], February [19–23], 1996), pp. 36–42.

Baumann, F., 2013. *Freeconomics: Do Consumers Tend to Discriminate Pay-Models for Information Goods?* GRIN Publishing, Munich.

Beck, R., 2018. Beyond Bitcoin: The Rise of Blockchain World. *Computer* 51, 54–58.

Behal, P., 2022. Listen-To-Earn: How Web3 Can Change the Music Industry. *SSRN Journal*. https://doi.org/10.2139/ssrn.4150998

Benhamou, F., Farchy, J., 2014. *Droit d'auteur et copyright*. La Découverte, Paris.

Bodó, B., Gervais, D., Quintais, J.P., 2018. Blockchain and Smart Contracts: The Missing Link in Copyright Licensing? *International Journal of Law and Information Technology* 26, 311–336.

Böhme, R., Christin, N., Edelman, B., Moore, T., 2015. Bitcoin: Economics, Technology, and Governance. *Journal of Economic Perspectives* 29, 213–238.

Boyer, M., 2017. The Economics of Private Copying. Working Papers no. 17-845, Toulouse School of Economics. URL https://publications.ut-capitole.fr/id/eprint/25701/1/wp_tse_845.pdf (accessed 6.20.21).

Büsges, M., Designbüro, 2014. English: Open Content – A Practical Guide to Using Open Content Licences. URL https://commons.wikimedia.org/wiki/File:Open_Content_A_Practical_Guide_to_Using_Creative_Commons_Licences_web-29.png (accessed 6.25.23).

Casey, M., Vigna, P., 2019. *The Truth Machine: The Blockchain and the Future of Everything*. Picador: St. Martin's Press, New York.

Castells, M., 2002. *The Internet Galaxy: Reflections on the Internet, Business and Society*. Oxford University Press, Oxford.

Chalmers, D., Matthews, R., Hyslop, A., 2021. Blockchain as an External Enabler of New Venture Ideas: Digital Entrepreneurs and the Disintermediation of the

Global Music Industry. *Journal of Business Research* 125, 577–591. https://doi.org/10.1016/j.jbusres.2019.09.002

Ciechoński, T., 2021. Opłata reprograficzna będzie rozszerzona. Obejmie m.in. komputery, tablety, pendrive'y [WWW Document]. Gazeta Prawna. URL https://www.gazetaprawna.pl/firma-i-prawo/artykuly/8162767,oplata-reprograficzna-podatek-smartfony-komputery-tablety.html (accessed 6.19.21).

Ciriello, R.F., Torbensen, A.C.G., Hansen, M.R.P., Müller-Bloch, C., 2023. Blockchain-Based Digital Rights Management Systems: Design Principles for the Music Industry. *Electron Markets* 33, 5. https://doi.org/10.1007/s12525-023-00628-5

CISAC, BIEM, deThuiskopie, 2020. *Private Copying Global Study*. CICAS, BIEM, de Thuiskopie, online.

Ciupa, K., 2019. Blockchain – zdecentralizowany system o scentralizowanej logice. *Bank i Kredyt* 50, 295–328.

Cooke, C., 2015. Dissecting the Digital Dollar. Part One. How Streaming Services Are Licensed and the Challenges Artists Now Face. *Music Managers Forum*.

Cooperative, L., 2018. A Preliminary Review of Blockchain in the Music Industry. https://doi.org/10.2139/ssrn.3280838

Czetwertyński, S., 2019. *Morfologia nieautoryzowanego kopiowania*. Wydawnictwo Uniwersytetu Ekonomicznego, Wroclaw.

De Filippi, P., 2015. Blockchain-based Crowdfunding: What Impact on Artistic Production and Art Consumption? *Observatório Itaú Cultural*. URL https://hal.science/hal-01265211/document (accessed 3.4.21).

De León, I.L., Gupta, R., 2017. The Impact of Digital Innovation and Blockchain on the Music Industry. Inter-American Development Bank. (November 2017). URL https://publications.iadb.org/en/impact-digital-innovation-and-blockchain-music-industry (accessed 6.23.20).

Demsetz, H., 1967. Toward a Theory of Property Rights. *The American Economic Review* 57, 347–359.

DigWatch, 2021. European Commission Issued Guidance on Article 17 of the DSM Directive. URL https://dig.watch/updates/european-commission-issued-guidance-article-17-dsm-directive (accessed 6.27.23).

Doctorow, C., 2020. A Plan to Pay Artists, Encourage Competition, and Promote Free Expression [WWW Document]. Electronic Frontier Foundation. URL https://www.eff.org/deeplinks/2020/05/plan-pay-artists-encourage-competition-and-promote-free-expression (accessed 6.23.21).

DotBlockchainMusic, n.d. About [WWW Document]. BC Media. URL http://dotblockchainmusic.com/about/ (accessed 6.10.21).

Dziuba, D.T., 2018. Technologia blockchain crowdfunding: zastosowania, korzyści i oczekiwania. *Annales Universitatis Mariae Curie-Skłodowska, Sectio H Oeconomia* 52, 61–69.

EEC, 1993. Council Directive 93/98/EEC of 29 October 1993 harmonizing the term of protection of copyright and certain related rights, OJ L.

eMusic, 2019a. eMusic. Redefining Music Distribution Through Blockchain.

eMusic, 2019b. eMusic White Paper [WWW Document]. URL https://token.emusic.com/assets/pdf/eMusic_White_Paper_EN.pdf?d=1688039072817 (accessed 6.29.23).

eMusic, n.d. Discover and Download Music | eMusic [WWW Document]. URL https://www.emusic.com/nfts/about (accessed 6.29.23).

Etherscan. Token Gramatik [WWW Document], n.d. URL https://etherscan.io/token/0x1db42ceba6bdebf86d287e11b159ff97b083b8af (accessed 9.27.20).

FCForum, 2015. Qué es. URL https://2015.fcforum.net/que-es/ (accessed 6.17.21).

Finck, M., Moscon, V., 2019. Copyright Law on Blockchains: Between New Forms of Rights Administration and Digital Rights Management 2.0. *IIC* 50, 77–108. https://doi.org/10.1007/s40319-018-00776-8

Fisher, W.W., 2007. An Alternative Compensation System, in: Fisher, W.W. (Ed.), *Promises to Keep: Technology, Law, and the Future of Entertainment*. Stanford University Press, Stanford, CA, pp. 199–258.

Fogel, K., 2006. The Surprising History of Copyright and the Promise of a Post-Copyright World – Question Copyright. Question Copyright. URL https://questioncopyright.org/promise (accessed 6.23.23).

Ghildiyal, A., Sharma, S., 2021. Music Genre Classification Using Data Filtering Algorithm: An Artificial Intelligence Approach, in: 2021 Third International Conference on Inventive Research in Computing Applications (ICIRCA). Presented at the 2021 Third International Conference on Inventive Research in Computing Applications (ICIRCA), pp. 922–926. https://doi.org/10.1109/ICIRCA51532.2021.9544592

Gorkhali, A., Li, L., Shrestha, A., 2020. Blockchain: A Literature Review. *Journal of Management Analytics* 7, 321–343.

Gratz, J., 2004. Reform in the Brave Kingdom: Alternative Compensation Systems for Peer-to-Peer File Sharing. *Minnesota Journal of Law, Science & Technology* 6, 399.

Halgamuge, M.N., Guruge, D., 2022. Fair Rewarding Mechanism in Music Industry Using Smart Contracts on Public-Permissionless Blockchain. *Multimedia Tools and Applications* 81, 1523–1544. https://doi.org/10.1007/s11042-021-11078-6

Handke, C., 2013. Empirical Evidence on Copyright, in: Towse, R., Handke, Christian (Eds.), *Handbook on the Digital Creative Economy*. Edward Elgar, Cheltenham, Northampton, pp. 249–261.

Hatch, O.G. [R.-U.], 1998. S.505-105th Congress (1997–1998): Sonny Bono Copyright Term Extension Act.

Heap, I., 2017. Blockchain Could Help Musicians Make Money Again. *Harvard Business Review*.

Henriksson, T., Janowska, A.A., 2023. Production Networks in the Cultural and Creative Sector: Case Studies from the European Music Industry. CICERONE Horizon 2020. URL https://zenodo.org/record/6885744#.ZEqwrHbP1PY (accessed 6.30.23).

Hirsch, P.M., Gruber, D.A., 2015. Digitizing Fads and Fashions. Disintermediation and Glocalized Markets in Creative Industries, in: Jones, C., Lorenzen, M., Sapsed, J. (Eds.), *The Oxford Handbook of Creative Industries*. Oxford University Press, Oxford, pp. 421–435.

IFPI, 2018. *IFPI Global Music Report 2018*. IFPI. URL https://www.ifpi.org/ifpi-global-music-report-2018/ (accessed 6.21.23).

IFPI, 2008. *IFPI Digital Music Report 2008*. IFPI. URL https://www.scribd.com/document/431110111/ifpi-2008-pdf (accessed 4.27.21).

IFPI, 2007. *Global Release Identifier (GRid) Standard* [WWW Document]. IFPI. URL https://www.ifpi.org/wp-content/uploads/2020/08/GRid_Standard_v2_1.pdf (accessed 6.21.23).

Isherwood, M., 2011. *Global Repertoire Database* [WWW Document]. World International Property Organisation. URL https://www.wipo.int/export/sites/www/meetings/en/2011/wipo_cr_doc_ge_11/pdf/isherwood_grd.pdf (accessed 6.21.23).

Ito, K., O'Dair, M., 2019. A Critical Examination of the Application of Blockchain Technology to Intellectual Property Management. *Business Transformation through Blockchain* II, 317–335.

Janowska, A.A., 2011. „Ekonomia własności" a „ekonomia daru". Nowy model promocji i dystrybucji muzyki. *Prace i Materiały ISM* 39, 179–204.
Kazi, N., Bhatia, S., 2013. Various Artificial Intelligence Techniques for Automated Melody Generation. *International Journal of Engineering Research & Technology* 2, 1646–1652.
King, A., 2019. Warner Music Joins $11M Investment In Cryptocurrency Start-Up. Digital Music News. URL https://www.digitalmusicnews.com/2019/09/13/warner-music-dapper-labs/ (accessed 6.30.21).
Kinsella, N.S., 2008. *Against Intellectual Property*. Ludwig von Mises Institute. URL https://cdn.mises.org/15_2_1.pdf (accessed 6.23.23).
Krzysztofek, K., 2006. Status mediów cyfrowych: stare i nowe paradygmaty. *Global Media Journal - Polish Edition* 1, 1–15.
Ku, R.S.R., 2002. The Creative Destruction of Copyright: Napster and the New Economics of Digital Technology. *University of Chicago Law Review* 69, 263–324.
Kumar, L., Goyal, P., Kumar, R., 2020. Creativity in Machines: Music Composition Using Artificial Intelligence. *Asian Journal for Convergence in Technology (AJCT)* ISSN-2350-1146 6, 36–40.
Landes, W.M., Posner, R.A., 1989. An Economic Analysis of Copyright Law. *The Journal of Legal Studies* 18, 325–363.
Latrive, F., 2007. *Du bon usage de la piraterie*. Découverte, Paris.
Leonhard, G., Kusek, D., 2005. *The Future of Music. Manifesto for the Digital Music Revolution*. Berklee Press, Boston, MA.
Lessig, L., 2008. *Remix: Making Art and Commerce Thrive in the Hybrid Economy*. Penguin Books, New York.
Lessig, L., 2004a. Free Culture: How Big Media Uses Technology and the Law to Lock Down Culture and Control Creativity [WWW Document]. URL http://www.free-culture.cc/freeculture.pdf
Lessig, L., 2004b. Free (ing) Culture for Remix. *Utah Law Review* 961–975. URL https://heinonline.org/HOL/LandingPage?handle=hein.journals/utahlr2004&div=43&id=&page=.
Lunney Jr, G.S., 2001. The Death of Copyright: Digital Technology, Private Copying, and the Digital Millennium Copyright Act. *Virginia Law Review* 9, 813–920.
Maj, M., 2009. Zamiast odcinać, będą dziękować za pobieranie muzyki [WWW Document]. Dziennik Internautów. URL http://di.com.pl/zamiast-odcinac-beda-dziekowac-za-pobieranie-muzyki-26193 (accessed 6.16.21).
Marinescu, A.-M., 2018. The Private Copy Remuneration System. *Challenges of the Knowledge Society* 771–779. URL https://www.proquest.com/openview/656e68abfd8effb832114bc40dddd861/1.pdf?pq-origsite=gscholar&cbl=2036059.
Massa, C., 2022. The Digital Markets Act between the EU Economic Constitutionalism and the EU Competition Policy. *YARS* 15, 103–130. https://doi.org/10.7172/1689-9024.YARS.2022.15.26.5
McConaghy, M., McMullen, G., Parry, G., McConaghy, T., Holtzman, D., 2017. Visibility and Digital Art: Blockchain as an Ownership Layer on the Internet. *Strategic Change Strategic Change* 26, 461–470.
MKiDN, 2022. MKiDN skierowało do konsultacji implementację dyrektywy o prawie autorskim i prawach pokrewnych - Ministerstwo Kultury i Dziedzictwa Narodowego. URL https://www.gov.pl/web/kultura/mkidn-skierowalo-do-konsultacji-implementacje-dyrektywy-o-prawie-autorskim-i-prawach-pokrewnych (accessed 6.27.23).

MKiDN, n.d. Opłata reprograficzna - rekompensata na rzecz uczciwej kultury - Ministerstwo Kultury, Dziedzictwa Narodowego i Sportu. URL https://www.gov.pl/web/kulturaisport/oplata-reprograficzna-rekompensata-na-rzecz-uczciwej-kultury (accessed 6.19.21). https://www.gov.pl/web/kulturaisport/oplata-reprograficzna-rekompensata-na-rzecz-uczciwej-kultury (accessed 6.19.21).

Mulligan, C., Scott, J.Z., Warren, S., Rangaswami, J.P., 2018. Blockchain Beyond the Hype. A Practical Framework for Business Leaders (White Paper). *World Economic Forum, WEF.*

MusicAlly, 2016. Blockchain: Music without the Middlemen?. URL https://musically.com/wp-content/uploads/2016/05/blockchain-report.pdf (accessed 6.9.21).

Musicoin Project [WWW Document], n.d. Musicoin Project. URL https://musicoin.org/ (accessed 6.29.23).

Mycelia, n.d. Our Mission Is... [WWW Document]. Mycelia for Music. URL http://myceliaformusic.org/ (accessed 9.27.20).

Nakamoto, S., 2008. Bitcoin: A Peer-to-Peer Electronic Cash System. URL https://bitcoin.org/bitcoin.pdf (accessed 6.27.23).

Netanel, N.W., 2003. Impose a Noncommercial Use Levy to Allow Free Peer-to-peer File Sharing. *Harvard Journal of Law and Technology* 17, 1.

Nicholls, S., Cunningham, S., Picking, R., 2018. Collaborative Artificial Intelligence in Music Production. Conference Paper Presented at the Audio Mostly 2018 on Sound in Immersion and Emotion. URL https://glyndwr.repository.guildhe.ac.uk/id/eprint/17411/1/GURO_392_SteveN_AM_camRdy_FINAL.pdf (accessed 6.22.23).

Nikoltchev, S., 2011. *Who Pays for Private Copying? European Audiovisual Observatory.* European Audiovisual Observatory. URL https://rm.coe.int/1680783bc7 (accessed 3.4.21).

O'Dair, M., 2018. *Distributed Creativity: How Blockchain Technology Will Transform the Creative Economy.* Springer, Cham.

O'Dair, M., Beaven, Z., Neilson, D., Osborne, R., Pacifico, P., 2016. Music on the Blockchain (No. 1). Middlesex University, London.

Oksanen, V., Valimaki, M., 2005. Copyright Levies as an Alternative Compensation Method for Recording Artists and Technological Development. *Review of Economic Research on Copyright Issues* 2, 25–39.

OPI, n.d. About [WWW Document]. Open Music Initiative. URL https://open-music.org/about (accessed 6.10.21).

Opłata reprograficzna - fakty i mity [WWW Document], 2021. Legalna Kultura. URL https://www.legalnakultura.pl/pl/prawo-w-kulturze/prawo-w-praktyce/news/3595,oplata-reprograficzna-fakty-i-mity (accessed 6.19.21).

Orlikowski, P., 2021. Opłata reprograficzna. Polacy mówią "nie", a rząd upiera się przy swoim [WWW Document]. www.money.pl. URL https://www.money.pl/gospodarka/oplata-reprograficzna-polacy-mowia-nie-a-rzad-upiera-sie-przy-swoim-6643938788092033v.html (accessed 5.29.21).

Panay, P., 2016. Why Us, Why Now: Convening the Open Music Initiative [WWW Document]. Berklee College of Music. URL https://college.berklee.edu/panos-panay-open-music-initiative (accessed 6.12.21).

Pereira, A.L.D., 2017. Levies in EU Copyright Law: An Overview of the CJEU's Judgments on the Fair Compensation of Private Copying and Reprography. *Journal of Intellectual Property Law & Practice* 12, 591–600.

Play Fair. [WWW Document], 2015. Resonate. URL https://resonate.coop/ (accessed 6.29.23).

Pons, J., 2017. Blockchains and Smart Contracts in the Culture and Entertainment Business. *Réalités industrielles* 3, 81–90.

Poort, J., 2013. Copyright Levies, in: Towse, R., Handke, C. (Eds.), *Handbook on the Digital Creative Economy*. Edward Elgar, Cheltenham, Northampton, pp. 235–246.

Ranaivoson, H.R., 2012. Licensing Music Works and Transaction Costs in Europe. Final Report. KEA/Vrije Universiteit Brussel, Brussel.

Resnikoff, P., 2021. PurpleThrone Wants to Solve the Streaming Royalty Mess With Cryptocurrency. Digital Music News. URL https://www.digitalmusicnews.com/2021/06/06/purplethrone-streaming-royalty-mess/ (accessed 6.30.21).

Revelator Pro Platform [WWW Document], n.d. URL https://www.revelator.com/product/revelator-pro (accessed 6.29.23).

Rifkin, J., 2015. *The Zero Marginal Cost Society: The Internet of Things, the Collaborative Commons, and the Eclipse of Capitalism*. St. Martin's Press, New York.

Roads, C., 1985. Research in Music and Artificial Intelligence. *ACM Computing Surveys (CSUR)* 17, 163–190.

Sabatini, F., 2019. Culture as Fourth Pillar of Sustainable Development: Perspectives for Integration, Paradigms of Action. *European Journal of Sustainable Development* 8, 31–31.

Sanchez, D., 2017a. Has Blockchain Arrived? Spotify Makes the Biggest Move Yet. Digital Music News. URL https://www.digitalmusicnews.com/2017/04/27/spotify-blockchain-deal/ (accessed 6.23.21).

Sanchez, D., 2017b. Will AudioCoin Change the Music Business and Get Artists Paid? Digital Music News. URL https://www.digitalmusicnews.com/2017/11/06/audiocoin-cryptocurrency-music-industry/ (accessed 6.30.21).

Savelyev, A., 2018. Copyright in the Blockchain Era: Promises and Challenges. *Computer Law & Security Review* 34, 550–561.

Schwab, K., 2016. *The Fourth Industrial Revolution*. World Economic Forum, Geneva.

Senftleben, M., 2020. Institutionalized Algorithmic Enforcement—The Pros and Cons of the EU Approach to UGC Platform Liability. *Law Review* 14. https://doi.org/10.25148/lawrev.14.2.11

Sitonio, C., Nucciarelli, A., 2018. The Impact of Blockchain on the Music Industry, in: 29th European Regional Conference of the International Telecommunications Society. Presented at the Towards a Digital Future: Turning Technology into Markets?, ITS, Trento.

Sony, 2018. Sony Develops Rights Management System for Digital Content Utilizing Blockchain Foundation [WWW Document]. Sony Group Portal - Sony Global Headquarters. URL http://www.sony.com/en/SonyInfo/News/Press/201810/18-1015E/index.html (accessed 6.29.23).

Stankovic, M., 2020. Can Blockchain Save the Creative Industry? Medium.URL https://mimi-stankovic.medium.com/can-blockchain-save-the-creative-industry-5c212bb52ac2 (accessed 3.4.21).

Sturm, B.L.T., Iglesias, M., Ben-Tal, O., Miron, M., Gómez, E., 2019. Artificial Intelligence and Music: Open Questions of Copyright Law and Engineering Praxis. *Arts* 8, 115. https://doi.org/10.3390/arts8030115

Tapscott, D., Tapscott, A., 2018. *Blockchain Revolution: How the Technology Behind Bitcoin Is Changing Money, Business and the World*. Pengion, London.

Tasca, P., Thanabalasingham, T., Tessone, C.J., 2017. Ontology of Blockchain Technologies. Principles of Identification and Classification. *SSRN Electronic Journal* 10. URL https://allquantor.at/blockchainbib/pdf/tasca2017ontology.pdf (accessed 6.8.21).

Thetsidaeng, C., 2019. *User-Generated Content and Copyright Dilemma in Web 2.0 Era*. Uppsala Universitet, Uppsala.

Throsby, D., 2010. *The Economics of Cultural Policy*. Cambridge University Press, Cambridge, New York, Melbourne, Madrid, Cape Town, Singapore, Sao Paulo, Delhi, Dubai, Tokyo.

Torbensen, A., Ciriello, R., 2019. Tuning into Blockchain: Challenges and Opportunities of Blockchain-Based Music Platforms. Presented at the Twenty-Seventh European Conference on Information Systems (ECIS2019), Stockholm-Uppsala, Sweden.

Towse, R., 2008. Why Has Cultural Economics Ignored Copyright? *Journal of Cultural Economics* 32 (4), 243–259.

Towse, R., 2001. *Creativity, Incentive, and Reward: An Economic Analysis of Copyright and Culture in the Information Age*. Edward Elgar, Cheltenham.

US Copyright Office, 1790. Copyright Act of 1790 | U.S. Copyright Office [WWW Document]. URL https://copyright.gov/about/1790-copyright-act.html (accessed 6.23.23).

Verma, M., 2022. Integration of Blockchain in Music Industry. *International Journal of Trend in Scientific Research and Development* 6, 687–690.

WEF, 2015. *Deep Shift. Technology Tipping Points and Societal Impact*. WEF. URL https://pdf4pro.com/amp/view/global-agenda-council-on-the-future-of-software-amp-1267de.html (accessed 6.8.21).

Wikström, P., 2020. *The Music Industry: Music in the Cloud*. John Wiley & Sons, New York.

Wilson, E.J., 2006. *The Information Revolution and Developing Countries*. MIT Press, Cambridge, MA.

Xu, M., Chen, X., Kou, G., 2019. A Systematic Review of Blockchain. *Financial Innovation* 5. https://doi.org/10.1186/s40854-019-0147-z

Yang, T., Nazir, S., 2022. A Comprehensive Overview of AI-Enabled Music Classification and its Influence in Games. *Soft Computing* 26, 7679–7693. https://doi.org/10.1007/s00500-022-06734-4

Zhao, H., Coffie, C.P.K., 2020. The Applications of Blockchain Technology in Crowdfunding Contract or https://doi.org/10.2139/ssrn.3133176. SSRN: https://ssrn.com/abstract=3133176. https://doi.org/10.2139/ssrn.3133176

Zhaofeng, M., Weihua, H., Hongmin, G., 2018. A New Blockchain-Based Trusted DRM Scheme for Built-in Content Protection. *Journal on Image and Video Processing* 2018, 1–12. https://doi.org/10.1186/s13640-018-0327-1

Ziemska, A., 2021. Opłata reprograficzna nie od smartfonów [WWW Document]. URL https://ksiegowosc.infor.pl/wiadomosci/5247915,Oplata-reprograficzna-nie-od-smartfonow.html (accessed 5.29.21).

Conclusion

Is it time for a new revolution?

The analysis of the recording industry's evolution or even revolution under the influence of rapidly changing external conditions, especially digital technologies, suggests that recorded music has significantly lost its value. Record companies argue that unauthorised copying and new business models, particularly streaming, have contributed to a drastic decline in their revenues. This raises the question of whether recorded music still holds the same value for consumers and if they will ever be willing to pay as much as before.

Considering the broad concept of value, analysed in disciplines such as axiology, philosophy, aesthetics, sociology, psychology, and economics (Marshall, 2019), it is challenging to provide an in-depth analysis of recorded music's value in this publication's conclusion. However, in light of ongoing changes in the industry and the associated problems, it is important to highlight key issues related to music's value.

Throsby (1998) highlights that when it comes to cultural goods, we can talk about both economic value and cultural value. Within the latter, aesthetic, spiritual, social, historical, symbolic, and authenticity values are distinguished. In terms of economic value, it was traditionally understood as utility value, meaning its ability to satisfy human desires and needs, and exchange value, which refers to the number of other goods that someone could sacrifice to acquire a given unit of the commodity. Both types of value are considered inseparably linked since a higher cultural value of a good can influence a consumer's willingness to pay for it.[1] However, this approach has been criticised, arguing that the economic value of culture, including music, is incomparable to the value of other goods in the market and should not be considered in an economic context (Behr et al., 2016, p. 416). Artists, in particular, have often opposed the commodification of culture.

Recorded music, however, is undeniably a commodity subject to market exchange processes. This does not mean, though, that the price or revenues from sales of companies or the entire industry reflect its cultural and economic value. Analysing the evolution of the recorded music market, it is inevitable to conclude that as its value drastically declined at the turn of the 20th and 21st centuries, the value of recorded music itself also decreased. But what kind of value? The history of the phonographic industry's development

DOI: 10.4324/9781003414605-6

shows that the value of phonograms has always been a unique matter, and various external circumstances have meant that the cultural value of music does not always translate into economic value (Marshall, 2019, p. 147).

Besides the recorded music market value decline, prices for music products have also dropped. In the pre-digital era, CDs with several songs cost around €10–20, while digital albums were at least 50% cheaper. Presently, individual users pay about €10 for monthly access to streaming platforms with unlimited music offerings. This suggests the decline in the value of music reflected in the decrease in prices. Is it a decline in cultural value? Or also economic value? Additionally, the higher cost of CDs compared to digital albums and the belief that digital music should be cheaper indicate that the main value resided in the medium rather than the music itself.

At the beginning of the 20th century, recording companies viewed recordings as complementary goods to boost sales of home music devices. As consumer demand for records increased, companies shifted their focus solely to recording. Simultaneously, radio emerged, driving the need for recorded music for broadcast. However, it was primarily used to attract advertisers who, as part of the so-called two-sided market (Doyle, 2010), financed radio stations' operations, primarily through appealing music that would also attract listeners. Although radio stations paid rights holders, often record companies, for the use of music (performance rights), it was distributed on the airwaves free of charge to consumers who were supposed to pay attention to advertisements. Moreover, recorded music played on the radio and later on television, through sampling or exposure effects, served sales and promotion on popular formats of the time (vinyl, tapes, CDs) and promoted concerts. Thus, its value functioned mainly as a promotional tool.

It may seem puzzling why consumers, who could listen to music for free in the media or at concerts (which are separate products with their own values), still bought music on physical formats for home listening. Undoubtedly, this option satisfied a different need of consumers, particularly those who placed greater importance on music and desired the freedom to listen to it anytime and anywhere. Engaged fans could satisfy their emotional connection with their idols through purchasing albums, while collectors could showcase their refined vinyl music collection, even if not always listened to. This however elevated their social status. Marshall (2019, p. 150) highlights that albums radiated more symbolic value, encompassing various social meanings, than the music itself.

The same recordings could have different utility value for consumers in different segments. However, it did not reflect exchange value or cultural value since album prices in the market were unrelated to production costs or artist reputation (Elberse, 2010). Prices were determined through agree ments among major labels, based on the principle of non-price competition. A newly released album by an international star had a similar price to that of a new album by a lesser-known local artist, signalling to consumers that price was a matter of convention and did not necessarily correlate with value.

The use of recorded music as a driving force to sell other products has always been present in the music industry. CDs in supermarkets were treated as loss leaders to encourage the purchase of other items. When Apple launched the iTunes music platform, the music was intended to boost sales of the complementary product, the iPod. Mobile network operators made agreements with music platform owners or launched their own platforms, providing free access to music as part of their offerings. Phone manufacturers, such as Nokia and later Samsung, also offered music as an addition to their mobile devices. Car manufacturers and sellers also proposed free access to music services as part of their packages. These actions conveyed to consumers that music was merely an add-on that didn't necessarily require payment.

Similarly, even in the pre-digital era, artists themselves treated recorded music in a similar manner. Research shows that most musicians, except for a few stars, didn't rely on album sales for substantial income. Albums served as archives of their artistic work and tools for image-building. Signing with a well-known record label, such as a major label, signified success both within the artistic community and among consumers. Recording and selling albums helped gain recognition, attract concertgoers, and facilitate merchandise sales.

Recognisability could lead to the use of an artist's music in other cultural and creative products, such as films or video games, which could potentially generate much higher revenue. It could also be leveraged by companies selling other products to enhance their value. An example of this is Jay-Z's contract with Samsung, offering modern smartphones along with access to his music.

The digitisation of music and information and communication technology development enabled mass file sharing, reflecting the belief that recorded music can be accessed for free. Unauthorised distribution channels provided free access, similar to radio or music bundles added as bonuses to smartphones. However, the difference was the absence of a business intermediary who would pay rights holders for commercial music use. Streaming platforms emerged as institutional intermediaries, offering ad-supported or premium experiences for unlimited music access. The situation for artists and musicians has remained largely unchanged. Their earnings from recorded music have remained low, both before and during the streaming era, as exchange occur between institutional participants in this market, namely intellectual property rights holders and commercial users.

In light of the above, the proposals in Chapters 3 and 4 offer a sensible solution to the crisis in the recording industry. However, implementing them requires a paradigm shift, a new revolution based on effective cultural policy to protect culture, creators, and artists. It would also need to recognise that the average uninvolved consumer does not have to pay for recorded music, as D. Bowie predicted when he described it as flowing ubiquitously and accompanying various activities. This would fulfil the principle of universal access to culture as a fundamental human right, as stated in the Universal

Declaration of Human Rights (United Nations, 1948), which asserts that "Everyone has the right freely to participate in the cultural life of the community, to enjoy the arts and to share in scientific advancement and its benefits." A new revolution in the approach to the value of recorded music for consumers and monetisation methods could alleviate the existing conflict within the industry between consumers, creators, and intermediaries.

Post scriptum

The recent development of the most exciting tool, the artificial intelligence (AI) has brought about significant advancements and possibilities and raised new questions about the condition of the recording industry, copyright and particularly creativity. On one hand, AI offers exciting prospects for the creative process in music production. It can assist musicians by providing advanced tools for composition, arrangement, and production, allowing for enhanced creativity and experimentation. AI algorithms can generate musical ideas, analyse trends and patterns in music consumption, and even mimic the styles of renowned artists. This opens up new avenues for innovative music creation and expands artistic possibilities.

Moreover, AI-powered recommendation systems have transformed the way music is discovered and consumed. Streaming platforms utilise AI algorithms to curate personalised playlists and recommendations based on user preferences and behaviour. This enables a more tailored music experience, enhancing user engagement and potentially increasing exposure for emerging artists.

However, the rise of AI also poses significant challenges to the recording industry, particularly in the realm of copyright. The use of AI-generated content raises questions about ownership and originality. As AI algorithms become capable of creating music that closely resembles human compositions, the distinction between human-made and AI-generated works becomes blurred. This poses challenges for copyright protection, as it may be difficult to determine the rightful ownership and attribution of AI-generated music.

Additionally, the ease of replicating and distributing music in the digital realm raises concerns about piracy and unauthorised use. AI-powered tools can facilitate the creation of counterfeit or derivative works, potentially infringing on copyright holders' rights.

However, while record labels may focus on the threats AI poses to copyright and the potential dilution of streaming volumes, there is a more exciting prospect at hand. AI has the potential to empower consumers by making music an expressive medium for all, rather than mere passive consumption. This paradigm shift would redefine the distinction between creation and consumption in the music marketplace. In this future landscape the emphasis shifts towards a more inclusive and participatory music experience.

What will be the value of music in this context?

Are we ready for such a revolution?

Note

1 The classical approach was, of course, revised within other economic theories. However, here the aim is not to analyse the concept of value but rather to highlight the issue concerning the value of music for different stakeholders, the income for creators, and the willingness of consumers to pay for music. Hence, reference is made to the proposition of the leading cultural economist – David Throsby.

Bibliography

Behr, A., Brennan, M., Cloonan, M., 2016. Cultural Value and Cultural Policy: Some Evidence from the World of Live Music. *International Journal of Cultural Policy* 22, 403–418.
Doyle, G., 2010. Why Culture Attracts and Resists Economic Analysis. *Journal of Cultural Economics* 34, 245–259.
Elberse, A., 2010. Bye-Bye Bundles: The Unbundling of Music in Digital Channels. *Journal of Marketing* 74, 107–123.
Marshall, L., 2019. Do People Value Recorded Music? *Cultural Sociology* 13, 141–158.
Throsby, D., 1998. *Economics and Culture*. Cambridge University Press, Cambridge.
United Nations, 1948. Universal Declaration of Human Rights [WWW Document]. United Nations. URL https://www.un.org/en/about-us/universal-declaration-of-human-rights (accessed 6.20.23).

Index

Note: **Bold** page numbers refer to tables; *italic* page numbers refer to figures and page numbers followed by "n" denote endnotes.

For Product Safety Concerns and Information please contact our EU
representative GPSR@taylorandfrancis.com
Taylor & Francis Verlag GmbH, Kaufingerstraße 24, 80331 München, Germany

www.ingramcontent.com/pod-product-compliance
Lightning Source LLC
LaVergne TN
LVHW022212200926
848481LV00006B/1945
* 9 7 8 1 0 3 2 5 3 9 8 3 6 *